SOCIAL CLASS, POLITICS, AND URBAN MARKETS

SOCIAL CLASS,

POLITICS, AND URBAN MARKETS

The Makings of Bias in

Policy Outcomes

Herman L. Boschken

STANFORD UNIVERSITY PRESS
Stanford, California 2002

Stanford University Press
Stanford, California

Library of Congress Cataloging-in-Publication Data
Boschken, Herman L.
    Social class, politics, and urban markets : the makings of bias
in policy outcomes / Herman L. Boschken.
      p. cm.
    Includes bibliographical references and index.
    ISBN 0-8047-4413-0 (cloth : alk. paper)
    1. Local transit—Government policy—United States.   2. Local
transit—United States—Finance. I. Title.
HE4461 .B67 2002
320′.6′0973091732—dc21

                                2002004724

Original Printing 2002

Last figure below indicates year of this printing:
11 10 09 08 07 06 05 04 03 02

Typeset by G&S Typesetters, Inc., in 10/13.5 Sabon.

To a bountiful future as it unfolds
in the lives of my grandchildren:
Jennifer, Christopher, James,
         and my grandchildren not yet born.

Contents

Tables and Figures

Tables

Figures

Preface

This book is about public agency policymaking in American cities. It is the result of a decade of research that incorporates many actors, many processes, and many disciplines. The work can be read at two levels. On the surface, it is about urban mass transit in America and the factors that drive this industry's policy outcomes toward one public-interest bias or another. At an even more important level, though, it is a book about the value of social science theory in making sense of urban processes and government's policymaking responsiveness in a plural society. Through an empirical weighing of "rival theses," it analyzes the applicability of competing concepts in political science, economics, administrative theory, sociology, social psychology, and urban planning to understanding the forces that mold policymaking in American cities.

In many ways, the work has prompted a return to my intellectual roots cultivated more than three decades ago during my student years at Berkeley and the University of Washington. In those days, my interests spanned many seemingly unrelated subjects: Camus's existentialism, Veblen's leisure class, the federalism of our Founding Fathers, "materials balance" and the use of resources, and the study of administrative institutions. These ideas were spawned in the twentieth century and before but in retrospect were the precursors of our modern-day understanding of the urban habitat in an age of globalization. Yet for all that those early university years contributed to exploding my youthful naivete, they were characterized mostly by the untidiness of loose ends—loose ends that have remained with me for several decades.

As for many of us in academia, my pursuit of a larger integration was put on hold partly because of the need to launch an academic career and produce publishable research in definable disciplines. This meant fragmenting my work into several fields, most of which shared little in the way of a common set of peers. With this book, however, I pick up many of those seminal loose threads and try to integrate them into an interdisciplinary whole. I have always believed this approach to be the most productive for those who really want to discover the competing forces that forge the life and institutions around us. I only wish I had started this adventurous work earlier.

From the standpoint of one's professional career, the interdisciplinary approach remains a risky venture. In his bestseller *The Lexus and the Olive Tree*, Tom Friedman reminds us of something the Nobel laureate Murray Gell-Mann once said:

> Unfortunately, in a great many places in our society, including academia and most bureaucracies, prestige accrues principally to those who study carefully some [narrow] aspect of a problem, a trade, a technology, or a culture, while discussion of the big picture is relegated to cocktail party conversation. That is crazy. We have to learn not only to have specialists but also people whose specialty is to spot the strong interactions and the entanglements of the different dimensions, and then take a crude look at the whole. (quoted in Friedman 2000: 28)

Although the fear of not being understood or recognized by one's discipline-confined peers afflicts all interdisciplinarians, I think the intellectual rigidity that has straitjacketed research for the past half-century is passing. In part, we see this in public policy, especially regarding urban affairs, where there is a growing reception and appreciation for alternatives that bring the larger picture into focus.

Although this is a work on public policy, some might still dismiss it because its coverage is not specifically and primarily focused on a particular discipline. On the one hand, it is policy analysis, but it does not employ economic cost-benefit theory. It deals with civic culture and government, but it is not carved only from political science. It contains a large component of interorganizational theory, but the research is only selectively known by the administrative science crowd. It has elements of sociology in it, but it also contains theory that reaches well beyond a sociologist's mantra. Some will recognize the essence of social psychology, but I am not known as a psychologist. On the other hand, discussions at academic conferences have shifted dramatically over the past few years to such interdisciplinary paradigms as the "new political culture," "new institutionalism," "new urbanism," and of course globalization. It is in these emerging interdisciplinary traditions that this book on policymaking will most likely find its place.

In the course of researching and writing this book, I benefited greatly from the collegial advice and contributions of some very important people. First among them are Jim Doig of the Woodrow Wilson School at Princeton University and Terry Clark, a sociologist at the University of Chicago. To my great advantage, both discovered my work early on and have offered substantial support for many years by critiquing early stages of the research and reading prepublication drafts of several articles in addition to this book. Aaron Wildavsky of U.C. Berkeley was also an enthusiastic early contributor to my thinking until his untimely death. I am deeply indebted to these scholars and to others, including Deil Wright of the University of North Carolina, George Frederickson at the University of Kansas, and Todd LaPorte at U.C. Berkeley, all of whom provided useful comments on some of the work leading up to this book. For all that these people have offered me, I remain solely responsible for any errors in thought or oversights that remain.

In addition to these colleagues, I express much gratitude to research assistants Suann Shumaker and Dave Budenaers for the huge collection of data and materials underlying this study. I also want to thank my Stanford University Press editors, Muriel Bell, Amanda Moran, Judith Hibbard, Janet Mowery, and Kate Wahl, for their diligent efforts in keeping the editing and production processes on track and on time.

Several institutions along the way also made this project possible. First is the Institute of Transportation Studies at the University of California, Davis, where I began my research during an adjunct professorship in 1989. I am especially grateful to Dan Sperling, the institute's director. Second, the CIES Fulbright Program and the University of New Brunswick Center for Property Studies provided me the opportunity to edit and revise the manuscript during my stint as a 2000–01 Fulbright Distinguished European and Canadian Chair. I also acknowledge the financial support provided by San Jose State University and the California State University system.

In addition, I want to recognize the many transit-agency executive directors and planning and budgeting managers for cooperatively sitting through hours of interviews, offering candid insights, showing me the ropes of transit management, and providing agency data. In a time when the public often perceives them as faceless bureaucrats, I found nearly all to be highly dedicated, professional, and public-regarding civil servants. We are lucky to have them doing the public's business.

Finally, I am eternally indebted to Irene, who watched and supported the progress of this scholarship even as months turned into years, and to my beloved blue-eyed Persian, Sasha, who was always there urging me to come out to play during those long days and nights of analysis and writing. Their presence and loving patience were priceless.

H.L.B.
Davis, California

SOCIAL CLASS, POLITICS, AND URBAN MARKETS

1   *Skewing Outcomes in Agency Policymaking*

1 Urban Settings: The Origins of Bias in Policy Outcomes

For all that we claim to be as a democratic society, the United States is not a nation of "presumed equals." Neither equality of condition nor equality of access can be found in the way people live, work, or collectively receive the fruits of government policy. This is largely due to the fact that America is fundamentally a diverse plural society and a nation of many overlapping governments. It is also due in some measure to the ability of wealthier, institutionally connected people to exert greater influence on politics than the less well-off. Although these sources of difference diminish any real prospects for a monolithic equality, we nevertheless expect comparable treatment and fair distribution of outcomes from our institutions. This expectation aside, distributing public benefits across a plural society is often a dicey proposition, involving inherent subjectivity in judging the legitimacy of competing public perspectives and making necessary but awkward tradeoffs from which policymaking bias is brewed.

In the case of government agencies, the quest to satisfy multiple constituencies invariably incurs daunting paradoxes in public purpose. Doing right by some interests is usually coupled with doing wrong by others. At the end of the day, policy choices are made that allocate benefits unequally and incomparably. Yet in solving the paradoxes there appear to be few "industry" standards or common patterns in the way policymakers bias agency outcomes to benefit one public or another. Why do we see such pattern variance among agencies? What are the important taproots of bias in policymaking? How does the pattern of outcomes correspond to the American mosaic of public interests?

Nowhere are the paradoxes more apparent and these questions more urgent than in the policymaking experiences of urban government. It is here where government actions are the most discernible to Americans and where policy outcomes have their greatest and most direct impact on daily lives. Yet much of policy research in urban affairs has overlooked these paradoxes and the questions they elicit. Traveling the less beaten path, this book is about the determinants of bias in policy outcomes of agencies operating in the urban milieu of contemporary America. Specifically, it looks at the case of urban transit. At its center is a neutral investigation of rival theses concerning political influence and civic engagement, institutional exchange, and the socioeconomic dynamics of an urban setting in which agency policymaking is done.

In taking a neutral stance, the study tries to avoid many of the ideology-fueled popular misconceptions about "bad" government and "good" government, but at times it must walk a thin line between oversimplification and informed understanding. For example, the research assumes that to understand the origins of bias in policymaking it is not sufficient to see urban outcomes as the result of a "back channel" of power elite. Nonetheless, it would be equally shortsighted not to expect socioeconomic status and urban structure to play an enduring role in skewing those outcomes to favor some interests over others.

Hence, at its roots, this book is a comparative treatise on the adequacy of theory. If we are to understand the ties between policymaking and an agency's differential impacts on competing constituencies, we must first reach out for conceptual clarity on the subtle but integral forces that make up the web of politics, markets, and the urban conditions they foster and perpetuate. What is in question here is the design of conceptual models that allow a more robust foretelling of which policy outcomes are likely to be emphasized among the pattern of alternatives. With knowledge that a similar set of agencies (those within the same public sector) tend to bias the pattern of outcomes differently, the research is set up to look for empirical differences in the complex world of urban policymaking that give hint of what theories are durable.

Critical to analyzing the roots of policymaking bias in a plural society is recognizing that different and often competing perspectives exist in judging the legitimacy of agency results. Policy outcomes, after all, are about *consequences* differentially felt and are perhaps best understood as the positive and negative impacts on those claiming to have a derivative stake in the agency's allocational processes. As such, policy outcomes are not the same as organizational outputs (such as number of clients served per day or cost per service unit produced), the latter of which contains little information on consequences or who gets what from the process. The question of legitimacy requires much more than a presentation of outputs:

> It is one thing to hold a police department responsible for expending its procurement budget (an input) without fraud or waste, for making a certain quota of arrests (outputs), and for achieving these objectives in conformity with prescribed procedures (process compliance). It is quite another to ask whether the department has made the city a safer place (the outcome people really care about). . . . Most accountability mechanisms in government focus on inputs, outputs, and process compliance, which are typically much easier to monitor than genuinely important outcomes. Increasingly, however, citizens and overseers want outcome answers. That is, they want to know whether public programs are accomplishing objectives that citizens value. (Altshuler and Parent 1999: 2)

Policy outcomes have been of long-standing importance to the study of politics and administration. In part, this is because outcomes are the primary means for judging the consistency of bureaucratic actions with governmental mandates, and in part because they provide the principal means to observe how agencies behave toward and satisfy the diverse public demands of a plural society. For example, by comparing one outcome with another, we may determine how and to what extent policymakers target the allocation of resources that skews outcomes to favor some stakeholders over others. In short, the comparison of outcomes goes to the heart of policy analysis because it provides evidence of *proportionality* in measuring who gets what and how much from representative bureaucracy (Levy, Meltsner, and Wildavsky 1974; Fried 1971). It must be noted, though, that skewed outcomes are not just the result of goal-driven policymakers or face-to-face struggles among stakeholders, but are caused by a variety of other urban and institutional forces as well. The shape or pattern of outcomes, therefore, does not always reflect what policymakers individually or mutually desired or intended.

Since agencies produce multiple and often paradoxical outcomes, it should be no surprise that they seldom address different policy aims with equal emphasis. After all is said, bias remains an unavoidable condition of policymaking. What is of greater interest, though, are the "causes" for the bias in emphasis. Why, for example, are some agencies able to emphasize their bureaucratic eminence and budgetary size at the expense of taxpayers' desires for smaller government? Why do some achieve highly efficient operations to the detriment of other outcomes? Why do other agencies favor effective social programs at the expense of operational efficiency? Why is it that only a few agencies achieve both operational efficiency and effective organizational and social-program outcomes? What are the makings of policy bias?

Rival Theses

Answers are not easily forthcoming, but many theses have been proposed. Indeed there is a long-standing debate about whether political or socioeconomic variables matter more (Dye 1998; Lewis-Beck 1977). For instance, in the case of policy outcomes skewed to deemphasize efficiency, traditional political answers have been that "bureaucrats have too much political and administrative autonomy" or that they are not subject enough to "market conditions." Sometimes the answer is simply a belief that bureaucrats are politicians disguised as administrators and are no professional match for their market-oriented business counterparts.

A similar range of arguments exists for outcomes emphasizing the agency's bureaucratic stature or its social-program effectiveness. Some see strategically minded agencies as having an "innovative management style" that propels them to effective outcomes. Others see strategic effectiveness as a function of resource availability allowing wealthier agencies to "spend to the limit of their tax bases" whether it be to achieve marketworthiness or political accolades. In contrast, some argue that robust emphases on social-program effectiveness and bureaucratic stature occur in agencies that serve populations with a disproportionally high number of disadvantaged people exercising their "political entitlements."

This study cannot address the whole plethora of rival theses offering explanations for why policy outcomes are skewed. It instead examines those that have been central in controversial debates in the social sciences regarding the urban context of policymaking. Its intent is not to prove or disprove a line of reasoning but to see which are more influential in explaining policy bias. It will show that while skewed outcome patterns are the result of both intentional and unintentional policymaking designs, they are probably more heavily influenced by conditions external to the agency. This is not to say that administrators are slaves to their urban settings or that organizational form does not matter—far from it. But the study shows empirically that certain socioeconomic, political, and urban spatial influences play an inordinately powerful role in "pushing" agency policymakers toward strategic choices that favor certain outcomes over others and constrain managerial flexibility in pursuing preferred courses of action. Certainly some of these influences may be interactive with management discretion, but others are wholly outside the control of agency discretion.

Along these lines, one of the more provocative rival theses posits that a significant influence on policy-outcome bias is attributable to the symbolism of socioeconomic status (SES). Specifically, an anonymous upper-middle-class (UMC) "genre," mirroring a prevailing culture in an agency's constituency population, is thought to cast a comprehensive influence over agency policymaking. Like artistic and literary types, a UMC genre is understood to be a distinctive cultural symbol of lifestyle, form, and content. Varying in prevalence from one area to another, the genre's cultural influence is strengthened and reinforced by enlarging the proportion of UMC individuals in an agency's population base.

This symbolic SES influence is said to operate in two ways. First, the anonymous genre exerts a "systemic power" (Stone 1980) over policymaking by providing subliminal cues of a socially and politically correct culture that conveys a basis or structure for an agency to use in contemplating specific policy emphases. The genre appears to represent to many Americans the inspirational (sometimes enviable) "good life," thus giving greater weight to policy choices that correspond to enhancing UMC culture and habitat. Second, the genre operates through other more visible means (including media advertising, lending credence to certain kinds of activities and property ownership) that influence aggregate consumer behavior in the agency's markets.

This thesis may sound as if it springs from the traditional "power-elite" literature (Mills 1956; Domhoff 1967), but it does not. Contrary to the notion of direct manipulation by individuals with power and position, the thesis suggests that systematic collusion or even direct communication among individuals is *not* necessary for an upper-middle-class genre to affect the course of policymaking. Indeed it may have become a replacement for flagging "civic engagement," individual citizens' withdrawal from traditional face-to-face involvement in government policymaking (see Skocpol and Fiorina 1999).

One rival to the UMC thesis places urban spatial form at the forefront of influences on policy outcomes. The spatial dimensions and physical layout of cities are reflections of the human exchanges and socioeconomic activities that make up the urban scene. The resultant physical pattern may range from an urban area dominated by a single dense activity center (like Chicago) to one characterized by level sprawl with no focal point (like most of the metropolitan basin consisting of Los Angeles, San Bernardino, Riverside, and Orange Counties). The concept is not new to urban planners focused on outputs, but its application to policymaking in a plural society breaks new ground in the quest for understanding causes of bias in policy outcomes. Depending on where along the centralization scale an urban area best fits, its spatial form may constrain the flexibility with which policymakers pursue outcomes that they might otherwise prefer. Los Angeles wanted desperately to make heavy-rail transit work as an effective, marketworthy alternative to the automobile, but this was made impossible by the basin's layout: the places where people live, work, and play are too scattered.

This study includes other theses as well. One of these addresses market conditions as determinants of outcome bias. In the urban affairs literature, a market thesis takes a back seat to the focus on politics and welfare economics. Public choice theory incorporates a role for market exchange, but principally from the perspective of relative operational efficiencies derived from contracting and privatization. This study looks at a different thesis of market transactions—that involving the structure of markets and the competitive conditions that confront public agencies operating on the supply side of market exchanges. In this instance, the degree of competitiveness among service providers (public and private) and a public agency's access to technology are seen as determinants of outcome skewness. Under the thesis, for example, the existence of an oligopolistic consortium, bent on limiting market access and choice, may substantially constrain an excluded producer (in this case, a public agency) from exercising its entrepreneurial ability to grow its organization and achieve the scale necessary to offer effective programs.

In politics and administration, of course, one of the most venerable bodies of theory is about the public agency's institutional setting of intergovernmental actors. This area of determinants is huge and supported by a diverse literature, but not all are relevant here. Indeed this vast literature poses less of an obstacle than it appears, since our interests focus more narrowly on the critical issues of intergovernmental exchange between dissimilar and potentially conflicting political actors. This takes us to a more recent thesis in the field called "new institutionalism." Sometimes associated with political economy theory, this thesis points to the structure of institutional power and agency autonomy in intergovernmental exchange. It holds that the number and variety of intergovernmental exchanges and institutional actors provide a context for policymaking bias. Greater numbers of players, for example, may induce agency policymakers to skew outcomes in favor of social programs at the expense of administration-centered norms of efficiency.

Although other political theses may seem to be forgone in the research, some arguably are captured in new institutionalism. For example, elected officials (mayors, council members, county supervisors, and state legislators) are shown to be part of the institutional apparatus of intergovernmental exchange. Along with government administrators external to the focal agency, they exercise their roles of political representation and leadership through the formal and informal apparatus of exchange. Although this book does not deal explicitly with the literature on elections and political leadership, it is indirectly accounted for by the scope and intensity with which these folks come to the intergovernmental table to engage agency policymakers. Furthermore, because this study focuses on the generic strength of their exchange presence, theory about the specific content of their demands (e.g., environmental quality, business development, antipoverty programs) is not of particular relevance here. Issue content is left for others to investigate.

Political parties and interest groups are not incorporated in the model either. Because they are usually tangential quasi-government actors without official portfolio or stature in the intergovernmental process at the urban level, they can be only loosely associated with agency outcomes. Downs, for example, argues in the "median voter" thesis that "political rationality leads parties in a two-party system to becloud their policies in a fog of ambiguity" (1957: 135–36). This led Dye to conclude that parties and party competition "may not matter much" (1998: 309). Attempts to specify hypotheses and empiricize variables for an analysis of their policymaking influence are therefore elusive and most likely unproductive. Though not addressed here, the party thesis applied to policy outcomes is taken up in a recent journal article (Boschken 1998a).

There are also other theses entirely left out of the model that nevertheless may have some significance in explaining policy outcomes. One of these targets the role of an agency's organizational structure in contributing to outcome bias. The reason for its exclusion is that in this study *all* the organizations in the sample appear to be designed around the same principles of bureaucracy. This structural hegemony is perhaps best explained as the result of "isomorphism," which is the emergence over time of a common structure and approach among organizations in the same field (DiMaggio and Powell 1983). Isomorphism, in fact, may have been hastened in transit and other sectors by the popular practice of "benchmarking," which serves to unify bureaucratic behavior around what organizational behaviorists call "best practices" as exemplified by industry leaders.

This mimicking process aside, some marginal differences in structure existed, and interviews with executives confirmed the presence of two variations within the bureaucratic model. For believers in the traditional operations-oriented organization, lines of bureaucratic authority were clearly defined and the chief administrative officer (CAO) was firmly in charge of decision-making responsibilities. For believers in managerial "empowerment," bureaucratic authority was only marginally relaxed to encourage some team activities and self-initiative (see Peters and Waterman 1982). Both mindsets, however, saw classical bureaucratic behavior as essential to success. Even agency advocates of the empowerment paradigm believed the first principles of management were an "emphasis on chain of command" and "unequivocal discipline" (Gambaccini 1993: 8). No major efforts at decentralization were observed.

Although a distinct literature in policy exists on the role and influence of agency governing boards, a thesis about these organizational actors is not included in the research model. Instead, boards are often construed as political microcosms or conduits of the agency's surrounding family of local governments whose influences on policy outcomes are included in the institutionalism thesis mentioned above. Moreover, even if a board's internal deliberative processes were to exert an independent influence on agency outcomes, nuances of board processes and their interactions with bureaucrats are often hidden, too subjective to verify quantitatively, and prohibitively expensive to gather data on.

Unions are external agents that might seem relevant in determining bias in policy outcomes. Nonetheless, a union thesis is not a part of this study because the variance in union impact on the study's agency sample is negligible. Unions matter but exhibit only minor intercase variation (probably because union locals morph into each other with the aid of their national leadership), and most of that is associated with agency size (a variable accounted for in the research model). Finally, because the analysis of rival theses is designed to examine policy outcomes as a long-term phenomenon, no attempt is made to account for short-term political issues and economic cycles.

The Setting: Urban Transit

This study's lens is trained on large metropolitan areas of the United States, where agency policy outcomes are overwhelmingly framed by the needs and circumstances of a complex urban population. It is here that government operates at the level of "the people" and where most of American government's vast assemblage of administrative agencies are located. These urban agencies hold domain over the most critical public services, ranging from K–12 education, community health, and development planning to police, fire-fighting, and infrastructure. Nevertheless, it would be hopeless to carry out a study like this that attempted to aggregate agencies or generalize results across all these different service areas.

To reduce the methodological risk of comparing apples and oranges, the comparative analysis is restricted to a particular type of government agency and to a sample of agencies within a particular urban service area. First, the study limits the scope to agencies that fit the widely used "public enterprise" model. This choice was made because their political and administrative structure is the most suitable for examining policy outcomes from a multiple-perspectives framework. This type of agency operates with more institutional autonomy and toward balancing both *administration*-centered aims for sector/industry stature and efficiency, and *politically* mandated social programs (J. Mitchell 1992; Boschken 1988; Walsh 1978).

Second, regarding service area, the study's focus is on urban transit. This choice was made because transit, like other infrastructure, is at the heart of so many of the most difficult and complex problems found in urban America. Whether speaking of our nation's public schools, clean water and sewerage agencies, county medical centers, or transit systems, infrastructure policymaking is faced with mediating the prospects of social isolation and the declining civic engagement of an aging population, dilapidation caused by deferred maintenance, declining fiscal support for capital funding, downsizing of services, incomplete planning for regional economic development, and "reengineering" of government. All the problems and many of the opportunities for better government come to the fore in this type of "enterprise" agency and in the provision of transit services. Moreover, what is found here may have important implications for other public sectors as well.

Unlike its foreign counterparts, which are mostly operated by national bureaucracies or ministries, the typical American transit agency operates as a locally formed public authority. Its jurisdiction may span an entire region (like the New York City metropolitan area) or may be one of several in a balkanized and mostly uncoordinated system of transit services (as in the San Francisco Bay Area). In addition, its legal form may be one of several alternatives, including a joint-powers agency, a regional special district, a multistate arrangement covering a common metropolitan region, a department of city government, or a metropolitan agency of state government. As hybrids of the business firm and a government bureaucracy, nearly all operate as semiautonomous public enterprises.

Usually separate from other local governments, the administrative autonomy of the transit agency is ostensibly maintained by the independence of its board of directors. Sometimes agency boards act like their corporate counterparts, but more often they behave as intergovernmental conduits for local and regional politicians. For example, the general manager of the Bay Area Rapid Transit (BART) agency compared Philadelphia's highly politicized appointed transit board with BART's elected board (he had been at these and other districts). He saw BART as "a flat-out business" because of its constituency-elected board, but he noted that in Philadelphia "the board was powerless to do anything. . . . Politicians behind the scenes wouldn't let [business decisions] happen. So, SEPTA [Philadelphia] was a political tool and could not be run as a real business" (F. Wilson 1990: 6, 14).

One factor related to a board's political independence is funding.

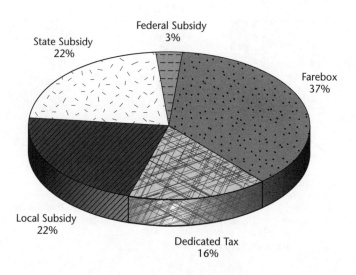

State Subsidy
22%

Federal Subsidy
3%

Farebox
37%

Local Subsidy
22%

Dedicated Tax
16%

FIGURE **1.1**   Sources of Transit Operating Funds (U.S. Public Transit Agencies, 1984–1996)

SOURCE: Data from the American Public Transit Association (1998).

An enterprise's autonomy tends to be reinforced if it has multiple sources of funds, a majority of which should come from self-generated and other nonpolitical sources. In the case of BART, nearly all revenues are acquired from a very high "farebox recovery ratio" (fee-for-service as a percentage of costs) and a dedicated local sales tax. By contrast, Philadelphia has a much lower farebox recovery ratio and received most of its funding for operations from the federal government and the state. As shown in Figure 1.1, the industry norm narrowly favors organizational autonomy with a multiple-sources mix that is about evenly split between agency-generated funds (including "farebox" and locally dedicated transit taxes) and local, state, and federal subsidies. Except for funding of new capital projects (typically rail-based), the federal government does not have a national transportation policy and is no longer an instrumental provider of operational subsidies. Its retreat from urban policymaking has left budgetary politics in transit mostly to locals and the states.

There are nearly 6,000 transit agencies in the United States, but fewer than 100 of them operate in the large metropolitan areas where more than 85 percent of all transit passenger trips occur. Of the agencies

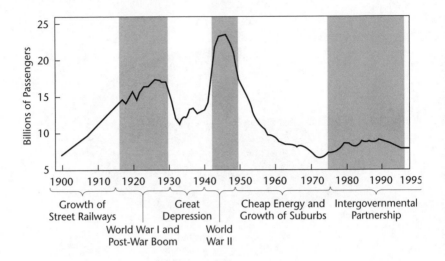

FIGURE **1.2**   Historical Trend in Public Transit Ridership (U.S. Metropolitan Areas, 1900–1995)

SOURCE: Data from the American Public Transit Association (1998).

in these larger areas, more than half operate systems that consist principally of buses. During the study period, only about fifteen operated rail systems as a major mode of transit service. Although transit is a very visible part of the urban cityscape and metropolitan politics, it accounts nationally for only about 5 percent of urban passenger trips; automobiles account for 87 percent (American Public Transit Association [APTA] 1998). Even though operating an automobile costs more than twice as much as riding transit, the vast difference in market share is chronic. As shown in Figure 1.2, transit ridership for the industry as a whole continued to slide relative to population growth for much of the last half of the twentieth century and into the current period of intergovernmental partnerships when public funding has been most plentiful.

Policymaking in transit agencies takes place in many kinds of market, technological, and political venues. Although the industry mean for transit's market share of urban passenger trips is only 5 percent, the range for agencies in this study varied widely from a low of 1.5 percent to a high of nearly 40 percent. Some agencies, such as the New York City Transit Authority, WMATA (Washington, D.C., area), MBTA (Boston), and CTA (Chicago), are powerful market providers of urban passenger transportation. But for others, such as those in Phoenix, Los Angeles, and De-troit, the commuter market is so heavily dominated by the automobile and freeway system that transit serves mainly a small transit-dependent segment of disadvantaged clients. The public perceives these less market-advantaged agencies principally as marginalized or supplemental welfare agencies.

Technologically, transit agencies are like most government orga-nizations in following, not leading, the private sector in entrepreneurial initiative and product innovation. This lagging market position has given the corporate consortium of automobile manufacturers, oil firms, and highway producers a free hand to set the terms of competition with em-phasis on speed, style, and "creature comforts." Thus, over the years, public transit has fallen further behind auto transportation in offering technological alternatives and in developing products that would lead to broader use.

For example, because a consumer's decision to purchase an auto is heavily influenced by socioeconomic status considerations, many transit agencies invest heavily in technologies that add glitz to the service (e.g., futuristic rail-car design) rather than route flexibility or improved access (such as client information systems and proximal stops). Although infe-rior in route flexibility and cost, the more aesthetically attractive rail-based system, especially light rail, is the mode many transit officials feel compelled to adopt instead of better-designed buses to match automobile appeal and functionality.

Compounding their disadvantages in market leverage and techno-logical entrepreneurship, transit agencies are government bodies legiti-mized in part by political considerations that dampen unbridled initiative. In the acquisition of half its revenue from nonmarket sources, the average transit agency enters into numerous exchange agreements with a web of federal, state, and local government actors who require the provision of specified services to transit-dependent and disadvantaged clients (usually without regard to cost). In addition, all must adhere to more global po-litical mandates, including the Americans with Disabilities Act (ADA), the Clean Air Act Amendments of 1990 (which require planning for air qual-ity as well as mobility), federal and state laws mandating drug and alco-hol abuse programs, and cooperative policymaking with metropolitan planning organizations (MPOs) and other agencies, specified by the Intermodal Surface Transportation Efficiency Act of 1991 (ISTEA) and its 1998 reauthorization (TEA-21).

Transit, then, shares with other sector agencies a common urban setting where conflicting stakeholder demands precipitate policy dilemmas resulting in beneficial outcomes that are seldom evenly distributed across contending interests. To bring empirical weight to the inquiry, this study uses a statistically significant database consisting of a cross-sectional sample of forty-two transit authorities operating systems in large metropolitan areas (greater than 500,000 population). Data on the sample were extracted from high-quality standardized nationwide reporting systems compiled by the U.S. Department of Transportation's (DOT's) Federal Transit Administration (FTA), the U.S. Census Bureau, and several transportation research centers. Subjects in the sample were identified from FTA's directory of transit agencies (Urban Mass Transportation Administration [UMTA] 1988). Data for all variables are specific to each agency or the population within each jurisdiction. Most data on policy outcomes are from the FTA's annual Section 15 reporting system, which is mandated for federal funding of transit agencies and contains self-reported data on agency finances, costs, and service levels.

The Concept of Skewness: Policy Outcomes from Multiple Perspectives

The notion that competing stakeholders derive different benefits from agency outcomes is a serious consideration for anyone seeking to evaluate how well and for whom governmental agencies perform. The research on government performance, however, seldom adopts a multiple-constituencies approach in connecting policy outcomes to questions of agency bias or to the "publicness" issue (Boschken 1994). Instead, much of the conventional literature advocates measuring agency outcomes according to a single standard of public welfare for society at large. Although couched in the venerable tradition of Progressivism, this approach has become increasingly problematic for policymakers for at least two reasons. First, because public welfare is defined in the context of society at large, competing interests are subordinated to a "majority" view in a priority "pinnacle" of public good. Second, although competing interests exhibit a variety of social, economic, environmental, and political preferences, policymakers are usually left to determine outcome benefits for all according to a single *economic* standard, usually functional efficiency. The result is that competing interests are forced into a cost-benefit analysis that creates a single-column calculation of "net benefit" to society or the community at large.

The major casualty of straitjacketing outcome analysis into a single, bottom-line structure is a loss of association between agency impacts and particular constituencies within a plural society. Although cost-benefit analysis seeks to incorporate all public issues (ranging from health and environmental quality to economic mobility and jobs) within its formulation of a net benefit, stakeholders cannot easily disaggregate the at-large calculations to associate specific outcomes with their particular interests.

Worse still, in making comparisons across agencies, the net-benefit calculation leads to ranking agencies on a best-worst scale, when achieving the public good in a plural society would require comparisons to be made from multiple perspectives. Hence a classic policy analysis problem is the impossibility of estimating the "goodness" of outcomes in an urban setting of contentious publics by sizing up outcomes from a single-standard at-large approach.

To avoid the quagmire, this research pioneers a different approach and method for evaluating policy outcomes. It asks not what agency is best according to a single standard or calculation, but which of the multiple constituency perspectives an agency's outcomes favor. This alternative framework, which we shall call a multiple simultaneous outcome indices (MSOI) analysis, does not rank the agency performers in order from best to worst. Instead, it identifies which agencies skew policy outcomes in what directions so as to enable independent judgments about the distribution of outcomes by competing stakeholders.

For the purpose of making transparent what interests are affected and in what ways, the framework places different outcome perspectives in a direct comparative context structured by two dichotomies found in the policymaking literature. One of these pits administration-centered interests against social-centered interests. In this dichotomy, policymakers appear at once as vested stakeholders seeking organization-enhancing outcomes that boost their executive status and career potential, and as servants of the public seeking to provide for politically prescribed social programs. The other dichotomy distinguishes a dual level of policymaking concerns. At a strategic level, policymaking is focused on outcomes that positively affect the overall context and long-term sustainability of the agency and its social programs. At an operational level, policymaking considerations go to the functional and immediate impacts of producing the agency's services. The four-celled "field" of perspectives resulting from these dichotomies allows a shift in analysis from single-scale comparisons to a concentration on varying patterns of outcome emphasis.

Although many patterns can occur within the four-celled MSOI structure, the resulting outcome skewness should not elicit black and white interpretations. Instead, skewness is the condition of an asymmetrical pattern in which a "bulge" of emphasis represents a disproportional apportionment to one of the four outcome perspectives. For example, differences in patterned asymmetry may show in one case that an agency pays higher returns to resource contributors (such as transit operators and other unionized wage earners) while another delivers higher operating efficiencies; or in another case, an agency may emphasize its organizational eminence (bigger budgets or deeper commuter-market penetration) while another pursues effectiveness in social-program delivery (mobility for the transit-dependent or regional economic development).

Such interagency differences in emphasis are not inherently the result of paradoxical outcomes, but the evidence will show that skewness is most often made up of tradeoffs that resolve a policymaking paradox. This notwithstanding, the MSOI analysis as a research tool is intended to view asymmetry with neutrality. We make no a priori judgment about whether a disproportional pattern is more or less "good" than a pattern of equal portions or that one disproportion is better or worse than another. The MSOI results certainly can be used by affected interests to make practical judgments about agency results, but here its purpose is solely to make evident interagency differences in outcome patterns for use in comparing the durability of rival theses.

The Research Model

As an inquiry into how and why public agencies emphasize different policy outcomes, this book also implicates a larger issue of government representation in a plural society. In much of the existing policymaking literature, the temptation is to ignore constituency diversity and assume that a monolithic consensus can be reached among policymakers over what or who matters most. With this leap of faith, past research often proceeded with a policy analysis that sought conclusions about why some agencies achieved high conformity to a preordained pinnacle objective while others strayed from the course. In contrast, this book reaches no conclusions about good and bad performance. Instead, it distinguishes different ways agencies address their publics, noting that policymaking involves making tradeoffs that result in outcomes that seem equitable to some constituencies but unfair to others.

In walking down this less-traveled road, I hoped to learn what determines different kinds of policy bias in the pursuit of managing agencies in the public good. I looked for answers in many places but was ultimately guided by a fragmentation of partial theses found in past urban affairs and public policy research. Although this previous research speaks more to individual performance than to a pattern of outcomes, it nevertheless provides instrumental insight into different pieces of the multiple-perspectives puzzle. One of the more difficult aspects of dealing with a collage of other nonaligned research is identifying specific threads of wisdom that can be used to formulate representative theses. This involves the sometimes daunting task of bringing together diverse writings into a single cohesive and concise thesis. When successfully accomplished, the weaving of these original thoughts into a thesis often brings their creators' contributions to life in a new state of relevance. The end result, though, will be to identify thematic central tendencies that resonate across a body of writings and outweigh individual differences in focus and intent.

Even though interpretations and interpolations must be made to adapt these theses to the focus on bias in policy outcomes, the various conceptual contributions are all treated as equally likely rival theses. Figure 1.3 introduces this nonrecursive model of multiple causation by (1) identifying asymmetry in the outcomes pattern as the effect, and (2) grouping rival theses into related categories of independent determinants. Conceptually, skewness is composed of a pattern of outcome emphases and deemphases spread over a field of alternative policy perspectives defined by the four-cell MSOI model. As dependent variables, each perspective, represented by an MSOI cell, contributes to an overall pattern of policy outcomes that is, to varying degrees, *asymmetric*. Indepen-

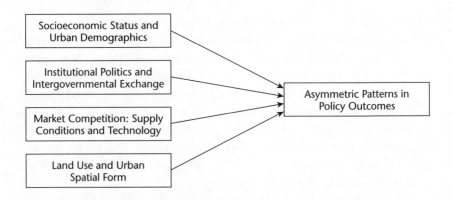

FIGURE **1.3** Determinants of Asymmetry in Policy Outcomes (Public Agencies in Urban America)

dent variables prescribed by theses, including socioeconomic status, institutionalism, market conditions, and urban spatial form, are brought to bear in explaining pattern asymmetry in policy outcomes.

Socioeconomic Status and Urban Demographics

Like all organizations, public agencies are affected by the socioeconomic setting in which they are found. In large metropolitan areas, where people are more concentrated, social demographics play out through personal and impersonal communications and interactions and through anonymous images and stereotypes formed on an urban stage of public events and activities and reinforced by the media. People find status identity and association according to socioeconomic characteristics and frequently make decisions or attribute outcomes to personal and anonymous social distinctions. Of the many demographics studied, the ones most discussed as potentially significant to agency policymaking are socioeconomic status, aggregate wealth of the urban area, and race and poverty.

SES is the most complex because it is composed of several interrelated characteristics. SES typically distinguishes individuals on the basis of education, career path, income level, and other acquired personal resources. Moreover, whereas SES can certainly be conveyed through interpersonal interaction and civic engagement, some aspects may be communicated anonymously through the exertion of a "systemic power" over society and public institutions (Stone 1980). For example, scholars have long postulated that an "upper middle class" image, acting as purveyor of cultural esteem in the social structure, surreptitiously affects policy outcomes in ways compatible with perceived aspirations and a lifestyle attributed to the genre (Veblen 1948; Whyte 1956; Riesman 1961; Clark 1998).

Wealth and poverty are other urban social conditions thought to affect an agency's policy choices. In the case of area wealth as a public resource, agencies experience urban affluence in the form of their tax base. Some theorists, for example, argue that policymaking, especially related to agency spending, is constrained by tax revenues and that greater taxable wealth begets larger agency budgets (Dye 1966). In terms of allocating resources across policy outcomes, wealthy-area agencies like MUNI (in San Francisco) and WMATA (greater Washington, D.C.) measure high on budgets and programs, whereas less-wealthy agencies like Bi-State Development (St. Louis) and Niagara Frontier RTA (Buffalo) score lower.

A thesis about race and poverty involves a more complicated logic than the one for the UMC but suggests that urban areas with predominantly affluent white populations will withhold resources from impoverished minority populations. This effect is complicated by the fragmentation of governmental jurisdictions in a metropolitan area and the degree to which suburbs are incorporated into the urban core. For example, SEPTA (the transit agency for metropolitan Philadelphia) is a joint-powers authority made up of several suburban cities and counties and the City of Philadelphia. This transit agency's experience has been that the more affluent white suburbs provide only limited budgetary expenditures for transit services to the core city's underclass. SEPTA is a big commuter system but offers relatively little mobility for the disadvantaged and transit-dependent poor. In contrast, MUNI in San Francisco exists as a department within a single consolidated countywide government whose poor and wealthy constituencies are marbled throughout the area. It ranks among the highest in providing for the disadvantaged underclass.

Institutional Politics and Intergovernmental Exchange

In American federalism, no agency of government is entirely autonomous in representing and exercising the will of the people. All exist in an intergovernmental setting of political actors and overlapping federal, state, and local authorities. However, the sharing of power and the degree of agency autonomy vary widely. In the urban environment, some agencies (such as BART in the San Francisco Bay Area) are able to act more independently because they exist as consolidated regional special districts that are fiscally and politically separate. This may not increase their autonomy from federal and state oversight, but it frequently reduces their exposure to the area's local politicians and lessens the obligation to negotiate policy with a maze of local governments. For many agencies, though, organic statutes and state laws limit such local independence, requiring "metapolicy" solutions that synthesize diverse mandates into actions that yield a variegated pattern of outcomes.

Among the theses that speak to intergovernmental influence on policy outcomes, perhaps the most promising is found in a branch of institutionalism called "transactional exchange" theory. The concept (found both in political economy and in administrative theory) argues that agencies incur transaction costs when they negotiate with other governmental actors and that these costs increase in proportion to the number of overlapping jurisdictions and type of intergovernmental authority exercised (Williamson 1990). That is, the magnitude of such political transaction costs is determined largely by the distribution of intergovernmental power and the degree of agency autonomy. Agencies are driven to minimize these costs by "horse-trading" or conceding ground in exchange for bilateral and multilateral agreements on policy and intended outcomes. In short, an agency will respond to intergovernmental exchange according to its relative institutional influence by adjusting its policy-outcome emphases accordingly.

Although an agency may also realize the benefits of "safety in numbers," institutional regularity, and strategic partnering with intergovernmental actors, the continuous interaction and attendant higher intergovernmental transaction costs diminish agency autonomy. Along with this loss is an expected shift in policy emphasis to outcomes that agency policymakers might not otherwise vigorously pursue. An example illustrating the thesis is the Americans with Disabilities Act, which requires wheelchair access on transit vehicles but without providing a budgetary subsidy to implement and maintain the social program. Few transit executives embraced the program, and some agencies avoided compliance with the requirements for many years. In the end, however, full implementation was achieved at most major agencies (albeit in different ways) after years of intergovernmental negotiation.

Market Competition: Supply Conditions and Technology

The role of markets and economic behavior has only recently become a mainstay in public organization theory, but their influence in analyzing policymaking performance varies widely from sector to sector. In sectors with little or no exposure to competitive conditions (police, urban parks, building inspection, and sewage treatment, for example), the market paradigm may be trivialized or barely visible. In others (garbage collection, utilities, or schools), market theses assume a much larger presence and include the concepts of consumer behavior, competition, and contracting. Transit lies somewhere in between.

Large urban transit systems are seldom privatized except for marginal services, but all operate in markets where the automobile and freeways provide substantial competition for commuting and noncommuting travelers. Although autos hold the dominant share in virtually every urban market, the competition varies widely, giving some agencies more opportunity than others to exhibit marketworthiness. Some survive by carving out a supplemental niche focused mainly on heavily subsidized transit-dependent riders, while others engage in mainstream competition for paying customers.

According to a market thesis, what differentiates the prospects of marketworthy agencies from marginalized or supplemental transit agencies are competitors' responses to consumer behavior. For example, market alternatives that address rider preferences for widespread travel-mode access to urban activities, congestion-caused variability in travel time, and technologies providing comfort and style are said to be at the core of consumer choice. Not surprisingly, then, the degree and manner in which agencies are immersed in market competition are important determinants in skewing policy outcomes to favor some stakeholders over others.

Land Use and Urban Spatial Form

To many, land use is an important consideration in agency policy-making, but in urban transit, it is central to explaining how service is laid out and how much the system is used by commuters and transit-dependent riders. The different facets of land use include (1) the physical conical form of an urban area that results from urban development over time, and (2) the transportation pattern that links residential, social, and economic activities over the metropolitan area. Although these two aspects of urban spatial form would seem compatible, viewing form from one or the other may cause one to hypothesize different effects on policy outcomes.

All American cities have become blends of their older central cores and suburban sprawl. Nevertheless, there are distinctions among them. They range from a *monocentric* pattern of rings surrounding a core of compact tall structures (as in greater Chicago) to a *polycentric* pattern commonly referred to in its most extreme form as randomly distributed urban sprawl (as in most of the southern California basin). Between these conical poles, spatial form may tend toward the monocentric except for the addition of high-rise corridors emanating from the core (as in greater Washington, D.C., especially in Virginia); or it may tend toward the poly-centric form but appear as a more leveled pattern of disassociated "urban villages" or "edge cities" (as in the areas surrounding Kansas City and Phoenix).

With respect to journey-to-work patterns, land use appears as con-duits along which people carry on social and economic activities. Patterns can be seen in the volume of traffic flows on main arteries and city streets. Traffic volumes may paint a land-use pattern different from the built cityscape because the overall physical structure cannot be reconfigured in the short run to match constantly shifting concentrations of use. As a con-sequence, some old metropolitan areas may appear spatially to have a vi-tal core-city cone while intraurban traffic patterns show a more isolated core that has long since lost its activity to the near suburbs and outlying areas (as in the downtowns of Los Angeles and San Jose).

According to a spatial-form thesis, policy outcomes should be skewed by the degree and array of concentration in urban activities. For example, density and conical shape have been historically associated with economic development potential. Even though many contend this relationship has been weakened by twentieth-century transportation and communications technologies, some scholars have recently found that spatial form matters in the variegation and development of economic activity (see, e.g., Suarez-villa and Walrod 1997).

As the model in Figure 1.3 indicates, all rival theses are directed at an inquiry into the external setting and conditions that seem to hold the greatest potential as determinants of policy outcomes. Of course, internal bureaucratic considerations probably have interactive effects with some environmental influences, but the analysis of results, which supplements regression statistics with agency executive interviews and other qualitative materials, indicates that intraorganizational considerations are secondary. Furthermore, preliminary analysis found that organization structure, the use of strategic planning, managerial compensation, and professionalism probably have roles in skewing outcomes but were similarly employed by all agencies studied, thus leaving little variance to analyze.

Executive leadership style and managerial culture are two exceptions. The sample interviews show important variance from agency to agency in the openness and entrepreneurial character of chief administrative officers. They also suggested that the culture in some agencies was more egalitarian and sympathetic to disadvantaged stakeholders; in others it seemed to be more business-oriented. But these distinctions are more the result of external socioeconomic conditions than of being isolated intraorganizational determinants of policy outcomes. In the case of leadership, transit is an industry where CAOs enjoy a very short tenure (typically about three to five years), which perhaps gives them time to set changes in motion but seldom enough to leave a permanent imprint without precursor momentum from external sociopolitical forces. Likewise, internal managerial culture seldom persists unless it is compatible with the surrounding political culture.

Methodology

To test the significance of rival theses in explaining variance in outcome patterns, the research employs multiple regression. This statistical technique provides a basis for analysis by showing the effect of independent variables on each outcome perspective, making for a total of three regression model results (a fourth is eliminated because urban scale alone proved to be the only significant determinant of agency variance). A comparison of the effects of independent variables according to each outcome perspective reveals the cause of outcome skewness specific to the pieces of the overall asymmetric pattern. Moreover, because the determinant variables would not hold the same significance of effect across all pattern components, this approach allows determinants to be seen in the more complex role they play in policymaking bias.

Organization of the Book

This book is an empirical study of applied social science theory. It first lays out testable hypotheses that might explain why or how public agencies design policy outcomes that favor the interests of some publics more than others. It then engages in an analysis using both the quantitative results of multiple regression and qualitative information from agency interviews and other documentary materials. Part I reviews the meaning of governmental performance in the context of a plural society; Part II describes rival theses purporting to explain the policymaking bias; and Part III analyzes empirically the relative explanatory significance of the rival theses in explaining the bias in policy outcomes.

Chapter 2 defines the study's dependent variables. It focuses first on problems of measuring and interpreting policy outcomes in a political economy of diverse constituencies. The chapter raises the fundamental problem of judging governmental performance with a biased eye and makes essential distinctions between two ways to conceive of performance evaluation. One of these is a single-standard method that judges agency results on a monoscale of best to worst; the other is a multiple-perspectives method that judges outcomes relative to different constituencies. The chapter proposes a formal framework for comparing and empirically analyzing the patterns of bias found among a class of agencies in a particular public sector.

The three chapters of Part II are devoted to a grouping of the rival theses described above. Their purpose is to make an accounting of the theoretical constructs found in the literature that bring relevance to the issue of patterned bias in policy outcomes. The concept descriptions are used to draw appropriate hypotheses that are tested as part of the model offered in Figure 1.3. Chapter 3 develops rival theses of a socioeconomic nature, including an upper middle class genre, regional wealth, and the underclass. The core concepts here come from economics, sociology, and social psychology. Chapter 4 develops theses about the nature of federalist government and develops the notion of intergovernmental power and agency autonomy. The core concepts here are from interorganizational exchange theory found in the "new institutionalism" literature. Chapter 5 introduces theses about competitive markets and the spatial dimension of the urban setting.

Part III analyzes the results. In Chapter 6 the focus is principally on interpreting the regression statistics, reporting initial results on what variables matter directly in skewing outcomes. Chapter 7 revisits the initial findings of Chapter 6 but continues with an analysis of indirect relationships. Using a path analysis, it seeks to identify relationships among the rival-thesis variables that would provide new insight beyond the initial results. Chapter 8 paints a larger picture of what the direct and indirect relationships mean by synthesizing the theses and drawing out implications for further study. It is here where several previously unexplored relationships emerge to invigorate future thinking about variances in the way policymakers skew outcomes. The book concludes with Chapter 9 as a note on how "globalization" plays into the discussion of policymaking bias in an increasingly "transterritorial" world.

2　Policy Outcomes from a Multiple-Constituencies Perspective

Much has been said about the American public's penchant for "accountable government" and its concomitant distaste for bureaucracies. Even more has been written about how to "reengineer" public agencies to make them perform more efficiently and professionally. For many, the dominant theme has been that, if reformable at all, the public sector needs agencies modeled after corporate business. This persuasion argues that government should provide a kind of "product assurance" that agency outcomes are compliant with a set of "customer demands" defined as *the* public interest. Yet in a plural society, whether an agency has done well for its constituencies can never be known from a single or monolithic perspective. When policy outcomes affect many different publics and policymakers skew agency results by emphasizing one over another, accountability takes on a character vastly different from how the term is applied today, especially in its use as an ideological weapon against government legitimacy.

Contrary to the many indictments on bureaucracy, this book finds the problem of accountability and legitimacy to be mostly a matter of perception rather than government resistance to imitating corporate America. That is, if accountability is about the consequences of government action on different people's lives, then performance will always seem problematic because judging outcomes cannot be done from a single prism of consensual neutrality. We must always ask: accountability from whose perspective? Agency performance lies in the mind of the beholder, and in a plural society there are many public minds with which to reckon.

Moreover, concerns about accountability are really just symptoms of policymaking bias resulting from an agency's response to societal diversity and scarce resources. Hence we are compelled to ask: What does it mean to say a public agency performs well or that its policy outcomes are legitimate? If an agency operates efficiently, is it successful? If it is inefficient, does it necessarily lack a basis for good performance? Can a parity be struck among contending performance objectives, or do evaluations of outcomes inherently require prioritizing to a single bottom line? Is the problem a case of administrative mismanagement or a case of multiple ways to legitimately weigh policy outcomes? In a plural society full of disagreements over what values matter more, should we expect to reach consensus about what our public agencies do for us?

I begin this study on policymaking bias with an outcomes model that assumes being a public agency requires addressing many different and often contradictory interests. Once legitimized by political processes, these contending interests form a comparative structure of multiple competing stakeholder perspectives. Since good and bad policymaking is subject to wide interpretation in a plural society, the purpose of a multiple-prisms approach is to concentrate on how agencies vary in their outcome biases rather than on making hegemonic or monolithic value judgments about the character of outcomes. In light of diversity and scarcity, three situations or occurrences obviate the questionable value of judging outcomes from only one perspective.

First is the adverse political impact of sacrificing legitimate policy considerations. Agencies have grown accustomed to being examined by oversight committees, scholarly researchers, and the public looking for a bottom line on which to base findings and grievances. The overarching standard most often applied by these observers to judge performance is efficiency. To wit, during the last decades of the twentieth century, urban public agencies operated under severe fiscal constraints enacted in response to "antigovernment" forces bent on cutting waste and making bureaucracies more efficient.

This approach was often supported by the scholarly community, where studies came to prominence because they highlighted scandalous overpayments for an agency tool or a subcontractor's services or uncovered noncompliance with budgets (Downs and Larkey 1986; Grizzle 1984). However, the popularity of this monolithic standard resulted in the deemphasis of other valued and legitimate outcomes, causing frequent budget crises and service interruptions. Given a diverse society often entrenched in divisive conflicts, a single standard for judging outcomes neither captures agency dilemmas regarding policy tradeoffs nor reflects how performance criteria vary across a field of multiple stakeholders.

Second, with rapidly diminishing fiscal resources, urban agencies that were formerly loosely coupled have pooled resources and become parts of tighter intergovernmental webs of policymaking and coproduction. Public problems have become the joint responsibility of agencies with very different mandates and stakeholders. The result has been that agencies find themselves in a far more complex and conflicting "metapolicy" environment (Gustafsson 1983), where each must consider policies from many more perspectives and design programs in light of their overlapping or reciprocal impacts on each other. Such a setting involves paradoxical and interdependent views on expected policy outcomes. In transit, for example, taxpayers expect the administrative agency to use quantitative business methods to achieve efficient operations. Other constituencies insist the agency develop policies that meet the needs of the transit-dependent poor and that are consistent with nontransit demands for cooperative land-use planning, retrofitting for the handicapped under ADA, providing de facto homeless shelters, and cost-sharing of urban development projects collateral to transit. Even if one were to remove efficiency from consideration, being effective across all these social-program areas requires enormous resources, which agencies seldom have available.

Third, most reengineering advocates have focused the search for evil on internal administrative processes when the pattern of policy outcomes may be more frequently the result of external influences (see, e.g., Osborne and Gaebler 1992). Ignoring the politics and nature of public goods, they often assume agencies can produce clearly defined services sold through market exchanges involving a homogeneous set of paying clients. Reengineering agency policies around "customers," packageable goods, and corporate organizational processes misses most of what is legitimately political in public policymaking in a federalist system. As a common shortcoming, the reengineers are barking up the wrong tree by advocating solutions for which they have yet to find the problem. Concluding that agency administrations need to adopt a business mentality badly misconstrues the nature of policy outcomes and the inherent ambiguities of performance evaluation in public organizations.

With these three difficult situations in policymaking, we begin the twenty-first century with vastly different visions of government bureaucracy than our Progressive forefathers did at the beginning of the previous century. Then as now, the performance focus was on efficiency and promoting innovation. But unlike in the present, optimism about "good government" flourished and hopes abounded that the nation's public agencies would lead the way, alongside business, in making capitalism work for all people. Over the course of the century, that optimism was rewarded with the development of a robust public sector economy that helped build huge electrical power systems, provide essential social and economic safety nets to maintain long-term job security and consumer confidence, lead the world in designing new institutions of higher learning for the masses, provide research funding and delivery systems for vast improvements in world health, build the world's most cost-effective transportation infrastructure, and provide countless other achievements requiring competent, innovative, and professional public policymaking.

Today much of that optimism is replaced with cynicism based on real or supposed government waste together with many inane rules that restrict the human innovative spirit. According to polls, most Americans have a profound distrust of government bureaucracies, and it seems most citizens have turned their backs individually and collectively on the plight of public economy providers. This shift in public sentiment is surely more than a spontaneous change in perceptions. But what are its sources? Much occurred during the twentieth century that might explain the public's growing apprehension about bureaucratic performance, including bureaucratic malfeasance.

Ironically, though, chief among the seminal causes is the triumph of the new order of business-government partnerships that had its intellectual roots in American Progressivism. In the early part of the twentieth century, most citizens, politicians, and scholars were concerned about a transformation of society from agrarian subsistence to urban affluence. Even though cultural tradeoffs and uncertainty about the ensuing changes made many anxious about their individual prospects (Wiebe 1967), most bought into the promise of a better life and higher standard of living. With government's central role in providing services and infrastructure for the new urban socioeconomic vision of modernization, belief was widespread that public agencies exercised a legitimate and productive purpose in promoting "welfare-at-large."

Indeed, for most of that century, this term was sufficient to justify the outcomes of public policymaking and agency programs without attaching specific performance criteria to those outcomes (see, e.g., Pinchot 1910 on managing national forestlands; or Goodnow 1900 and Willoughby 1919 on urban administration). The nation had come to accept an abstract single standard for its governmental agencies just as it had embraced corporate profitability. Aside from a small community of scholars and muckraking journalists (see Veblen 1948; Steffens 1931), few asked how government operated or corporate profits were made. Why should they query public agencies about the specifics of how policy outcomes met the welfare standard? Equity and egalitarian values seemed to be satisfied by some abstract calculation of the "greatest good for the greatest number over the long run" (Pinchot 1910).

During the rise of Progressive achievements, few (at least among the voting public) found substantial reason to question the calculation. Until the 1960s the economic system was viewed mostly as a successful partnership of business and government that together had been responsible for the massive (though periodically interrupted) spread of affluence throughout society. Although restlessness in some academic circles brewed from the beginning, societal seeds of discontent were more likely sown by the triumph of Progressivism itself. The singular belief in the means of prosperity had ushered in an "end of ideology" (Bell 1960) and produced a society that seemed remarkably homogeneous in aspirations, lifestyle, and culture. However, as first demonstrated by discontented youthful baby boomers in the 1960s, the spread of affluence freed many to aspire to new and variant lifestyles. But the triumph of Progressivism also stretched the scale of affluence, where most of the newly affluent were leaving less-well-off minorities and newly arrived immigrants further behind.

For public agencies this meant a proliferation of specialized constituencies where before there had been mainly economic distinctions between haves and have-nots. In urban transit, for example, the middle-class paying commuter was pulled away to the suburbs by the automobile and partly replaced by a variety of mostly nonpaying clients (minorities, the aged, the poor, the handicapped, and the homeless). Where transit had been seen principally as a vital service to a healthy metropolis (we still see nostalgia-inducing film clips of early transit), it eventually also came to be viewed as a necessary evil to maintain the labor supply for core-city employers and inadvertently provided access for criminals to invade the suburbs. Not even environmentalists could see transit in a common beneficial light.

With a widening role for urban services in an increasingly affluent society, political actors came to have "significantly different expectations about bureaucratic performance" (Gruber 1987: 142). Public agencies found themselves trying to please many masters, most of whom disagreed among themselves as to what policies were legitimate for the public sector. In transit, was it appropriate for a public agency to compete with the private sector for "customers," or should it only supplement automobile commuting by providing services mainly for indigent or disadvantaged "clients"? Although the differences between business management and public administration provide for a rich intellectual discussion, business is distinctly different in its lexical ordering of profitability as its pinnacle objective. Although we speak of business "social responsibility" as a desirable secondary objective, public sector organizations must perform according to multiple legitimate stakeholders, many of whom are nonpaying clients but hold contending political status in agency policymaking.

Policy Outcomes as Agency Performance: Conceptual Foundations

With traditions in both politics and administrative science, urban policy research might be expected to have produced a robust literature on multiple-perspective valuation of outcomes. But generally, this is not the case. In administrative science, some developed frameworks that abstractly relate outcome performance to multiple constituencies (Quinn and Rohrbaugh 1983; Quinn and Cameron 1983; Cameron 1986), but their work is difficult to operationalize empirically. For example, Quinn and Rohrbaugh developed a framework for classifying the organizational performance literature around generic conceptualizations, but not for empirically grounded research on comparing organizations. In political science, most constituency-based research on policy outcomes is in the form of case studies (e.g., Pressman and Wildavsky 1973; Sayre and Kaufman 1965; Danielson and Doig 1982). Only a few studies have attempted intersubjective methodologies to identify what constituencies exist for an organization (Tsui 1990; Grizzle 1984), and none until recently successfully derived a framework for large-scale empirical analysis associating different stakeholder-based outcomes with patterned bias in policymaking (see Boschken 1992).

One reason for the oversight is that, while recognizing multiple constituencies, the literature tends to focus on prioritizing performances by advocating a single or "pinnacle" standard of evaluation that leaves important constituencies out in the cold (for a review, see Boschken 1994). This approach resolves the paradox by determining a public interest representing the "greater good," which takes precedence over multiple particularized interests. This penchant for determining a single index for evaluating policy outcomes begs a question central to urban politics and agency policymaking: Why does so much of the esteemed literature adopt this approach when it is clearly at odds with the competing values of American pluralism?

Two answers are evident. First, it is easier to understand the value of an agency's performance from a single standard because it reduces equivocation. Conflicting or contradictory outcomes of equal standing are messy for those seeking to compare agencies on a best-worst continuum of performance. Second, public organizations have developed under the shadow of Progressivism, which held that a single public interest should be culled from the many interests of society so as to provide clear guidance for agencies striving to achieve the welfare of society at large (Boschken 1982; Warren 1966; W. Wilson 1887).

The single-criterion logic notwithstanding, a multiple-perspectives analysis is not only more consistent with classical notions of pluralism (Lindblom 1977; Dahl 1961) but is also superior in at least two respects for analysts interested in policymaking bias. First, it provides a comparative framework that associates policy outcomes with respective stakeholder perspectives; and second, it allows an evaluation of tradeoffs among outcomes that shows an agency's relative emphasis in satisfying some interests over others. It does not speak to the determination of best-worst performing agencies, but rather to *skewness* in the *pattern* of outcomes that result from policymaking choices. Hence, in selecting a method for analyzing bias and responsiveness in a plural society, the focus should be on the asymmetric pattern created by the tradeoffs made in choosing among the agency's many stakeholder perspectives.

The idea of multiple perspectives has a long tradition in governmental studies and is also found in administrative theory, where it embraces the notion of organizations having many competing stakeholders upon which they are dependent for resources (Pfeffer and Salancik 1978). In this resource dependence view, public resources include not only revenue (i.e., legislated for statutory clients or won in market competition), but also management skills and experience, production labor, intergovernmental agreements, and other necessary contributions to organizational processes that potentially may be withheld. Constituencies today, then, include stakeholders who depend on the agency to realize their objectives and on whom the agency is dependent for resources.

According to Freeman (1984), constituencies may be both "generic" stakeholders common across most public sector organizations (e.g., executive and operational administrators, other metropolitan agencies with overlapping authority, environmentalists, taxpayers) and "specific" stakeholders unique to a particular public sector (in urban transit, e.g., statutory welfare riders, middle-class commuters, the federal Department of Transportation [DOT], urban economic-development interests, vehicle operators). In this sense, we may recognize public agencies as "coalitions of interests that face an environment of competing, frequently conflicting, demands which need resources from that environment" (Pfeffer and Salancik 1978: xii). Because constituencies are legitimized by political and other institutional processes, they can be identified through an analysis of applicable legislation, intergovernmental fiduciary relationships and agreements, service delivery systems used, labor contracts, and environmental impacts and regulations.

The MSOI Framework

Legitimized stakeholders and policy outcomes are categorized and associated according to conceptual traditions in policymaking and administration. As shown in Table 2.1, the framework employed in this study is constructed as a four-cell categorical matrix of multiple simultaneous outcome indices (MSOI). It is bounded by two orthogonal and dichotomous dimensions that provide an analytical structure that "weeds out the overlap and gets down to the core variables" (Campbell 1977: 39)

TABLE 2.1 A Multiple Simultaneous Outcome Indices (MSOI) Model
A Categorical Framework of Policy-Outcome Perspectives

| | Policy Legitimacy | |
Policy Focus	Administration-Centered (Economic Considerations)	Social-Centered (Political Considerations)
Strategic Outcomes	CELL I Outcome Perspective: **Organizational Effectiveness** • Are we marketworthy? • How much organizational eminence do we hold in our public sector?	CELL III Outcome Perspective: **Social-Program Effectiveness** • How well are we meeting legitimate political mandates?
Operational Outcomes	CELL II Outcome Perspective: **Operational Efficiency** • Are we minding the shop?	CELL IV Outcome Perspective: **Reciprocal Effectiveness** • What amount of value are we reciprocating to resource contributors?

for comparison of agencies within the same service delivery sector (e.g., urban transit, county mental health, K–12 education, or water resources). One dimension's significance is derived from a conceptual tradition in political science, the other from a convention in administrative science.

The first dimension dichotomizes legitimacy of authority by distinguishing the policymaking focus of any organizational activity as either *administration-centered* or *social-centered*. In dealing with the long-standing "publicness" issue and the sources of legitimate administrative authority, Bozeman argues that "organizations are not wholly public or private but are more or less public in respect to particular aspects of organizational activity" (1987: 86). He goes on to identify two separate sources of legitimated authority that determine the degree of publicness in the policy outcomes of those organizational activities.

The first source is economic authority and prescribes the organization's marketworthiness and ability to grow and maintain itself in a resource-dependent setting. This administration-centered legitimacy is the perspective of agency bureaucrats who have career and institutional interests that may not be entirely congruent with their agency's formal political missions (Moe 1990: 143). Political authority is the contrasting source and refers to the agency's public-regarding obligation in responding to social needs spelled out by organic statutes and other legislative mandates, intergovernmental agreements, and public opinion. Similar dichotomous distinctions in this tradition are also found in the literature on market-centeredness and social progressivism (Kantor, Savitch, and Haddock 1998; Logan and Molotch 1987), on efficiency and effectiveness (Downs and Larkey 1986; Pfeffer and Salancik 1978), and in the study of bureaucracy and politicians (Aberbach, Putnam, and Rockman 1981; Niskanen 1971).

In the MSOI matrix, constituencies and policy outcomes classified as administration-centered (cells I and II) address two perspectives. First is effectiveness in growing the agency's organizational stature by either capitalizing on market opportunities or acquiring broader (or dominant) jurisdictions and bigger shares of revenue from intergovernmental exchanges. The second is efficiency in operating service-delivery activities. Those classified as social-centered (cells III and IV) address effectiveness in satisfying the agency's political mandates by providing beneficial social programs and reciprocating value to resource contributors.

The second dimension is derived from a convention in administrative studies (Ansoff and Brandenburg 1971) that dichotomizes policy outcomes into *strategy-focused* and *operations-focused* categories. Strategic outcomes (cells I and III) address the well-being of the organization as a whole where vested stakeholders include executive management and external political actors seeking to articulate and achieve the agency's role and purpose in the public economy. They are concerned with the objectives of the organization as a public institution and who its legitimate social-program clients are.

Here, effectiveness in outcomes is determined either by how competitive an agency remains in acquiring the necessary resources to grow or by the design of client entitlements and how services fit social demands (Kaufman and Jacobs 1987). By contrast, operational outcomes (cells II and IV) address subpart functions of the organization and its external operational contributors. More functional and less global than strategic outcomes, this focus is on how resources are acquired and utilized to produce or deliver services. It is of primary concern to middle and lower-level managers seeking operational performance and to external resource providers (e.g., production workforce, subsidizing taxpayers) expecting to receive some return for their contributions to the agency process. It is also where environmentalists fit with their perceived role of protecting the natural ecology.

The two MSOI dimensions define the four cells as categorical policy perspectives, where each cell is distinct and necessary to understand the range of mindsets that bear on the agency's policymaking choices and allocation of resources. Together the four cells summarize the great issues of accountability and performance in public organization theory. All cells are assumed to hold equal legitimacy in the policymaking process, and no weights should be assigned to give one perspective preeminence over another. This allows pattern skewness to be entirely a reflection of emphasis in an outcome perspective's numerical values for each agency in the sample. According to the two dimensions, each cell's outcome perspective is defined in the following way.

Outcome I: Strategic Organizational Effectiveness

Outcomes in cell I represent degrees of "organization-wide effectiveness" (Campbell 1977: 36) in achieving strength, intensity, and scope in the organization's overall economic position (Nutt and Backoff 1997;

Niskanen 1975, 1971; Downs 1957). The perspective is most often as-sociated with an agency's senior management, which is focused on the marketworthy stature or budgetary size of the organization as a whole. For example, Niskanen argues that although senior bureaucrats may be motivated in the public interest, they are primarily focused on the sys-tem maintenance issues of the "whole budget" rather than the value of individual social programs that are part of the agency's budget (1971: 38–39).

With its professional stake, this constituency is charged with "identifying new strategies and new projects that will add to the organi-zation's overall strength" (Doig and Mitchell 1992: 22). This strategic po-sitioning may regard competing for market share or acquiring greater public appreciation in the public economy. Measures of this outcome fit a standard of strategic effectiveness because they show "the ability of an organization to exploit its environment to obtain resources, while main-taining an autonomous bargaining position" (Mindlin and Aldrich 1975: 382). The essential concerns of this perspective for policymakers are two: Are we marketworthy? And, how much organizational and fiscal stature do we possess in our public sector?

Outcome II: Operational Efficiency

Cell II outcomes are about an organization's "efficient ways of bringing services to the public" (Doig and Mitchell 1992: 21) and rep-resent goodness by minimizing cost per unit through "adherence to en-gineering standards [and] accounting rules" (p. 25). The perspective is focused on "a level of detail useful for managers with operating or super-visory responsibilities, but of scant usefulness for top level officials who have to determine organizational objectives and goals" (Schick 1970: 41). Moreover, though many presume this perspective to be compatible and synchronized with outcome I, the MSOI does not exclude a paradoxical relationship. The essential concern of this perspective is: Are we function-ally minding the store?

Outcome III: Social-Program Effectiveness

Outcomes in cell III demonstrate strategic effectiveness in design-ing services for mandated welfare clients. Natural market demands fail to occur for social programs because either (1) those who want certain outcomes do not have the means to pay, or (2) the costs and benefits of such outcomes cannot be meaningfully related to each other in market transactions. Since not all political demands are legitimate and worthy of government response, strategic public-regarding objectives and criteria for social-program effectiveness are usually determined by legislative mandates, interagency agreements, and an agency's traditional public role. For example, an Orange County Transit manager said, "I still believe a major traditional function of a transit agency is to provide mobility to those who cannot afford an automobile. It keeps them off the welfare rolls, so from a tax-base standpoint, it pays for itself even though the agency doesn't recover the savings" (Catoe 1989: 11). The essential concern of this perspective is: How well are we meeting legitimate political mandates?

Outcome IV: Reciprocal Effectiveness

The outcomes in cell IV encompass the reciprocal impacts of operations on external contributors who view themselves as voluntary or involuntary resource providers to the agency's service delivery process. The essential distinction between this cell's program-based reciprocal effectiveness and internal efficiency outcomes lies in the referent authority. An external stakeholder in cell IV holds politically legitimized concerns about what it is getting for its resource contribution, whereas a managerial referent in cell II holds economic authority to control the cost structure in producing services. Outcomes regarding reciprocal effectiveness are associated with the agency's production workforce, taxpayers, and a class of involuntary constituencies concerned about minimizing their exposure to the organization's externalities (i.e., pedestrian and vehicle accidents, pollution, and blight). The essential concern of this perspective for policymaking is: What amount of value are we reciprocating to resource contributors?

Each of the four MSOI cells represents not a single stakeholder but groups of constituencies who hold a common or generic interest in a particular policy perspective for a class of agencies. Constituencies are matched with a cell concept according to the agency's source of legitimating authority and the constituency's policy focus. Empirical measures for each cell are derived from an analysis of constituency demands and form the basis for constructing an index value for each cell. Empirical analysis of MSOI involves comparing the index value for each cell in the matrix to observe a pattern or profile. In seeking a pattern skewness among the four cells, the framework relies on an index of multiple measures because it offers greater validity than any single measure.

Values for the cell indices are determined by a two-stage methodology. In the first stage, each performance measure making up a cell index is calculated using a regression technique that produces residuals estimating outcome "frontiers" for the agency sample adjusted for scale (i.e., all agencies are made equal according to scale). In the interest of producing scale-equivalent agency values, this technique incorporates more global factors than nonregression techniques (e.g., ratio analysis), making it the best linear unbiased estimator of comparative data for policy outcomes. The resulting residual values for each agency are scattered according to the frontier that represents the upper boundary of achievable performance for the agency sample. In other words, one agency's performance relative to another's is based on its deviation from this frontier. For a detailed description of the technique, see Appendix B.

For the second stage, values for each measure are standardized (residuals divided by standard deviation [s.d.]) to provide a common scale for summing measures within cells and making them comparable across cells. The resulting four indices are the data representing policy outcomes that are used in this study as dependent variables in the analysis of pattern skewness. Each agency in the sample has four values from which a pattern of emphasis or bias is apparent relative to other agencies. Any pattern that shows emphasis (or deemphasis) in one or more outcome perspectives (i.e., an asymmetrical pattern) constitutes some type of *outcome skewness*. In other words, as deviations from intercell equity, the resulting pattern represents the outcome perspectives that are relatively more or less advantaged by agency policymaking choices.

The usefulness of the MSOI framework and its methodology, however, is limited by five considerations. First, because any conceptual framework establishes an analytical focus in its design, MSOI may be idiosyncratic to those not interested in metapolicymaking at the macroorganizational level. For example, those less likely to find value in it would include economists who prefer the single-issue or programmatic focus of cost-benefit analysis and human resource specialists focused on analyzing personnel performance. Second, MSOI is designed for application within a specific public service activity. Agencies from different sectors (e.g., transit, K–12 education, or police) cannot be pooled into the same sample for comparison because outcome-cell indices are based on sector-specific empirical measures.

Third, the degree of difficulty in applying the framework varies by sector. The easiest application is made to service sectors dominated by public enterprise agencies; the more difficult is to regulatory sectors dominated by line agencies. Fourth, MSOI cannot tell us whether sectorwide levels of performance are acceptable, mediocre, or bad. It is therefore of little use to those seeking to determine the "goodness" of a whole government sector. Fifth, the matrix consists of categorical cells, but this does not entirely eliminate the temptation to see some measures in a cell index as applicable to more than one cell concept. In the analysis of urban transit, every attempt has been made to deal with these limitations or make them irrelevant.

MSOI Application to Urban Transit

Since the early 1980s, transit has experienced both opportunity and fiscal constraints initiated by federal cutbacks during the Reagan and two Bush administrations. What emerged is a dual consciousness of the transit agency as both a distinct organizational unit or "business" and a more tightly coupled intergovernmental actor providing social programs related to regional mobility, employment opportunity, and economic development. The head of MARTA in Atlanta reflected on this, saying, "I operate on the basis that my job is to manage this organization as a business. We must market our service like an enterprise in contrast to traditional governments who do not. At the same time, we are a government agency and provide a vital service to the transit dependent. We've had a good balance between being a social agency and a business enterprise" (Gregor 1990: 18–19).

As a result of the many impinging external forces, agencies began to think more strategically about planning *alongside* their traditional concerns for daily operations (Fielding 1987; Perry and Babitsky 1986; Wachs 1985). But strategic management was not fully implemented by most agencies. Characteristic of this nouveau-awareness, the head planner at Orange County (California) transit said the agency was "trying to get more of a formal approach to strategic planning, but we're not far enough along to know how its going to function. Initially, we will hire a consultant to do the first strategic plan for the agency" (Van Sickel 1989: 12). At MARTA in Atlanta, an assistant general manager admitted, "We had no strategic planning to speak of at all until a department for this function was created by an agency reorganization in 1989" (Olson 1990: 12).

Furthermore, relative to the literature underlying the MSOI framework, the transit literature often misconstrues the relationship between strategic planning and policy outcomes. Specifically, much of urban transit research maintains either a narrow focus that usually emphasizes operational efficiency or a mass-measures approach that provides little structure for theory-based analysis. In the first instance, some leading transit observers maintain that "performance analysis for strategic management purposes should rest on efficiency measures" (Fielding 1987: 116). This leaves the impression that transit organizations have a single, clear objective around which general agreement should exist for all constituencies. It does not overtly recognize the question of outcome skewness; neither does it include performance emphasis in other than operations despite the strategic reference.

In the mass-measures approach, performance is represented by multiple measures allocated according to a fuzzy three-legged framework of "service inputs," "service outputs," and "service consumption" (UMTA 1988: 83; Fielding 1987; Perry and Angle 1980). This approach may seem broadly defined and theory-based, but it leaves considerable ambiguity about how measures relate as a pattern to each other and fosters confusion over which measures are relevant to what constituencies. Because the measures are about inputs and outputs, they do not represent outcome perspectives, leaving unaddressed the consequences of pattern skewness.

Advancing beyond these inadequacies, the MSOI framework is consistent with a multiple-perspectives assessment. This can be seen by revisiting the MSOI model (Table 2.1). In responding to competitive influences and in addressing social-program demands, transit agencies must answer to both economic and political authorities. Strategically, executive management's focus on urban commuter markets and the agency's

organizational stature (cell I) is contrasted with political mandates by local and state governments and the Federal Transportation Administration's (FTA) social-welfare agenda for the "transportation disadvantaged" (cell III).

With FTA and many state mandates, transit-dependent users include the working poor, urban-core employers and retailers, the low-
income elderly, the handicapped (ADA), and the nonworking poor who
rely on transit "mainly for noncommutation purposes" (Altshuler 1979:
299). Local elected officials and urban governments are also in the social-
program cell representing these constituencies as well as regional economic development proponents. As a consequence, many transit managers feel a need to place "a bit more emphasis on [social effectiveness]
because we're in a fishbowl and have to deal with accountability and the
taxpayers' dollars" (Reichert 1989: 10).

Operationally, specialized functional management units look after
production-flow outcomes (cell II), including route schedules, vehicle and
facilities maintenance, and capital equipment replacement. Also at the
operational level are those seeking reciprocal benefits for their contributions (cell IV). Labor and taxpayers track policy outcomes according
to their contributions as vehicle operators, maintenance personnel, and
taxpayer advocates. In addition, this reciprocating perspective includes
pedestrians, motorists, and environmentalists concerned about safe and
pollution-reducing operation of transit vehicles.

Policy Outcomes in Transit

Each of MSOI's four policy outcome indices is an aggregation of
three performance measures commonly used in urban transit (for detail
in calculating the twelve transit-specific performance measures, see Appendix B). Values for each of the forty-two agencies in the sample fall
along these continuum-scaled indices, which represent the comparative
degree of emphasis an agency places on each outcome cell. Table 2.2 reports clusters of agencies at the scale extremes for each of the outcome
emphasis cells. Extremal clusters of emphasis and deemphasis vary in
number of agencies included and show which agencies distinctively lead
and lag the sample for each cell index.

TABLE **2.2** MSOI Cell Emphasis: Extremal Clusters
Urban Public Transit, 1987–1991

	Outcome Perspective Cell			
	I: Organizational Effectiveness	II: Operational Efficiency	III: Social-Program Effectiveness	IV: Reciprocal Effectiveness
Top-Cluster Agencies (*emphasis*)	N = 4	N = 6	N = 6	N = 5
	Philadelphia	Los Angeles	BART*	Chicago
	Washington, D.C.	Houston	Washington, D.C.	Houston
	San Francisco	Seattle*	Atlanta	Atlanta
	Boston*	San Antonio*	San Francisco	Los Angeles
		St. Louis	Los Angeles	St. Louis
		Philadelphia	Chicago	
Bottom-Cluster Agencies (*deemphasis*)	N = 2	N = 2	N = 4	N = 4
	St. Louis	Boston	Dallas	Dallas
	Los Angeles**	Washington, D.C.**	Buffalo**	Boston
			St. Louis	Cleveland**
			Denver**	Seattle**

NOTE: * = Agency appears in only one emphasis cluster.   ** = Agency appears in only one deemphasis cluster.

The table shows no common pattern of outcome skewness for the sample as a whole. However, most agencies in emphasis clusters (69 percent) are leaders in two clusters (Los Angeles has three emphases). This pattern suggests that some outcome perspectives are combined by some groups of agencies (i.e., two-cell combinations sharing a common side of the matrix's dichotomous dimensions). For example, Philadelphia leads in the emphases of two administration-centered cells, while Chicago and Atlanta share dual emphases in social-centered perspectives. San Francisco and Washington, D.C., share dual emphases in strategic policy cells, while Houston and St. Louis lead in both operational policy perspectives.

Further, a significant minority of the agencies in extreme emphasis clusters (38 percent) are also found in extreme deemphasis clusters, suggesting that many depend on outcome tradeoffs to achieve emphasis leadership. For example, at the time of this study, WMATA (Washington, D.C.) was an extremal emphasizer of strategic effectiveness (cells I and III) and achieved this aggressive focus while deemphasizing efficiency. The agency's assistant general manager acknowledged WMATA's strategic preoccupation, saying, "Our primary goal is to increase ridership and revenue. So we market to both the private and public sectors. We also are one of the leading agencies in the country to own and operate commercial development at our metro stations. . . . We are very customer oriented" (Mitchell 1993: 1–2). However, it was due to this extremal tradeoff of efficiency for effectiveness that the agency brought in David Gunn, the renowned transit efficiency reformer, as its CAO during the study period. Reflecting on the extreme tradeoff, he noted: "They knew they were going to hit the wall sometime. Costs were out of control" (Gunn 1993: 11).

In contrast to emphasis clusters, dual deemphasis patterns are less frequent, and most were due to individual circumstances. St. Louis, for example, is second only to Detroit as a manufacturing center for automobiles. Its extremal deemphasis of both strategic effectiveness perspectives is related to the population's focus on cars: "St. Louis is a big automobile town. People like their cars here, and big ones at that . . . even more than Californians do" (Stauder 1993: 10). As a result, transit is tolerated as a "supplement" to the automobile but is not indulged in. More characteristic of the sample, then, is a single deemphasis to shore up emphases. Sixty-seven percent of the forty-two agencies lag in only one out-

TABLE **2.3** The Dependent Variables Composing the MSOI Pattern
Descriptive Statistics and Intercorrelations for 42 Transit Agencies

Variable	Mean	s.d.	1	2	3	4
1. Outcome I	10.99	2.27	—			
2. Outcome II	13.01	2.74	−.56**	—		
3. Outcome III	12.29	2.53	.48*	−.38*	—	
4. Outcome IV	10.07	1.24	−.22	.23	.18	—

NOTE: $N = 42$. Two-tailed significance: * = .01 ** = .001. Outcome perspective cells: Outcome I = Strategic Organizational Effectiveness; Outcome II = Operational Efficiency; Outcome III = Social-Program Effectiveness; Outcome IV = Reciprocal Effectiveness.

come perspective. The twenty-six agencies not shown in Table 2.2 neither emphasize nor deemphasize outcomes in the extreme.

As the study's dependent variables, the four continuum-scaled indices are intended to be MSOI components shaping the pattern of skewness in outcome emphasis. As shown in Table 2.3, the outcome indices have significant intercorrelations, confirming that they are consistent with the MSOI concept of an interrelated profile of outcome perspectives. Data-quality tests indicate that two essential statistical conditions were satisfied for use in this study. First, according to descriptive statistics and a frequency analysis, each cell index contains data approximating a normal distribution. Second, three tests confirm that the outcome indices are statistically different from each other in means and variances. An analysis of variance (ANOVA) shows significant differences in index means (F value = 13.77 for four groups with three degrees of freedom). The F-test comparing the two outcome indices with the greatest differences in variance indicates significance (F = 4.85 at the .05 level). A principal components analysis shows that the indices are sufficiently different from one another as to require three indices to explain 94 percent of the variability.

Perhaps the best test of all, though, was the acknowledgment by many agency executives interviewed in this study who attributed accuracy to the MSOI data. For example, looking at the data found in Table 2.2, a Bi-State (St. Louis) executive said, "We would like to tell you that we do well in all four outcome perspectives, but in reality, emphasizing operational outcomes is where we belong. We were amazed at how someone who didn't know us, had never talked to us, or probably hadn't even been here could peg us so well. We had quite a bit of discussion about that in a staff meeting" (Stauder 1993: 24).

Given these statistical tests for data quality and independence, the results reported in Table 2.3 are reliable and consistent with the MSOI concept and structure. The samplewide correlation matrix shows three out of the six bivariate associations to be significant (outcome cell IV associations contain all of those not significant). One of the positive correlations is between the two strategy-focused policy cells ($r = .48$, signif. $= .01$). Irrespective of their individual association with operational efficiency, the strategic cells' intercorrelation may represent the effect of long-term planning in meshing the administrative and political missions of transit agencies. Pointing to a strategic mission directed at "a little of both" perspectives, one transit executive echoed the sentiment of many: "I see us in the business of providing transportation to a paying market, to be an asset to the community in terms of economic development, and providing transportation to those who cannot afford to own their own automobile. Kind of a mixed bag" (Sehr 1993: 8).

The other two bivariate associations show inverse (negative) correlations and represent a significant source of pattern skewness caused by tradeoffs among outcomes. These tradeoffs indicate difficulty in achieving equity among competing policy perspectives. The most significant of these is between the two administration-centered outcome perspectives—strategic organizational effectiveness and operational efficiency ($r = -.56$, signif. $= .001$). Although administrative theory sometimes poses that striving to be efficient should also enhance an agency's emphasis on organizational effectiveness, the data show this not to be an industrywide convention in transit.

Indeed, some interview evidence indicates that a logical reason for the tradeoff is a lack of resources to be strategically effective caused by an emphasis on efficiency. A strategic planner from an efficiency-emphasizing agency said, "We are not as innovative as we probably need to be because we are pretty well understaffed [owing to their emphasis on efficiency] and the situation is that every hour of every day is spent on the tasks immediately in front of us" (Stauder 1993: 17). This tradeoff, however, is not made by all agencies in the same direction. Some solve the paradox in favor of organizational effectiveness, others solve it favoring efficiency, and still others maintain the paradox by not emphasizing either perspective.

The other tradeoff is between social-program effectiveness and operational efficiency ($r = -.38$, signif. $= .01$) and was expected in light of the redistributive and regulatory nature of social programs. Again, though, agencies do not resolve the paradox by favoring one direction or the other. As shown even in the extreme cases of Table 2.2, some agencies, such as Bi-State Development in St. Louis, sacrifice social effectiveness for operational efficiency, while others, such as WMATA in Washington, D.C., emphasize social effectiveness and deemphasize efficiency.

In contrast with associations between the first three indices, all of the insignificant intercorrelations are found in associations with outcome cell IV. This is primarily because residual values for this index show only about half the variance (mean $= 10.07$, s.d. $= 1.24$) of the other three outcome indices. In effect, variance in emphasizing this cell's reciprocal effectiveness is principally a function of scale. According to bivariate regressions of the index's underlying three performance measures, 80 percent of cell IV's variance is determined by an agency's system size and jurisdictional population. Much of the residual 20 percent is probably due to normal statistical error, leaving little of substance to explain. Indeed, none of the many independent variables tested as potential determinants of outcome skewness were at all significant in explaining variance in cell IV. For this reason, the outcome perspective of reciprocal effectiveness was not considered further in this study. Size alone determines this perspective's inclusion in the patterned skewness of policy outcomes.

This chapter provides a foundation for conceptualizing different policy outcome perspectives and establishes the comparative dependent variables necessary to proceed with the analysis of rival theses. This concludes the description of MSOI and its application to policy outcomes in urban transit. In the search for what matters most in determining policy-making bias, the next part provides conceptual propositions from various literatures to form each of those competing theses.

II   *Rival Theses*

3 The Upper-Middle-Class Genre and Other Socioeconomic Influences

Socioeconomic data tell us a lot about urban lifestyle and the human condition. They reflect relative affluence of the population, social class, income stratification and poverty, cultural diversity, and myriad other factors that define the urban macro-fabric on which the daily lives of individuals play out. Through formally collected and experientially acquired demographic information, agency policymakers are said to sense contours in this societal fabric that have bearing on what policy options matter most. From a systems perspective, this socioeconomic backdrop contains aggregate influences that Easton (1965) describes as "intrasocietal" inputs with the capacity to determine how and what choices are made by organizational policymakers.

With respect to the skewing of policy outcomes, some scholars have argued that policymakers perceive and respond to demographics as a symbolic pattern of human needs and wants. However, the abstract or anonymous nature of demographics often leaves theories about the route of causation unclear and difficult to verify. Do demographic profiles act mainly as anonymous signs of the human condition that impact policymaking separately from that of individuals' actions in markets and political arenas? Or are demographics inert, requiring their influence to be felt through overt and focused political activism of individuals and groups? The debate is over whether socioeconomic determinants of policy outcomes can be a function simply of "being something rather than doing something" (Pitkin 1967: 67).

In this chapter, three theses are developed about how demographics, separate from their expression in political action, might influence the skewing of policy outcomes. The first of these brings together writings about an upper-middle-class (UMC) genre that is characterized as an anonymous symbolic representation of a lifestyle near the top of the social ladder. The UMC thesis argues that agencies skew policy choices in reference to an image of this influential social class. The second thesis deals with household wealth and argues that affluence of the metropolitan population brings to policymaking an issue of resource dependence. Here, the fiscal capacity to emphasize social-program effectiveness is said to depend on the magnitude of an urban area's tax base derived from income and property values. The third thesis is about an urban "underclass" and the role race and poverty play in policy choices regarding who gets what from the public economy. For each of these theses, hypotheses are drawn about specific effects on skewing policy outcomes. The chapter concludes with a description of operational variables for each of the socioeconomic theses.

The Upper-Middle-Class Genre

The upper middle class in American society is a highly permeable socioeconomic grouping, consisting of individuals whose status is tied to modern and postmodern institutions formed from the industrial and information revolutions of the twentieth century. Drawn together by these institutional roots, the UMC is "distinguished by its members' sharing a common culture" and "defined as the interaction patterns connecting a set of people" (Lindblom 1977: 223). The bonding agent is found in the sharing of a "similar spirit, similar experiences, even roughly similar aspirations" (Wiebe 1967: 113). By the late twentieth century, noted scholars such as Robert Reich were referring to the UMC as "the glass tower people" who were "economically ascendant, college educated and professionally employed" (quoted in Farney 1994: 1).

The UMC is not part of a traditional hierarchical social structure but the result of a "revolution in identity" (Wiebe 1967: 113). As a genre, the UMC is that segment of a stratified but fluid society that consists of urbane professionals whose lives derive meaning from the institutional venues in which they circulate and the positions of responsibility they occupy in large corporate, government, and nonprofit organizations. For those outside this genre, the UMC appears to be at the top of the socioeconomic pyramid. But it should not be confused with the much smaller "invisible" upper class whose transgenerational capital wealth and connections protect their members from social infiltration. Unlike an upper class, the UMC is composed of socially mobile individuals who must work or have worked to support their socioeconomic position and cosmopolitan lifestyle.

Such position and lifestyle, however, are often but wrongly measured by consumption patterns that foster yet another potential confusion about who is included in the identity. The UMC is a *resource-based* social class distinguished by its acquisition of intellectual, positional, and fiscal capital strategic to institutional identification (i.e., education, professional position, income growth). The genre, therefore, is not equivalent to the *consumption-based* Yuppie, which is probably composed partly of UMC but mostly of others attempting to emulate the social class by mimicking a transient pattern of material acquisition.

Although it is conventional to recognize UMC influence through political activism and civic engagement of individuals (Verba, Schlozman, and Brady 1995; Pitkin 1967), the picture drawn by this lesser-acknowledged thesis is not about the active tacit collusion of a "power elite" (Mills 1956; Domhoff 1967). Indeed, as Brint argues about a decline of the UMC, "Professionals tend to lose their distinctive voice in public debate" because they lack a strong sense of connectivity between politics and their professional knowledge (1994: 17). The theories of *purposeful and direct* political action notwithstanding, the UMC thesis is focused on the *indirect and contextual* influence of a social identity made visible to policymakers as an anonymous demographic genre but not "individualized" as known persons or interest groups (Berger and Luckmann 1966: 30–34).

As Dahl (1961), Stone (1980), and others suggest in the case of indirect contextual influence, it is not necessary for a passive "actor" to intend that its preferences be taken into account in policymaking or even to be conscious that a power relationship exists. The essential thesis, then, is that a consistent set of UMC characteristics stands out from other factors to exert a "systemic power" defined by Stone as "the impact of the larger socioeconomic system on the predispositions of public officials" (1980: 979). Like the opinion cues of other anonymous identities such as the "median voter" (Miranda and Walzer 1994; Downs 1957), the perceived political preferences and power of the UMC gleaned from the genre may give them influence with policymakers.

The notion of an anonymous UMC genre systemically influencing agency policymakers takes on additional salience in light of increasing political apathy and declining civic engagement in America. Some scholars have argued that democratic governments' ability to produce fair and equitable outcomes in a plural society is compromised by a profound decline in face-to-face civic engagement in community and politics (see Skocpol and Fiorina 1999). The decline in civic engagement is attributed to a variety of causes, but the most compelling appear to be the bureaucratization of life coupled with the imposition of media and information technologies. Brint and Levy (1999), for example, found that "compartmentalization" of bureaucracy in professional organizations causes a break in individuals' links to public society and a subsequent decline in the civic engagement of organization members in politics. Much of the civic engagement now comes from impersonal functional organizations, "largely run by advocates and managers without members and marked by yawning gaps between immediate involvements and larger understandings" (Skocpol and Fiorina 1999: 462).

From an agency policymaker's perspective, this bureaucratic intervention and concomitant disconnect from individual expressions present the problem of losing access to reliable, broad-based political cues on which to premise policy outcomes. Because the compartmentalized organization is more likely to promote narrow or extreme positions unrepresentative of mainstream constituencies (Brint 1999), policymakers may consciously or otherwise seek alternative sources for cues. One potential source is the anonymous UMC genre, which may stand in policymakers' minds as an inspirational icon of preferences for the good life.

In light of the genre's potential role as a surrogate for civic engagement, the perceived content of UMC identity becomes central to policy choices. As Reich suggests, the attributes of the UMC are institutional trappings and influence bestowed by positional status, rather than consumer mimicry found in Yuppie look-alikes. Moreover, at the outset of the twenty-first century, much of the UMC's distinctive features have become based on the control and use of organized technical and managerial information—the dominant feature of postmodernization that has emerged since World War II. Bell (1976), for example, saw that the bearers of specialized theoretical knowledge (e.g., managers, medical and legal professionals, educators, some artists, and engineers) were a particularly privileged social set whose status and salaries matched their strategic role in shaping the emerging postindustrial culture. Lindblom concurs with his discussion of the institutional origins of this American "socioeconomic class" (1977: chap. 17).

Although the genre is mostly a post–World War II phenomenon, the first association of a new UMC with modern large-scale organization came at the end of the late 1800s and in the early twentieth century when the great transformation ushered in an urban industrial system to replace agrarianism. Wiebe characterized the "new social class" as having attributes bestowed by the emergence of large-scale bureaucracy and the new living arrangements of urbanization. As the agrarian society crumbled, "The specialized needs of an urban-industrial system came as a godsend to [an emerging professional class]. Identification by way of their skills gave them deference of their neighbors while opening natural avenues into the nation at large. . . . The ability to see how their talents meshed with others in a national scheme encouraged them to look outward confidently instead of furtively" (Wiebe 1967: 113).

However, agreement has never been universal on the exact composition of the genre as a distinct category within stratified society (for an overview, see Giddens 1973; Smith 1996: chap 5). Moreover, some have emphasized one or another UMC characteristic such as professional status (Brint 1994), higher education (Kerr 1963), or income (Reisman 1964). Others see distinct groupings within the UMC caused by different institutional and social affiliations (Ehrenreich 1989; Gouldner 1979). Still others are impressed with the genre as a distinct political culture (Clark 1998; Brint 1984; Lineberry and Fowler 1967).

This study takes a broader focus in constructing the UMC thesis as an internally consistent composite of these marginally different but interrelated perspectives. It is an attempt to identify those common themes that resonate across a body of writings which give structure and definition to the thesis. Hence, as a symbol of institutional influence, the profile described here consists of distinctions based on the confluent contributions of professional status, education, and income.

Of the three distinguishing characteristics, *professional status* is the most commonly used central tendency in referring to an upper middle class. Part of the reason is that the growth in size and number of American institutions has inflated the ranks of people engaged in activities requiring the systematic application of a relatively complex body of knowledge. Brint refers to these activities as creating a "matrix of contemporary professionalism . . . requiring advanced training in a field of learning and non-routine mental operations on the job" (1994: 1, 12). Reich adds to the characterization by referring to this class of organizational employee as "symbolic analysts" (1991). As a result, the UMC is most easily identified by its members' institutional titles and positions of responsibility, which to Veblen collectively amounted to symbols of society's "general staff" (1948: 440).

Although some distinguish between professionals and managers on the basis of profit motive and property ownership (see Brint 1994; Freidson 1986), these differences have become increasingly invidious. As seen especially in the behavior of those in knowledge-based industries (e.g., high technology, international finance, global media, and biotechnology), professionals and managers share similar lifestyles and institutional settings as a common source of identity and influence. Both use their training in the systematic application of knowledge gained in a university setting to accomplish their roles, and neither professionals nor managers own much business property other than stock options and retirement accounts. For these reasons, the use of the term "professional status" applies to both professionals and managers who "are the ranking staff in radically different kinds of organizations" (Brint 1994: 13).

A *college education* is often seen as equally central in defining UMC status, even though much of the curriculum seems broadly defined and less directly focused on professional job training. Clark Kerr, the father of the modern University of California system, pierced this unaffiliated "liberal arts" notion of academic freedom in his book on "the uses of the university" (1963). His query about the "partnership" of the "multiversity" with institutions of corporate business and government provides an important insight for understanding the role of the university in linking SES to higher learning. As the repository of scientific, technical, and organizational knowledge, the university is where individuals acquire the character of the educated class imbued with concepts of functional expertise and institutional protocol. Along with conceptual and humanistic knowledge, education imparts a common language, set of symbols, code of conduct, and awareness of institutional processes not shared for the most part by the non-UMC (Waldo 1948; Hartz 1955; Whyte 1956; Scott and Hart 1979; Brint 1994).

Regarding the relative affluence of the UMC, high and rising *income* not only provides the means to display independence from the "drudgery" of physical work but also helps provide access to those exclusive social venues that concentrate these "significant people" in their glass towers and status enclaves (Veblen 1948; Scott and Hart 1979). Riesman (1964) saw these new meanings in income as the result of a whole society moving from the "scarcity psychology" of agrarian roots to an "abundance psychology" of postindustrialism. Likewise, Maslow (1954) perceived this evolving abundance as a means of freeing those with surplus income from pursuing subsistence to "self-actualizing" higher-order needs, including the pursuit of socioeconomic activities with influence on style and institutional character. Veblen (1948) gave social-class context to the high-income earner by pointing out the underlying motives for "conspicuous consumption" of the emerging "leisure class" of engineers and managers. In short, the writings suggest that income alone may not offer much in distinguishing the UMC, but when used to buy into the resources and venues of institutional influence (e.g., university education, professional associations and clubs, political access) and to achieve higher-order pursuits, income becomes a significant characteristic of the profile.

The writings often associate these characteristics with the UMC's greater urgency or intensity in maintaining the genre's distinction from other SES groupings. Unlike aspirants from other social classes who try to emulate the UMC as material look-alikes, UMC members exhibit an "other-directedness" toward each other (Riesman 1961). The underlying motive is to maintain an "associational position" (Stone 1980) that affirms membership in this influential social genre (Ashforth and Mael 1989). To this end, "Consciousness of unique skills and functions characterized all members of the class. They demonstrated this by a proud identification as [professionals] . . . and by an eagerness to join others like themselves in professional organization" (Wiebe 1967: 112).

Why should such institutional membership matter so much? Riesman points to the need for social structure, saying that without aristocratic ancestry or a psychological "gyroscope" to establish influential position, behavior protocol, or esteemed social connection, UMC members acquire status and approval through continuous "responsive contact" with each other (1961: 23). All people seek social identity with particular groups (Turner 1985), but the UMC is set apart by a preoccupation with positional influence and "the process of striving itself" (Riesman 1961: 21).

If that is true, why is a UMC genre not more distinct empirically in its material trappings and social ambiance? Partly, it may be that striving to be known as influential does not require or depend on verbal contact. Social psychology research shows that individuals "interact" with others in a similar social position even when they have no formal communications (Lazar 1995; Burt 1987). Using nonverbal cues, the formation of anonymous groupings is based on the exhibition of *structural equivalence* in socioeconomic status.

The term defines "a measure of an individual's status, where individuals are sensitive to what other individuals of similar status are doing, believing, etc." (Lazar 1995: 4). This sensitivity involves prior consensus on discriminating categories, which Turner (1985) argues to be prototypical characteristics abstracted from the grouping. The UMC's professional status, university education, and economic ascendancy are convenient for determining structural equivalence because they can be openly displayed without verbal communication. Moreover, as their symbols of institutional achievement indicate (titles, degrees, organizational position, compensation level, and strategic affiliations), the characteristics hold in common a trait of subtlety in facilitating an individual's estimation of structural equivalence measured across a wide field of institutions, private and public. Their symbols can be innocuously displayed and acknowledged publicly in the course of institutional life without overt self-promotion or civic engagement.

For the most part, the writings bring together these SES characteristics as interlaced dimensions of a core profile that empirically distinguishes UMC from non-UMC (see, e.g., Verba, Schlozman, and Brady 1995). At various times in the twentieth century, other attributes were prominent as well, including race and religion (e.g., WASP "membership"), mobility, consumption patterns, and age. But their lack of empirical salience over time in defining structural equivalence makes them peripheral to the genre's persistent core profile outlined here.

Beyond what it means for self-identification of UMC members, the genre is also said to exhibit greater influence on society than its proportion of the population would indicate. If one were subscribing to a median-voter model of citizen preferences, the conclusion might be that such small numbers in the population could not have much influence as a demographic phenomenon. However, from the view of "culture as history," Susman (1984) counters that a UMC genre has been disproportionally influential across the century in scripting American ways of living and thinking. Referring to the genre as a symbol of aesthetic and material abundance, he calls it "the ideal for a culture," made more visible by media and education serving as a "means to help all move toward the ideal" (p. xxii). Lindblom concurs, saying that the "decline of class conflict" in America "might in fact indicate a rise in a success with which [the UMC] and its allies win all classes over to endorsing certain of its own attitudes, beliefs, and volitions, despite other evidence that class distinctions may be declining" (1977: 229).

What, then, is the connection to policy outcomes? Stone theorizes that the UMC exercises an indirect influence that "is completely impersonal and deeply embedded in the social structure" (Stone 1980: 981). That is, merely perceiving a predominant presence of the genre at the apex of society's "diamond-shaped distribution" of socioeconomic status (p. 983) may be sufficient to exert a "systemic power" affecting policy outcomes. A detailed example of this effect in transit is found in the regime politics of MARTA in Atlanta (Stone 1989). Getting a new region-wide transit district off the ground in the 1960s and 1970s was very contentious and required the cooperation of many and often conflicting groups in the greater Atlanta area.

Resolution was eventually reached by a pact founded on certain informally understood assumptions among politicians about the composition of the MARTA regime. Among them was the insistence that member groups be accountable to UMC expectations. In subsequent years, a cross-section of the agency's board has had the outward appearance of socioeconomic diversity but always the substance of one political culture. MARTA's general manager explained it this way: "I don't tell the politicians who to appoint, but I do remind them of the person they need. Just before Andy Young left office as Atlanta mayor, I told him if you want a black chair for the MARTA board, you need to appoint a prominent black businessman, not a civil rights leader" (Gregor 1990: 26).

At the heart of the thesis, then, are an implicit systemic influence and a cultural deference that give the genre its policymaking visibility. Moreover, as a potential surrogate for declining civic engagement, the genre's symbolic presence should vary across the transit agency sample according to the proportion of UMC in an agency's metropolitan population. The following hypotheses associate this proportion with the three emphases composing the field of policy outcomes.

Strategic Organizational Effectiveness (Outcome I)

Answering why the UMC genre promotes emphasis on the organizational stature of public agencies involves a two-step logic. First, UMC motives are defined by organizational values that promote administrative processes as a way of life. As "a vast complex of interlocking management systems, sharing a common set of values" (Scott and Hart 1979: 5), organizations provide a common arena for expressing "associational position" (Stone 1980: 982) and measuring structural equivalence. It is this "distinctive *employment situation* for the majority of professionals" (Brint 1994: 12) and the interlocking hierarchies that provide empathy and mobility across all types of organizations and beyond to "organization man" communities (Whyte 1956).

Second, *public* organizations in this interlocking institutional system represent an extension of the field of business (W. Wilson 1887) and play an instrumental albeit indirect role in a UMC lifestyle. Simon (1995), for example, claims that government organizations are equal partners of the American institutional structure in that they contribute to social stability and economic growth. "Free markets thrive, not in splendid isolation, but in a context of large and productive business and government organizations," the latter of which provide "effectiveness of infrastructure and public goods" (p. 404). Stone (1980) emphasizes further that agencies providing public infrastructure, education, and public safety are likely to have even greater UMC support than purely redistributional welfare agencies.

Hence, although clouded by current antigovernment sentiment of the median voter, the case for UMC commitment to maintaining eminent public organizations is based in both empathetic and practical motives. In that public agencies may be viewed as part of the larger professional class culture of administrative protocol and professional competence, we may conclude (Hypothesis 1) that:

> H1: The greater the proportion of UMC in an agency's service-area population, the greater the emphasis an agency will place on performance stressing outcomes of strategic organizational effectiveness.

Operational Efficiency (Outcome II)

The UMC is often painted as having subordinate concern for organizational efficiency, even though this interpretation has not always applied to the genre. Before World War II this class consisted mostly of small-business owners, family doctors and lawyers, and leaders of a much smaller public sector. The educated organizational professional had not yet emerged to replace the robber barons and other nouveaux riches as influential in American institutions. With the dominance of large impersonal corporate and government organizations in the post–World War II political economy, the old-order UMC was replaced by educated professionals who acquired their values and attitudes from the white-collar milieu of their employment situation.

Often floors above or miles away from the physical work of operations, very few UMC have a first-hand notion of production workflow efficiency. Separated from the mechanics of physical work, the professional's "intellectually demanding work" (Brint 1994) also does not lend itself well to providing practical criteria on which efficiency standards are based. Of equal importance, though, is the UMC priority of interests. Consistent with Maslow's (1954) hierarchical pursuit of "self-actualization" and Veblen's (1948) "conspicuous waste," the culture of institutional professionals extends from "best practices" learned in their education and employment settings. These practices give preferential weight to lavish marketing of the organization, liberal belief in institutional expense accounts, and reliance on product development and revenue growth for success. Cost efficiencies, in contrast, may well be accorded less attention and urgency by these "symbolic analysts" (Reich 1991) except during periods of fiscal crisis.

Projected across all institutional forms, the UMC may see efficiency as secondary. As Clark and Goetz explain, the new-order UMC "stress social issues and consumption over economic and fiscal issues . . . [and] increasingly want to enjoy their surroundings, even if they 'lose money' by doing so" (1994: 110). The implication would seem to be that when viewing the performance of all institutional forms, including the outcomes of public agencies, UMC expectations for efficiency would not be given priority over effectiveness outcomes in a tradeoff. Hence we are led to the proposition (Hypothesis 2) that:

> H2: The greater the proportion of UMC in an agency's service-area population, the more likely the agency will deemphasize operational efficiencies in favor of strategic (higher-order) effectiveness outcomes.

Social-Program Effectiveness (Outcome III)

Social-centered policy outcomes matter to the UMC, but why should they, except negative fiscal issues and unemployment concerns? With few exceptions, the UMC is seldom very cognizant of its "use" or dependence on most specific public services like transit, and even less so for those provided to nonmarket users. It therefore would not seem to have a vested interest in an emphasis on social programs. One counter-argument from traditional class theory contends, however, that the UMC are "social trustees" (Brint 1994) who accept noblesse oblige. Wilson and Banfield expound further that a "public-regarding" UMC often supports social programs that seem at variance with the UMC's "self-interest narrowly defined" (1964: 876).

However, another and more plausible argument for the UMC's interest in social-centered outcomes is self-interest. The UMC's urban habitat serves as a nonverbal means to calculate the structural equivalence of social position in interurban comparisons. Hummon, for example, points to the UMC's metropolis as a "nonverbal medium for the communication of moral reputation, social rank, and other significant qualities of self" (1992: 258). Gottdiener says of this that "the urban image must be read . . . as an outcome of class society propelled by powerful forces of development and change" (1986: 216). In the case of transit, social programs that contribute a sense of vitality and connectedness about urban life lend a "world class" or cosmopolitan stature to a city's image, even though the UMC seldom use transit. As SEPTA's chief planner said about the surrounding communities of Philadelphia, "The [UMC] communities like public transit so long as the actual routes are not in my back yard" (Bickel 1993: 5).

As part of the urban makeup, social programs matter to the UMC because they contribute to a city's stature and allure, which figure unobtrusively in the UMC's quest for positional influence and their calculation of structural equivalence. Supporting this perspective, Clark (1996; 1994a) found that the UMC strongly favor taxes and social-program expenditures that improve the overall quality and cosmopolitan character of the urban milieu. Such stature carries with it an image of personal liberty, tolerance, and social justice, all of which make up the character of social liberalism often attributed to the UMC (Clark 1998; Clark and Ferguson 1983: chap. 7). Likewise, Hahn and Kamieniecki (1987) found that symbolic public accoutrements (a prominent airport, arts and entertainment venues, reputable schools, modern mass transit) are more important than economic issues in UMC voting. They concluded that the status benefits of effective social programs were seen as outweighing the associated costs of higher taxes.

This logic and supporting evidence leads us to the third proposition (Hypothesis 3) that:

> H3: The greater the proportion of UMC in an agency's service-area population, the more likely the agency will emphasize social-program effectiveness.

The three hypotheses compose a comprehensive thesis that anonymous UMC influence causes a skewed pattern of outcomes that emphasize strategic organizational effectiveness and social-program effectiveness, and a tradeoff that deemphasizes operational efficiencies. In short, skewness caused by the presence of a UMC genre involves asymmetry contributed by all three components of the policy outcomes pattern.

Wealth of the Metropolitan Polity

Unlike the UMC's combined effects on outcomes, metropolitan wealth would appear to have a more limited scope in skewing the pattern. As one of the oldest causal arguments about policy outcomes, the wealth thesis contends that agency budget size and expenditure levels are determined by fiscal resources of the local or indigenous population. Over the years, the weight of this thesis has risen with the popularity of systems theory, whose core premise is that environmental inputs flow across a public agency's organizational boundary. By noting the significance of permeable boundaries, systems theory concentrates analysis on exchanges and "flows of effects" resulting from "transactions" between an agency and its environment (Easton 1965). From these the wealth thesis extrapolates that in the course of political deliberations policymakers become informed about the level of aggregate constituency wealth (potential input) and design policy outcomes accordingly.

A refinement of systems theory that gives further weight and dimension to the wealth thesis is the "resource dependence perspective" (Pfeffer and Salancik 1979). This concept underscores the importance of wealth by focusing the analysis of causal inputs on tangible resources and who controls them. This is apparent, for example, in Dye's argument that the level of government activity is "closely related to the level of economic resources in society" (1998: 306; 1966). The importance of resource inputs to the wealth thesis is based on two "dimensions"—the proportion of total inputs represented by the resource in question and the "criticality" of the input to the agency (Pfeffer and Salancik 1979: 46). The latter refers to the ability of the agency to continue functioning in the absence of the resource. In the case of fiscal resources, urban agencies are heavily dependent on local wealth because it is usually a significant revenue source without which the agency could not operate.

A principal form of wealth relevant to an agency's dependence on fiscal resources is personal or household income and property. An agency gains access to that wealth for the purpose of establishing and maintaining budget levels through its ability to tax. Dye, for example, found in his classic study that both revenue levels and the ability to carry debt loads were significantly related to median family income (1966: 187–90). With reference to the "fiscal base of a local government," Peterson's famous argument on economic interests includes the corollary that "taxes on local sources" are an important component of a public agency's revenues and its fiscal well-being "requires continuing local economic prosperity" (1981: 29). Schneider (1989) echoes Peterson's claim but sees the importance of income and property taxation for revenue generation as more variable depending on the "flypaper effect" of intergovernmental transfers.

The central assumption of the wealth thesis is that governments spend to the limits of their fiscal capacity as determined by the tax base. Thus Schneider is led to conclude that because "taxes represent the extractive capacity of government, . . . higher taxes allow local governments to generate even bigger and more expensive government" (1989: 56). From this root assumption, numerous writings have theoretically and empirically supported the thesis that wealth is a crucial input variable that shapes the policy outcomes produced by government agencies (Schneider 1989; Peterson 1981; Niskanen 1971; Sharkansky and Hofferbert 1969; Dye 1966; Elliot 1965; Fisher 1964).

Although the relationship between wealth and agency expenditures is moderated by the effects of minor variations in tax rates among governments (Schneider 1989: 164; Peterson 1981: 32), consistency among these different findings suggests that a strong causal influence of the population's fiscal capacity should skew the pattern of policy outcomes toward social-centered outcomes. Nevertheless, a paradox in concept exists. Even though the resource dependence model associates agency spending with the level of community wealth, other research has established that increases in wealth carry with it an aversion to government spending. For example, Clark and Ferguson deduce from their multicity data that "in general, the more affluent the citizen, the less government spending he prefers, especially for poor-oriented services" (1983: 179).

Both sides of the paradox are supported empirically, but the deciding question is, Which matters more? Does the *availability* of known wealth beget the ability of government to acquire and spend it, or do *preferences* of wealthy citizens override or become those of the "median voter"? The answer may be that, except during exceptional times of heightened voter angst such as the "tax-revolt" era, the tendency is to tax using a standard method and a rate politically accepted across metropolitan areas irrespective of an individual area's wealth index. Hence, if a uniform calculus on taxing income and property prevails, a reasonable proposition would be that:

> H4: The greater the wealth of an agency's service-area population, the more likely the agency will find revenues available to emphasize social-program effectiveness.

Would the same be true for administration-centered outcomes, especially regarding the agency's organizational eminence? Since past research has only looked at expenditures of different kinds of programs, it does not directly speak to outcomes of strategic organizational effectiveness. On the one hand, greater population wealth would seem to enhance overall agency robustness and stature relative to agencies with more limited local resources. All other things equal, agencies in wealthy areas should have larger overall budgets and more market presence as the result of a bigger tax base. Schneider, for example, says, "Total expenditures . . . and the expansion of local government . . . are a function of community income" (1989: 60, 66). On the other hand, resource availability does not inherently yield marketworthiness or administrative adroitness at achieving respected organizational stature. Moreover, none of the wealth-thesis proponents address strategic enhancement of the agency as an organization. Hence, with the thesis silent on this policy outcome perspective, a hypothesis cannot be deduced with confidence regarding organizational effectiveness.

The Urban Underclass

The third socioeconomic thesis introduced here raises issues of racially based poverty and social hierarchy. Called the "underclass thesis," it derives significance from "social cleavages" (Lineberry and Fowler 1967), which separate groups hierarchically by making them conscious of class or status distinctions. As underclass members discover their shared disenfranchisement and the origin of their deprivation in social hierarchy, mobilization against a political regime becomes a feasible option (Clark 1996) even though impoverished minorities typically remain passive and apolitical. In the United States, hierarchical distinctions are often of a racial or ethnic nature. Hence, although Clark maintains that class and race are "partially separate empirical dimensions" (1996: 384), he argues that race has an impact on policymaking in America "the way that class and party do in Europe" (p. 382).

Like the wealth thesis, the underclass thesis hypothesizes a more focused impact on the pattern of skewness in policy outcomes than the comprehensive effects of a UMC genre. That focus is on social-program expenditures. However, unlike either of the previous two socioeconomic theses, the underclass argument does not contain writings and research that show high congruency on effect. For example, in reviewing the literature on "racial effects," Schneider saw two contending perspectives: "Given that blacks, on the whole, have lower incomes than whites, black concentrations might be associated with lower [public] expenditures. But given higher objective need for local services, blacks may demand more municipal services" (1989: 54).

In the first perspective, the maxim is "them that has, gets" (Lineberry 1977: 61), where a double standard causes the government to spend proportionally less on the underclass. This interpretation assumes a racially motivated "Machiavellian malevolence" in policymaking (p. 62), where zero-sum outcomes mean that the white majority elects to keep more of its discretionary income by expressing a preference for lower social-program expenditures. Lineberry is led to postulate "that the quantity and/or quality of urban services are positively related to the proportion of Anglos in a neighborhood population" (p. 66).

Many problems, however, beset this perspective. For one, the argument is directed principally at *intra*urban population demographics that compare service levels between segregated clusters of whites and non-whites. To extrapolate premises for *inter*metropolitan comparisons (as needed for this study), the thesis would require several additional behavioral assumptions. For example, are white regimes in urban areas with a high percentage of minorities indifferent about the appearance of their metropolitan area such that they forgo status-enhancing social programs for minority employment, education, and recreational facilities? In the reverse, are cities with a white majority likely to lavish themselves with social programs because they have few minority people with which to share services?

In contrast, the second perspective offers a clearer logic and empirical record. It holds that an underclass may have a less determinate effect on agency expenditures than other socioeconomic variables, but when it does matter it causes expenditures to be larger, not smaller (Clark 1996; Stone 1989; Dawson and Robinson 1965). The argument for higher resulting expenditures is rooted in the idea that the underclass represents a passive but potentially explosive political force in government policymaking. To ensure that the ethnic underclass cooperates with or accepts the larger urban and white-dominated political agenda, policymakers identify "anticipated reactions" (Stone 1980) of the underclass and preempt activism by impoverished minorities by providing additional expenditures for social programs. Stone, for example, argued under the guise of social equity for Atlanta's black underclass that the city's white power structure would have fared better over the long run if it had "improved transportation [to impoverished areas] . . . as a boost in mobility for residents in economically isolated areas" (1989: 205). Hence the more likely application of the underclass thesis to policy outcome bias is:

> H5: The larger the proportion of ethnic minorities in an agency's service-area population, the more likely the agency will emphasize social-program effectiveness.

The underclass thesis makes no mention of relationships with other policy outcome perspectives, so we are left with unanswered questions regarding whether to anticipate tradeoffs that would add to skewness in the outcome pattern. Since additional social-program expenditures are made principally for the purpose of securing underclass passivity or buy-in to the white-dominated agenda, does this result in greater operational inefficiencies for agencies? For example, as Stone (1989) surmised in his regimes treatise, if the Atlanta white coalition had adequately anticipated underclass reaction by incorporating MARTA transit routes for nonpaying black neighborhoods, would this not have disproportionally added capital requirements and operating costs to the transit agency's urban renewal efforts? Although the logic for an efficiency tradeoff is apparent, writings on the underclass thesis provide insufficient discussion to include a generalized hypothesis. An empirical analysis will be necessary to resolve the conceptual shortfall.

Operationalizing the Socioeconomic Variables

The three socioeconomic theses describe different causal relationships to policy outcomes. The UMC thesis postulates a subtle, more intangible set of relationships, while the wealth and underclass theses propose more visible connections. The UMC thesis poses far-reaching and comprehensive impacts involving all three policy perspectives; the other two propose more focused effects on pattern skewness. The most significant distinction, however, is with respect to empirical testing, where the UMC poses a greater challenge than the other two.

Many critics, in fact, would argue that because the systemic power of a UMC genre is "purely situational" (Stone 1980: 981), it is only an abstract estimation of a qualitative lifestyle. Without observable substance like that found in tangible wealth or abject poverty, the route of causation cannot be directly measured. Although the intangible or symbolic route may not be definitively "proven" by empirical means, numerous writings nevertheless have argued that it logically exists. If true, then any effect on policy outcomes that is significantly associated with the presence of a UMC genre, *independent of other socioeconomic agents and the political actions of individuals*, would provide strong inferential evidence that the thesis has explanatory power.

To operationalize the socioeconomic theses, variable definitions were extracted from the U.S. census and dimensioned according to the hypotheses. In the case of the *UMC thesis*, the conceptual discussion gives rise to four components that represent parts of the genre's profile. The first is *professional status*, which is defined as the percentage of individuals in the agency's metropolitan population who are employed in professional and managerial positions. The second is *college education*, which indicates the percentage of individuals who have finished four or more years of higher education. The third census variable is *high income*, defined as the percentage of households with 1989 income above $75,000 — a figure more than twice the national mean. The fourth variable is *income change*, which captures upward economic mobility and is defined as the percentage change in household income between 1979 and 1989.

Instead of using each of the four variables as independent components in regression analyses, the thesis is represented by a factor called *UMC genre*, which consists of the four as a set of interrelated discrimi-

TABLE **3.1** Agency Populations with the Highest and Lowest UMC Populations
Urban Public Transit, 1990

Ten Agencies with Highest Percentage of UMC	Factor Value	Ten Agencies with Lowest Percentage of UMC	Factor Value
1. WMATA	2.42	42. Pierce Transit	−1.37
2. CCCTA	2.19	41. M-DT	−1.33
3. MUNI	1.73	40. MCT	−1.22
4. Santa Clara	1.55	39. NFTA	−1.18
County Transit		38. Tidewater Regional Transit	−1.13
5. GGT	1.52	37. VIA Metropolitan Transit	−1.06
6. MBTA	1.23	36. IPT	−0.92
7. BART	1.18	35. GCRT	−0.88
8. MMS	1.06	34. Bi-State DA	−0.87
9. SamTrans	0.96	33. PT	−0.71
10. MARTA	0.81		

NOTE: See Appendix A for agency names.

nate SES parts. Choice of a factor fits the thesis that policy outcomes are influenced by the *whole* demographic profile and not the individual components acting independently. This choice is supported by a principal components analysis that determined a single factor accounting for 78 percent of the four-component variance (eigenvalue = 3.13). Correlations of the factor with its components are high and include professional status ($r = .93$), education ($r = .92$), high income ($r = .93$), and income change ($r = .74$).

Table 3.1 identifies from the factor values the agencies with the ten highest and ten lowest concentrations of UMC in the sample. UMC seem to be regionally concentrated in the far West and in the East; fewer are found in the Midwest and South. The remainder not shown on the list cluster more tightly around the distribution mean.

In the case of the *wealth thesis*, the conceptual discussion potentially involves several indicators, but *median income* of the population is the one most commonly used. It is defined as 1989 mean household income for the agency's jurisdictional population. In addition, real estate property is a key wealth indicator because local government taxation most often uses the value of residential assets as the basis for taxation. Hence a second variable called *property value* is extracted from the census and represents the housing price index for the metropolitan area

TABLE **3.2** Agency Populations with the Highest and Lowest Population Wealth
Urban Public Transit, 1990

Ten Agencies with Highest Wealth Base	Factor Value	Ten Agencies with Lowest Wealth Base	Factor Value
1. CCCTA	2.28	42. Regional Transit Authority	−1.47
2. Santa Clara County Transit	1.93	41. VIA Metropolitan Transit	−1.14
		40. Sun Tran	−0.98
3. WMATA	1.90	39. Jacksonville	−0.92
4. SamTrans	1.86	Transportation Authority	
5. OCTA	1.83	38. Pierce Transit	−0.91
6. GGT	1.45	37. Utah Transit Authority	−0.87
7. BART	1.20	36. GCRT	−0.81
8. AC Transit	1.07	35. MTA	−0.80
9. MUNI	0.84	34. IPT	−0.77
10. MTDB	0.81	33. Port Authority of Allegheny County	−0.77

NOTE: See Appendix A for agency names.

within the agency's jurisdictional boundary. Because wealth is most frequently held in the form of a home, it is not surprising that the two variables are very significantly intercorrelated ($r = .74$).

Hence, instead of using the individual variables as separate estimators of indigenous wealth, a factor composed of the two components is substituted. Called *population wealth*, it incorporates the notion that local taxation and ultimately the capacity for government expenditures are the result of personal income channeled to residential property. This choice is supported by a principal components analysis, which determined a single factor accounting for 87 percent of the two-variable variance (eigenvalue $= 1.74$). Table 3.2 identifies agencies with the ten highest and ten lowest wealth bases in the sample. Highest wealth is heavily concentrated in California and the lowest levels are found in the South and Southwest.

In the case of the *underclass thesis*, the conceptual discussion obviates two components of the underclass in America. The first is *race*, which Clark (1996) considers equivalent to European class in its effect on policymaking. To account for all racial minorities, it is defined here as the percentage of nonwhite persons in the population. The second component is *poverty*, which is defined as the percentage of the population receiving public assistance (Bureau of the Census 1992). This official status

TABLE **3.3** Agency Populations with the Highest and Lowest Percentage of Underclass Urban Public Transit, 1990

Ten Agencies with Highest Percentage of Underclass	Factor Value	Ten Agencies with Lowest Percentage of Underclass	Factor Value
1. M-DT	2.75	42. Utah Transit Authority	−1.18
2. SCRDT	2.09	41. Tri-Met	−1.15
3. Long Beach Transit	1.84	40. CCCTA	−1.10
4. MUNI	1.72	39. Metropolitan Transit	−1.05
5. Regional Transit Authority	1.64	Commission	
		38. MMS	−0.97
6. VIA Metropolitan Transit	1.32	37. NFTA	−0.91
		36. GGT	−0.91
7. AC Transit	1.29	35. MBTA	−0.89
8. BART	0.91	34. Regional Transportation	−0.88
9. CTA	0.86	District	
10. Sacramento Regional Transit	0.77	33. Port Authority of Allegheny County	−0.86

NOTE: See Appendix A for agency names.

is established for those below the poverty threshold, which in 1990 was $13,254 for a family of four (Bureau of the Census 1999). Since each variable is a component described by the underclass thesis, and probably shares a reciprocal association (r = .42), the two were combined into a factor called the *underclass* to represent a more holistic empirical estimation of the thesis. The factor is supported by a principal components analysis, which determined a single factor accounting for 71 percent of the two-variable variance (eigenvalue = 1.42).

Table 3.3 identifies from the factor scores those agencies with the ten highest and ten lowest concentrations of underclass in the sample. Those with the highest proportions of underclass tend to cluster in California and the southern states, while lower concentrations are most often found in the northern states.

We now reach closure on the three socioeconomic theses. In sum, this chapter provides a foundation for seeing how a culturally powerful social class, the influence of wealth, and a disenfranchised underclass may contribute to the skewing of policy outcomes. Acting independently of each other, they predicted different patterns of outcomes. With the prevalence of an upper middle class, the thesis argued for a tradeoff favoring two kinds of strategic effectiveness at the expense of operational efficiency. In the cases of income and the underclass, no tradeoff is expected. Instead, a single emphasis was hypothesized, and in both cases that was expected to be an emphasis on social-program effectiveness. With these theoretical underpinnings established, Chapter 4 turns to the question of institutional politics as this plays out through the direct use of authority in an intergovernmental setting.

4 Institutionalism and the Politics of Intergovernmental Exchange

As a comparative study of bias in policy outcomes, this book looks in many directions for rival theses about what matters most. Juxtaposed to the passive socioeconomic influences outlined in Chapter 3, institutional theory brings to the table considerations involving the influence of "political actors." At the root of this perspective is the notion that constituencies seeking policy congruency with their interests are represented by a system of fiduciary actors engaging in intergovernmental transactional exchanges. Because such exchanges are seldom found on a level playing field, the *relative institutional power* of these governmental actors may be central to explaining the asymmetrical distribution of policy outcomes we have called pattern skewness.

Attention to power is part of the study of institutionalism (or political economy) because power in exchanges is defined by the context of legitimated intergovernmental arrangements and constitutionally prescribed rules. It is the structure, regularity, and persistence of established protocol that bring to policymaking exchanges not only expectations about the use of power but also a sense of predictability in participants' behaviors. Moreover, with this emphasis on fiduciary political actors, institutionalism offers a rival thesis to the socioeconomic theses of the last chapter. It argues that *active engagement* in intergovernmental exchanges must occur for private interests to be represented in public policy outcomes (Meier and Stewart 1991; Eulau and Karps 1977; Pitkin 1967).

By contrast, the socioeconomic theses place the cause of outcome skewness on the *passive presence* of SES identities represented by their cultural prominence in the population. For example, the UMC thesis holds that the "felt" presence of this socioeconomic genre in an urban society is sufficient to skew policy outcomes toward UMC interests. Murray (1999) makes a similar claim for the cultural influence of the underclass. Institutionalism, in contrast, requires a demonstrated link, such as one or more persons from the genre "acting in the interests of the represented" to achieve such policy congruency (Pitkin 1967: 209).

Many institutional theorists have taken up this question of active and passive representation. For example, Verba, Schlozman, and Brady (1995) argue that because UMC persons are more politically active than those of other socioeconomic classes, policy congruency with UMC interests is the result of active rather than passive representation. In fact, by applying the theory of group socialization processes, Meier and Stewart (1991) claim to have found a link between "passive and active representation" that explains why socioeconomic factors might have influence through institutional exchange. The implication is that institutionalism supersedes the SES theses in explaining policy outcomes and that little is gained by treating SES variables as passive influences in policymaking separate from those of political actors.

This chapter trumpets that perspective. It puts forward a thesis about how political exchange influences the skewing of policy outcomes. Although institutionalism sprawls over many concepts in several disciplines (Powell and DiMaggio 1991), the aspects of relevance in intergovernmental exchange deal with a focal agency's relative autonomy to make policy choices in a constitutional setting of concurrent authorities and arrangements. The institutional exchange thesis drawn here argues that policy outcomes are a function of a focal agency's relative power in intergovernmental exchange where pattern skewness depends on the amount of autonomy held by the subject agency.

While the thesis identifies public agencies as the principal "political actors" of intergovernmental exchange, it also extends transactional involvement to legislators, mayors, other public officials, and at times the courts. It stops short, however, of including interest group theory in the discussion. Although interest groups and powerful private citizens may play a direct participative role, a separate interest group thesis centered on exchanges with nongovernmental actors is not carved out here as part of the institutional perspective.[1]

Agency Autonomy in Intergovernmental Exchange

Institutionalism is about how policy choices "are shaped, mediated, and channeled by institutional arrangements" (Powell and DiMaggio 1991: 2). It is not a new thesis, but recent versions focus attention on the emergence of distinctive authority structures, processes, strategies, and competencies as they form around intergovernmental exchanges (E. Ostrum 1995; Powell and DiMaggio 1991; Pfeffer 1990; Moe 1990; Williamson 1990; Chisholm 1989; Shepsle 1989; E. Ostrum 1986). Describing the nature of relations prescribed by institutional arrangements, Moe says the thesis is "fundamentally about actors who enter into exchanges with one another: they bargain, they haggle, they design . . . solutions to their mutual problems. The actors on both sides of the exchange have interests at stake, goals to achieve, information and resources to use on their own behalf, and strategies to formulate and follow" (1990: 129). In this sense they behave much like rational actors in a market except that the exchange is over policy outcomes rather than packaged private goods.

Regarding impacts on policymaking, specific attention is given to the power a focal agency holds relative to that of political actors with which it has intergovernmental exchanges (i.e., other agencies with overlapping authority, legislatures, court rulings). Much of this power and the motive to participate in exchanges are directed at a need to acquire essential but scarce resources (especially fiscal and statutory ones). The acquisition of such resources, however, involves incurring transaction costs, which all parties to the exchange want to minimize for themselves. In part, this cost minimization is achieved from the actors working together over long periods to normalize cooperative, stable, and predictable intergovernmental relationships. Indeed, Shepsle describes the resulting institutional arrangements as "ex ante agreements about the structure of cooperation [which] economize on transaction costs" (1986: 74).

Within this institutional context, then, policy outcomes of inter-governmental exchange reflect who controls which scarce resources. Since control of fiscal and statutory resources is likely to be unevenly distributed among intergovernmental actors, application of the institutional exchange thesis to intergovernmental behavior also incorporates the concept of "resource dependence" (Yamaguchi 1996; Pfeffer and Salancik 1978). Dependence on resources is the basis for interdependence among governmental actors who individually hold incomplete authority to act alone.

Central to this concept is the premise that relative power attributable to individual parties to an exchange is a function of the valued political and fiscal resources each actor brings to the table or holds under its control. In the case of a transit agency heavily dependent on subsidies, the formula might involve developing broad grass-roots political support to succeed in an exchange for intergovernmental funding. In Philadelphia, for example, SEPTA needed almost $5 billion to revamp its deteriorating transit system. The only intergovernmental actors large enough to supply such a sum were the federal and state governments. Instead of approaching them as a lone agency, SEPTA organized a grass-roots coalition of 400 Philadelphia-area organizations (businesses, unions, churches, and non-profit civic groups): "We literally took a SEPTA train, filled it up with people, and went to Washington a couple of times and Harrisburg [the state capital] a couple of times. There was a big rally when we arrived at each place. We tried to disperse our influence and lobby with respect to the agency. . . . We got the dedicated funding!" (Gambaccini 1993: 11). In Atlanta, MARTA assembled a similar political resource it called "the Committee of 50" to strengthen the agency's hand in securing intergovernmental funding (Gregor 1990; Olson 1990).

Attention to institutionalism in American public agencies goes back at least to Selznick's analysis of TVA (1948), or perhaps even earlier to Barnard (1938), who defined institutional authority in the context of cooperative relationships. However, more recent interest in its policy-making implications is introduced by Rosenthal (1984) and Elinor Ostrom (1986, 1995), both of whom characterized authority structure and competitive intergovernmental exchange as potent determinants of policy outcomes. From their perspective, other administrative agencies, elected officials, and legislatures are seen as a focal agency's institutional environment. This intergovernmental setting is structured by a protocol "of rules, procedures, and arrangements" (Shepsle 1986: 53) that mandate "prescriptions about which actions are required, prohibited, or permitted" (E. Ostrom 1986: 5).

Different from competitive market environments of private firms, the intergovernmental setting requires managerial skills based on contending struggles in a variety of frequently interlinked political arenas. In Atlanta, MARTA's general manager shared this distinction between business and public managers: "When public agencies took over private transit systems, they discovered that being a public manager required a set of skills that private managers seldom develop. You now had to deal with Washington, with a lot of local elected officials, and with state legislatures that you didn't have to deal with as a private firm" (Gregor 1990: 1).

Institutional exchange in the public sector can be unpackaged to produce hypotheses about specific connections between the distribution of governmental power and policymaking. For example, the thesis paints the picture of a focal agency embedded in an interactive "multi-organizational system" (Chisholm 1989) whose transacting actors are coupled by their individual dependence on resources. For a focal agency to prevail in emphasizing its preferred administration-centered outcomes in the face of this setting of interdependence, the thesis holds that policymaking is a function of the focal agency's positional power in intergovernmental exchanges (Yamaguchi 1996; Coleman 1990). Responding to what Shepsle calls a "game form" of policymaking (1989: 135), the agency makes and seeks concessions on policy outcomes based on its perceived power relative to other governmental actors with which it interacts (Shepsle 1986; Boschken 1988; V. Ostrom 1973).

In St. Louis, one of Bi-State's deputy directors illustrated this delicate connection:

> Our agency crosses so many political jurisdictions, it's much harder to get things done. Each municipality has its own politics and you have to be that much more careful not to disenfranchise any of the political entities. For a number of years, St. Louis County has been very strongly Republican and St. Louis city is very Democratic. But you need both [for subsidies], so you're walking a real thin line. . . . And it even gets more complicated. Our appropriations [request] in St. Louis city actually goes before the Board of Aldermen and has to be signed off by the mayor. With St. Louis County, we have to get a bill appropriated [each year] by

the county council and it has to be actually signed off by the county executive. (Douglas 1993: 11)

As intimated, this positional power has to do with an agency's control of (or lack of) specific resources needed to carry out its organizational strategies and manage its operational processes (Williamson 1990; Oliver 1991; Pfeffer and Salancik 1978). According to Yamaguchi (1996), such power is also contingent on the location of critical resources to each other in the field (i.e., whether critical resources are concentrated in the hands of a few or widely distributed) and on whether those resources have substitutable alternatives. The first condition is experienced by the focal agency as the structure of intergovernmental authority (measured along a scale between the archetypes of multiple overlapping, concurrent authorities, and a center-peripheral structure). The second condition is felt by the focal agency primarily as the kinds of substitutable fiscal resources available (i.e., intergovernmental grants, local taxation powers, user fees).

Referring to autonomy as a type of relative power, Benson defines the term as "a claim [by the focal agency] permitting the performance of activities independently, without supervision, direction, or shared authority by another agency" (1975: 232). In an intergovernmental power structure, the definition would mean the locus of power exists wholly or mostly within the focal agency. This absolute condition, however, is not reflective of American federalism, and the more likely occurrence is a sharing of power in such a way that an agency sees its policy "turf" as encompassing less than the fiscal and statutory resources necessary for it to act alone. On the basis of the resources needed by itself and others, the focal agency reaches explicit and implicit intergovernmental accords about its discretionary autonomy, the magnitude of which varies from one focal agency to another.

Emphasizing Administration-Centered Outcomes

The exchange thesis assumes agency policymakers hold preferred policy aims that emphasize administration-centered outcomes (Shepsle and Bonchek 1997; Yamaguchi 1996; E. Ostrom 1995). Thus the more autonomous agency also can be expected to pursue policies that maximize its continued access and use of critical resources, the most important of which take the form of organic enabling statutes and revenue. Even though some agencies, like those in urban transit, have a market venue that acts as a partial substitute to public sources of revenue, their resource dependence lies mostly in the intergovernmental environment.

What this dependence means for organizational effectiveness is that transaction costs associated with intergovernmental exchanges may dilute the agency's efforts to be a marketworthy provider of transit services. The chief planner of Los Angeles's regional transit agency put it this way: "A lot of our resources are devoted solely to working with other agencies, wrestling money from them, and responding and reporting to them. That decision-making process is time-consuming and costly—even more so in lost market opportunities" (Perdon 1989: 11–12).

Moreover, when a transit agency compromises quality or service to accommodate the demands or mandates of remote intergovernmental actors, the agency suffers some decline in market strength and public prestige. According to Los Angeles's chief planner:

> We're being held accountable by our riders. When our ability to make decisions is curtailed and decisions are made by others who don't have a transit-customer perspective, that hurts us. [Intergovernmental actors] are too far removed from the day-to-day problems of the customer. If things don't go right, the people who ride our buses don't get a vision of staff people in Washington, Sacramento, or local intergovernmental actors. They look at RTD [Rapid Transit District] as the guys who are screwing up. To make decisions from the user's perspective, you've got to have control. (Perdon 1989: 29)

Hence, by explaining the control of statutory resources that enhance agency autonomy, the institutional exchange thesis suggests a link to the agency's focus on strategic organizational positioning:

> H6: The greater the autonomy a focal agency has in policymaking exchanges with its web of intergovernmental actors, the greater the emphasis will be on its strategic organizational effectiveness (Outcome I).

With regard to operational efficiency, the thesis is more involved. For example, although Niskanen expects an administration-centered agency to seek both resource- and efficiency-maximizing outcomes in its negotiations with intergovernmental actors, he argues that "neither businessmen nor bureaucrats have any inherent motivation to be efficient" (1971: 209). What makes efficiency an administration-centered preference for bureaucrats are "specific conditions" found in most areas of today's public sector. Urban bureaucrats experience a "strain" on the agency's organizational system that stems from dwindling fiscal resources (Clark and Ferguson 1983).

In the event that they are unable to acquire funds through intergovernmental exchanges, they reduce the strain by improving operational efficiency. They "choose an efficient combination of production processes because efficiency is a characteristic of the budget-maximizing equilibrium. . . . [A] bureaucrat has a budget-maximizing incentive to identify and use more efficient production processes" (Niskanen 1971: 209–10). Hence, with the caveat that endemic fiscal strain forces the administration-centered bureaucrat to desire efficiency, the exchange thesis would hypothesize that:

> H7: The greater the autonomy a focal agency has in policymaking (resulting from sparse regulatory overlap and reduced intergovernmental funding sources), the greater the emphasis will be on its operational efficiency (Outcome II).

Combined, the two administration-centered hypotheses run counter to the tradeoff in policy emphasis between organizational effectiveness and operational efficiency as identified empirically in Table 2.3 of Chapter 2. However, the seeming contradiction between theory and empirical reality is not an unusual condition in multivariate statistics. Because the forces at play in skewing policy outcomes are hypothesized to affect individual MSOI components, some determinants may accentuate the tradeoff while others diminish it.

Social-Centered Outcomes

When the locus of intergovernmental power is outside the focal agency's reach and requires considerable sharing of policy discretion, autonomy is reduced. Moreover, when concurrent authorities are able to exercise veto power, the focal agency's resulting "compliance is a loss of discretion, a constraint, and an admission of limited autonomy" (Pfeffer and Salancik 1978: 95). As encroachment on focal-agency discretion affects more policy considerations, its policy emphasis will likely shift to social-centered outcomes. Downs and Larkey argue that numerous legislative mandates, intergovernmental agreements, and recurrent interagency exchanges force administrators to "function within a web of rules and statutes whose primary purpose is not to achieve [the agency's preferred outcomes] but to ensure stability of service, accountability, and equality of treatment" (1986: 45).

An administration-centered agency is not as motivated to adopt such measures without intergovernmental intervention because the outcomes may be only a tangential part of its organic mandate or not economically advantageous to its bureaucracy (i.e., they may raise operational costs without raising net resources). This can be understood in two lights. First, social programs seldom spring from market transactions among willing self-interested parties. Instead, they are found in the public domain of political exchange that results from intergovernmental mandates and funding opportunities. In Philadelphia, SEPTA's chief planner explained: "There's a philosophy among some people that if SEPTA were totally independent, it would act like a big brother and would do whatever it wanted. There is a certain justice in having the agency come hat-in-hand every year because that exerts control. Local governments can say 'in return for money, I want certain routes and services,' not just what SEPTA staff thinks is good" (Bickel 1993: 10).

Such intergovernmental demands usually are either regulatory or distributive, the latter of which Altshuler claims is "particularly attractive to politicians in a highly pluralistic system" (1979: 67; see also Dye 1998; Clark and Ferguson 1983: part IV). For example, to obtain a broader distribution of federal funds at the local level, the Intermodal Surface Transportation Efficiency Act of 1991 (ISTEA) tied federal capital funding for transit to a mandate requiring a 10 percent set-aside for nontransit expenditures. These collateral social programs cost the focal agency money, but the welfare benefits may be only vaguely associated with those costs. Hence, although the local agency has a choice not to take the federal funds (Clark and Ferguson 1983: part IV), *voluntary* adoption of such tangential programs by the focal agency would be unlikely without a federal requirement, especially when resources are tight.

A second deduction is that the greater the number of governmental agencies constraining the focal agency, the more likely broader representation of interests will occur in its policymaking (Buchanan and Tullock 1965; V. Ostrom 1973). Turk (1970), for example, found that a richly connected interorganizational network reduced agency autonomy and "broadened" the types of agency outcomes. In transit agencies, Fielding found that "taking care of the customer is important, but it is also essential to be attentive to the desires of [political actors]" (1987: 29).

Both applications of institutional theory suggest that more intergovernmental involvement and resource dependence reflect a locus of power outside the focal agency and result in reduced autonomy. Hence the implication for choice of policy resulting from intergovernmental exchange is that:

> H8: The lower the statutory autonomy (and/or the higher the fiscal dependence) a focal agency has in exchanges with intergovernmental actors, the greater the agency's emphasis will be on social-programs (Outcome III).

The three hypotheses constitute a thesis that high focal-agency autonomy in intergovernmental exchanges contributes to a skewed pattern of outcomes consisting of emphases on the administration-centered outcomes of strategic organizational effectiveness (Outcome I) and operational efficiency (Outcome II), and a concomitant deemphasis on social-program effectiveness (Outcome III). Low focal-agency autonomy leads to a pattern with a politicized emphasis on social-program effectiveness at the expense of administration-centered preferences.

Operationalizing Intergovernmental Autonomy

The institutional exchange thesis describes political power in a resource dependence context. From the agency's standpoint, power has to do with how much autonomy the agency maintains over policymaking by virtue of its granted statutory authority and control over fiscal resources. Transit agencies vary greatly in the mix of resources they control and in the intergovernmental environments to which they are subject. Even though the federal government appears to be a common intergovernmental actor to all, agencies experience different fiscal and regulatory treatment. Vast differences also exist in their state and local intergovernmental settings and the types of policy issues that constitute their exchanges.

For example, even though most states participate substantially in intergovernmental funding to transit agencies, two states—Missouri and Colorado—provide none at all. In some cases, as in Maryland and

New Jersey, the state directly operates urban transit agencies. Some locally formed agencies enjoy an areawide metropolitan monopoly and dedicated sources of tax revenue, while others exist in a balkanized metropolitan area of many transit authorities where fragmentation leaves each transit agency with a smaller scale of authority and fiscal resources relative to other intergovernmental actors.

Such wide variations in levels of autonomy should result in differences among agencies regarding how much policymakers are able to emphasize their administration-centered preferences. For example, arguing for the legitimacy of skewing outcomes toward administration-centered performance, Doig and Mitchell consider autonomy essential to a public authority's "primary mandate to . . . develop revenue-producing facilities in an atmosphere insulated from political pressures" (1992: 20). This highlighting of autonomy also leads the institutional theorist to consider any particular intergovernmental exchange to be part of a larger pattern of established expectations and assumptions about an agency's control of critical resources and prior intergovernmental agreements that support its bargaining position.

On this point, Benson (1975) argues that money and institutional authority are the most critical resources for maintaining autonomy in intergovernmental exchange. Hence, with respect to these resources, intergovernmental autonomy is operationalized by three resource-dependent variables. Using data extracted from FTA Section 15 reporting by individual agencies, the first two incorporate fiscal resources and are estimators of the degree of policymaking autonomy an agency has by virtue of its source of funds. Fiscally, transit agencies fall between general-fund agencies (which are heavily dependent on legislative resource providers) and independent government corporations (which rely mostly on agency-determined and market-sourced funds). The gray area in between allows for wide variation to exist in the degree of transit agency autonomy. With such variance having important policy implications, fiscal variables have been the focus of past research (Cervero 1984; Barnum and Gleason 1979), but not as in this study, which examines their effects in skewing policy outcomes.

The first of these two fiscal variables is called *revenue autonomy* and is measured by the proportion of total focal-agency revenues generated by user fees or through "dedicated" sources such as a permanent transit tax. Both sources impart budgetary independence to the agency

TABLE **4.1** **Agencies with the Highest and Lowest Revenue Autonomy**
Urban Public Transit, 1990

Ten Agencies with Highest Autonomy	Z-Score	Ten Agencies with Lowest Autonomy	Z-Score
1. Long Beach Transit	1.04	42. MBTA	−2.31
2. BART	1.04	41. M-DT	−2.11
3. MMS	0.91	40. Jacksonville Transportation	−2.03
4. SamTrans	0.85	Authority	
5. MARTA	0.82	39. Tidewater Regional Transit	−1.59
6. Santa Clara County	0.80	38. MCT	−1.40
Transit		37. WMATA	−1.39
7. Pierce Transit	0.79	36. Sun Tran	−1.39
8. Regional Transportation	0.77	35. MUNI	−1.29
District		34. Port Authority of	−1.27
9. GGT	0.77	Allegheny County	
10. Tri-Met	0.76	33. NFTA	−0.99

NOTE: See Appendix A for agency names.

where the higher the proportion coming from these sources, the greater the agency's autonomy over its use of revenues. Table 4.1 identifies in the sample those agencies with the ten highest and ten lowest levels of autonomy in securing and deploying operational revenues. Most of those with the least dependence on intergovernmental sources are located in Western states; most of those with the greatest dependence are located in the East and Atlantic South.

The second variable, called *capital autonomy*, is the proportion of an agency's capital funding sourced from municipal debt, user fees, or dedicated taxation and not dependent on recurrent legislation or repetitive interagency negotiation. Table 4.2 identifies those agencies with the ten highest and ten lowest levels of autonomy in securing and deploying investment capital. Those with the least dependence on intergovernmental sources are located principally in the East and far West, while those with the greatest dependence do not seem to exhibit a geographically skewed pattern.

The third intergovernmental variable is a surrogate for the focal agency's statutory autonomy. Regarding organic enabling statutes, most transit agencies exist as some form of chartered public authority, which generally means they have varying degrees of administrative discretion not characteristic of general-fund departments within city or county government. That is, they are free of most external political meddling in their

TABLE **4.2** Agencies with the Highest and Lowest Capital Autonomy
Urban Public Transit, 1990

Ten Agencies with Highest Autonomy	Z-Score	Ten Agencies with Lowest Autonomy	Z-Score
1. IPT	1.90	42. MCT	−1.39
2. MARTA	1.89	41. VIA Metropolitan Transit	−1.39
3. BART	1.86	40. Port Authority of	−1.39
4. MBTA	1.67	Allegheny County	
5. Sacramento Regional	1.64	39. Tidewater Regional Transit	−1.39
Transit		38. M-DT	−1.39
6. PT	1.18	37. Sun Tran	−1.39
7. Long Beach Transit	1.07	36. WMATA	−1.34
8. SCRTD	0.95	35. NFTA	−1.09
9. Mass Transit	0.90	34. DART	−0.99
Administration		33. Regional Transit Authority	−0.97
10. CCCTA	0.60		

NOTE: See Appendix A for agency names.

authority to carry on a "business" in a specific mandated public domain (Boschken 1988; Walsh 1978). Such independence, however, extends only to the agency's service domain authority specified by its enabling statutes, and not to a freedom from exchange with government actors who have separate but overlapping authority in policy areas such as urban land use and environmental quality. These other authorities make up the intergovernmental network that overlays transit agencies' jurisdictions. They are typically located at all levels of American government.

However, unlike accounting for fiscal variables, designing an empirical variable to adequately reflect statutory autonomy poses some difficult operational problems. The variety and robustness of a multilevel web of intergovernmental relations revolves around many nuances in formal and informal protocols that are not easily captured by quantitative measures. As mindsets or competing conventions about what constitutes the legitimate structure of intergovernmental authority, the protocols of intergovernmental networks vary from one metropolitan area to another and are not easily reducible to quantitative data even if one could determine a single intersubjective empirical dimension. Moreover, the protocols may be constantly in flux over what Moe calls a recurrent political struggle "to control how authority will be exercised" (1990: 121).

In one example of the difficulty in judging whether statutory or informal intergovernmental authority matters more, Tri-Met operates the transit system in the three-county Portland (Oregon) metropolitan area and formally holds great autonomy. However, even though the agency is a consolidated special service district having "very broad taxing authority without intergovernmental O.K.'s," agency policymaking defers to the area's protocol for operating "on a consensus model" where any affected government within Tri-Met's jurisdiction can participate and "kill a project" (Tri-Met 1994).

Nevertheless, estimating statutory autonomy is important to testing the institutional thesis, and the empirical variable designed to approximate this is called *intergovernmental (IG) interaction autonomy*. It refers to the focal agency's required legal couplings with intergovernmental actors, which subject the agency to varying degrees of jurisdictional overlap, oversight control, and negotiation (Wise 1990; Boschken 1976; V. Ostrom, Tiebout, and Warren 1961). Because concurrent authorities limit agency autonomy, Wise argues that in predicting agency outcomes one must "analyze the potential interactions between organizations at the various levels of government" (1990: 145). Reflecting the degree of mandated concurrence, intergovernmental interaction is the product of two components: *scope* and *intensity*. The first is defined as the number of intergovernmental actors involved in focal-agency policymaking; the second is the percentage of those involved that hold concurrent statutory approval/veto authority (as opposed to advisory authority only). Combined as an interaction variable, they estimate the range of specialized authorities and how tightly coupled they are with focal-agency deliberations.

Through a survey of policymakers at each transit agency, the two components of IG interaction were determined from management perceptions. For the scope indicator, the agency was asked for the name and authority of governmental actors (federal, state, and local; agencies and legislatures) with which it had ongoing exchanges in policymaking. The greater the number, the greater the scope of intergovernmental authorities represented. For intensity, the agency was asked whether each of those governmental actors named held only an advisory role or had statutory approval/veto authority over agency policymaking. The greater the percentage with approval authority, the greater the intensity of overlapping authorities.

On a continuous scale, the interaction of greater scope and inten-

TABLE **4.3** Agencies with the Highest and Lowest Interaction Autonomy
Urban Public Transit, 1990

Seven Agencies with Highest Interaction Autonomy	Z-Score	Seven Agencies With Lowest Interaction Autonomy	Z-Score
1. MCT	1.21	42. MTDB	−2.94
2. Regional Transit District	1.21	41. WMATA	−2.66
3. Utah Transit Authority	1.19	40. SEPTA	−2.59
4. MBTA	1.08	39. AC Transit	−1.26
5. MTA	1.01	38. GGT	−1.00
6. CCCTA	0.92	37. MUNI	−1.00
7. DART	0.79	36. NFTA	−1.00

NOTE: See Appendix A for agency names.

sity of statutory exchange represents increasing degrees of transactional involvement of the focal agency with intergovernmental actors. Since higher values mean lower autonomy, to be consistent with the hypothesis, data for the interaction autonomy variable is scaled as the mirror image of figures reported by survey respondents. That is, the Z-score data were altered by changing the signs (+ and −) on the IG interaction values. Table 4.3 identifies agencies with the seven highest and seven lowest levels of autonomy residing in mandated interaction. Fewer agencies are shown in the extremal clusters for this variable because variance outside the two clusters is low and the many ties in rank make a clean breaking point beyond the seven unattainable.

This chapter provides a foundation for the institutional exchange thesis (described here as a subfield of "new institutionalism") as it informs us about how intergovernmental exchange is expected to affect the skewing of policy outcomes. Generally, the combined effect of focal-agency autonomy on outcomes is predicted to accentuate a tradeoff between administration-centered outcomes and social-program effectiveness. Greater autonomy should allow for more emphasis on organizational effectiveness and operational efficiency, but at the expense of an emphasis on social programs. Less autonomy would create the opposite condition. With this theoretical underpinning for the thesis established, Chapter 5 considers two more theses about competitive markets and urban spatial form.

Up to this point in the discussion, proposed determinants of policy outcomes have covered mostly familiar conceptual territory for students of sociology, political science, urban planning, and public policy. The influences of socioeconomic factors and intergovernmental politics have been studied from a wide range of perspectives. One area that does not enjoy much intellectual currency in public organization and policy studies, however, has to do with the effects of markets, technology, and urban spatial form on policy outcomes.

Scholarly inattention to these influences has not always been the norm. Indeed, before the nation's preoccupation with Reaganomics, privatization, and reinventing government, interest in the determinant roles of markets and urban form on agency policymaking was more widespread. In the case of markets, a rich literature on public enterprise painted a picture of public agencies as corporatelike organizations immersed in an environment of technological change, competitive service providers, and multiple stakeholders (Boschken 1988; Walsh 1978). More often subject to a market environment than the line agency of a general-fund bureaucracy, the semiautonomous public authority is more likely to view policymaking from both market and political perspectives. But even more generally, the literature surrounding the "Tiebout Hypothesis" has argued that, for all public agencies, quasi-market competition among similar public agencies fosters different administrative behavior than that fostered by a monopolistic public economy (Tiebout 1956; Ostrom, Tiebout, and Warren 1961; Warren 1966).

In the case of urban spatial form, another rich scholarly tradition theorizes about different configurations of the built environment. Although dating back at least to Frederick Olmsted in the nineteenth century (Rybczynski 1999), this tradition was dominated for most of the twentieth century by University of Chicago sociologists (see, e.g., Burgess and Bogue 1967; Park and Burgess 1967). Today its currency is seldom found in urban administration or policy studies and is mostly limited to urban planning issues, where classical and contemporary discussions of the urban habitat revolve around two juxtaposed cityscapes (see Suarez-Villa and Walrod 1997; Bourne 1982; Timms 1971; Wingo 1963). Respectively called "monocentric" (center-peripheral form) and "polycentric" (multinucleated pattern), these two models potentially offer enormous insight into why an agency's policy outcomes are skewed in certain ways.

In this chapter, markets and spatial form are handled as separate theses, partly because concepts for each have evolved in separate scholarly domains. The market thesis argues that competition forms around consumer preferences to create conditions that stimulate the public agency to behave more strategically toward both market customers (Outcome I: Organizational Effectiveness) and mandated clients (Outcome III: Social Effectiveness). By contrast, the urban-form thesis explains skewed policy outcomes by arguing that the aggregate spatial configuration of the urban area creates a preexisting condition enabling or restricting agencies in their quest to be efficient and responsive to customers and social clients.

Public Enterprise, Markets, and Technology

Since most transit agencies operate as public enterprises, this chapter's description of a market thesis unavoidably emphasizes this organizational form even though a market thesis may be applied in varying degrees to most public organizations. The modern public enterprise is a hybrid of the traditional government bureaucracy and the private firm. Historically, its form and legitimacy in the urban milieu evolved largely from Progressive Era tenets, which began with a conceptual partitioning of politics and administration (Boschken 1988; Doig 1983; Walsh 1978). On the political side, expectations were for the use of partisan bargaining and mutual adjustment to produce policy mandates that met a test of social equity irrespective of whether service delivery costs were captured by user fees. On the administration side, legitimacy was based on the neutral competence of professional managers and their expertise in producing policy outcomes that meet administration-centered criteria of efficiency and effectiveness.

As originally formulated, this duality was to make the public authority more like a "business" in public matters but not to encourage it to enter markets reserved for private enterprise. Although a more complicated story emerges for transit (Jones 1985), the fact that we find public enterprises in competitive markets with business is in many instances because private firms enter the public sector to "cream" lucrative opportunities in service delivery. As a consequence of the collision between Progressive intent and opportunistic business intrusion, the modern public enterprise has inherited obligations to behave toward two strategic but competing forces: one focused on the politics of social good and the other on business efficacy.

Which of the two obligations should be the more important to a public enterprise has always been a source of discussion, but history has shown that even the business mandate does not necessarily promote public organizations as fit for the dynamics of consumer behavior and market competition. Indeed, a traditional view of the independent public authority sees it as principally for "the management of truly monopolistic undertakings" (Smerk 1979: 422). It may be for this reason that the larger purpose of most public enterprises was more often for constructing and managing projects of *great physical accomplishment* (e.g., public housing, airports, bridges, transit systems) rather than for services designed around *consumer choice*. In fact, the marketworthiness of many independent authorities has often been sacrificed to technological solutions with a dubious connection to market utility.

Public authorities also suffer from the perception that they are administratively inferior to private firms (Savas 1987). What makes public organizations seem to compete less effectively is that they carry political baggage and have the collective good to worry about. Unburdened by such issues, private firms have shown an ability to skim off the most lucrative services and clients, leaving public agencies to serve low-end users who cannot afford "Cadillac" services. Without the lucrative revenues from high-end users, these agencies also often cannot provide decent services to the underclass. Whether in transit, K–12 education, health care, or security, public agencies have found themselves in an inferior defensive position where government reform has more often sought to privatize public services than entrust their delivery to an independent public agency.

Nevertheless, the stodgy image may be misleading. A more refined look at public authorities shows considerable variance in their successful pursuit of consumer demands and in providing superior services to competitive markets. This leads one to wonder if marketworthiness in public agencies may be less a function of their preoccupation with "publicness" and more the result of the urban market environment in which they operate (Bozeman 1987; Rainey, Backoff, and Levine 1976). As shown in Table 5.1, two market characteristics are of particular interest in distinguishing competitive environments: (1) the level of competition (i.e., market structure) and (2) whether private firms or public enterprises are the dominant providers. The figure is intended to distinguish market environments in which public agencies are found, but is limited to those administrative situations where market transactions take place. That is, the categorical cells include only those environments where information is sufficient for customers to associate cost and benefit, and where services are "packageable" enough to price for a market transaction (Arrow 1977; Savas 1987). General-fund agencies with little or no market exposure are therefore excluded.

Those public authorities with the most challenging market environments are found in cell I, where the supply side of markets is open-ended and competition is intense and dominated by the legitimacy of private laissez-faire. Since maintaining a market foothold is key to public agencies surviving private-firm agility, it is in this cell where they have been singularly most aggressive toward their organizational stature and growth potential. Being most reflective of the "Tiebout Hypothesis," cell II has many of the same market attributes of cell I because consumer choice remains high and multiple producers maintain competitive substitutes. However, the cell's dynamics are governed by the legitimacy of a public purpose rather than of laissez-faire and do not include private firms

TABLE **5.1** Market Environments of Urban Public Agencies

Market Structure

Dominant Provider	Competition	Monopoly
Private Firm	CELL I • Transit Authorities • Public Housing and Redevelopment Agencies • County Medical Centers	CELL III • Municipal Utility Agencies (electric, gas, water) • Solid Waste Disposal Agencies
Public Enterprise	CELL II • Airport Authorities • Seaport Authorities • School Districts • State Universities • Parks and Recreation Districts	CELL IV • Sewerage Districts • Building Inspection • Fire Districts

as central entrepreneurial agents. Cells III and IV are market environments structured around legal monopolies where consumer choice is marginalized by a lack of service substitutes. The distinction between these two cells is determined by whether firms or public agencies dominate the provision of services. In cell III the public authority holds an exclusive franchise to serve consumers but is benchmarked against a private firm's performance. In cell IV it holds a monopoly position but enjoys a special legitimacy of public purpose.

Although constrained by public-purpose mandates and by limited entrepreneurial flexibility, public agencies operating in either cell I or cell II competitive settings behave more like private firms in that they "also seek to ensure their own success [i.e., emphasizing Outcome I effectiveness]. . . . Their motive is not so much greed for excess revenues as a desire for a secure cash flow and an eagerness to avoid . . . dependence on public appropriations" (Walsh 1978: 11).

For this study, the cell I environment most closely fits the circumstances under which urban mass transit agencies operate. It is here where agencies are subject to market competition but do not have special status that gives them a competitive edge. Being especially exposed to the conditions of market supply and demand, but also burdened by a public purpose, transit is frequently the underdog in a market dominated by the unfettered strategic alliance of private-public providers of the auto/roadway system (i.e., auto producers, oil companies, roadway construction firms, and federal and state highway departments).

Even though transit agencies have sought strategic alliances of their own with state Departments of Transportation (DOTs) and regional economic development agencies, the subsidies and the tenor of intergovernmental mandates often work to subordinate and discourage transit agency competitiveness. In Washington, D.C., for example, where government is the principal employer, parking subsidies that encourage auto use rather than parking surcharges are the rule. One WMATA transit executive complained, "We're trying to get local officials to think about their responsibility. . . . There are land use policies that don't support transit. At 37 percent of the federal facilities, their parking fees are reduced. So how can you say on the one hand you're pro environment, pro transit and still have these policies that do just the opposite?" (Mitchell 1993: 7).

Seen from the context of market choice, the more powerful influence determining transit's competitiveness with the auto/roadway consortium is consumer response to modal-supply alternatives (Bish and Nourse 1975; Sherman 1967). Users select a transportation mode according to the mode's net value in moving the traveler around a circuit of metropolitan activities. In making a modal choice, several specific consumer preferences are known to be primary considerations in judging the quality and availability of supply alternatives.

One of these is *access* to locations of urban activity (Cervero 1997), which may be perceived in a spatial dimension. Because people seldom live within walking distance of work and engage in other activities spread over a wide area, they must select a mode based partly on proximity of the mode's infrastructure to the traveler's points of origin and destination. The access question involves a comparison between car ownership, which places a vehicle at the traveler's immediate disposal (i.e., home garage, activity parking), and transit, which requires locating the nearest system entry point at origin and exit point at destination (i.e., rail station, bus stop).

Another and closely related consideration is *modal flexibility*, which has to do with a traveler's ability to use a mode to circumnavigate a circuit of origin and destination points at random and "on demand" at the traveler's convenience. The single-occupancy automobile and extensive network of areawide urban roadways made possible the ability to live and work in locations widely dispersed from each other and without reference to a common core. Meyer, Kain, and Wohl proclaimed in their classic study that "automobiles and suburban living space appear to be complementary superior goods" (1965: 12).

As a result, consumer preference for modal flexibility is heightened by urban sprawl. At the same time, since transit agencies depend on concentrated population corridors to maximize market penetration and efficiency, sprawl potentially leaves transit as an inferior substitute in providing equivalent flexibility. In fact, general agreement exists and research shows that roadway expansion and improvement (i.e., increasing market supply) creates the self-fulfilling prophecy of adding to auto demand at the expense of transit's marketability (Hansen and Huang 1997; Hansen 1975).

Travel time is a third consideration in modal choice. Because urban travel is seldom pursued as an end in itself and takes time away from desired socioeconomic activities, travel time may be perceived as the relative "annoyance" in using one mode over the other (Altshuler 1979).

Central to this annoyance is the uncertainty of waiting time: unreliable "headways" (i.e., frequency and cadence of service) for transit and roadway congestion for autos. Transit passengers, on one hand, must wait at stops for vehicle arrivals, endure multiple stops along their journeys, usually must transfer, and often must do considerable walking to complete their trips. Auto users, on the other hand, have the daunting burden of driving themselves through often heavily congested traffic and finding parking in lots where tickets or permits represent little more than "hunting licenses" for a space. Nevertheless, transit remains at a disadvantage because travelers place a higher psychological cost on the uncertainty of out-of-vehicle waiting than on time spent in a vehicle (Fisher and Rickeson 1994; Cherlow 1981; Wachs 1976). All things equal, people would rather be tied up in freeway congestion than waiting for a bus.

A fourth consideration is *modal attractiveness*. Transportation consumers have aesthetic preferences that involve feeling comfortable and safe in pleasant, familiar, and physically attractive surroundings. Autos provide much of this in the form of personal privacy and stylishly designed cars. Transit cannot compete on the privacy issue because route stops and in-vehicle environments cannot provide exclusive occupancy to riders. Instead the transit alternative relies more heavily on cleanliness, brightness, and a technologically advanced appearance, features that impart conviviality, provide comfort, and generate rider loyalty.

As part of these system-supply characteristics, the type of transit technology seems to matter in modal choice, at least symbolically (Altshuler 1979; Meyer, Kain, and Wohl 1965: chap. 12). Relative to the auto/roadway system, bus systems seem to hold less market esteem than more "picturesque" or "futuristic" rail-based transit (Meyer, Kain, and Wohl 1965: 309). Asked why or on what basis people distinguish between rail and bus modes, the general manager of San Diego's Metropolitan Transit Development Board (MTDB) found that the bus system "was not a well-respected operation in the community. The new rail system generally has a more positive perception which doesn't get bogged down with an old, behind-the-times image" (Larwin 1989: 6). The same question asked elsewhere received even more explicit responses. The head of operations for Baltimore's Mass Transit Administration (MTA) said, for example, "Rail systems have sex appeal. People who won't ride a bus will ride a rail car" (Buckley 1991: 270). At Orange County Transit, the chief planner proclaimed, "Rail is more glamorous" (Van Sickel 1989: 37).

A final consideration of modal choice is relative monetary *cost* to the user. In the choice between autos and transit, the cost differential favors the use of transit by a substantial margin. Lower costs are made possible in part by transit subsidies, which transfer funds from highway and gasoline taxes to underwrite uneconomic transit fares. Thus the direct costs of using a car (i.e., gasoline, maintenance, parking fees, tolls, insurance, auto-loan interest, and so forth) far exceed the nominal user fee charged by transit.

Nevertheless, much of the research regards the cost factor as less significant to modal choice than the other primary considerations (see Mogridge 1997; Cherlow 1981). This lesser significance may be due in part to the user's inability to accurately compare the cost of the two modes because automobile-use cost has many unrelated and often hidden components. In addition, the sunk cost of vehicle ownership is often ignored by those who see ownership as a necessary subscription fee to fully participate in American society.

Applying these modal-choice criteria to judging transportation supply-side characteristics establishes the market conditions under which transit agencies compete with the auto/roadway consortium in a cell I market environment (Table 5.1). For example, excess freeway capacity encourages greater use of autos because consumers prefer to minimize travel time and maximize route flexibility. Congestion does the opposite, encouraging instead more use of transit. Looking at congestion as a market opportunity for transit to acquire customers, an Orange County (California) Transit manager suggested this could be done by "providing a level of service that's attractive to those individuals who sit for hours on the freeway and don't go anywhere" (Catoe 1989: 11). In the case of modal attractiveness, supplying transit with state-of-the-art trains and shiny new buses encourages a shift to more transit use. Dingy, antiquated rolling stock marred by graffiti provides greater route flexibility than stylish rail or luxury express buses but is an undesirable substitute for those with a market choice.

However, unlike the auto/roadway consortium whose primary consideration is market conditions, transit agencies are also saddled with social-program obligations. Many transit riders do not have sufficient means to make market choices and require intergovernmental mandates imposed on transit alone to provide them with equitable transportation services. The resultant separation of policymaking into two domains (one market-based, the other political) creates a potential paradox between the need for a competitive market response and the need to reserve resources for subsidizing nonmarket demands. For example, in fulfilling a public good, the agency provides basic mobility to disadvantaged and transit-dependent persons (e.g., neighborhood routes with frequent stops and a dense matrix network), but this social service differs markedly from the agency's provision of "premium" service to a competitive market (e.g., express buses or rail transit for long-distance commuting).

Which policy outcomes win when "an inconsistency exists between policies which attempt to improve access for the transit-dependent and those which are designed to attract the auto user away from his car?" (Wachs 1976: 97). Do market conditions cause an asymmetrical pattern of policy outcomes to exist? In response, many market-condition hypotheses could be proposed, but for the sake of parsimony and with only a limited amount of quality data for some variables, only two are offered as indicative of the thesis.

The first hypothesis addresses consumer preferences concerned with travel-time differentials and comparisons of modal flexibility. The central question, here, is whether transit holds unilateral capabilities to compete with autos based on these preferences. Believing transit does, Cervero (1990), Cherlow (1981), and Wachs (1976) suggest transit could improve its market position by simply offering faster vehicles, having fewer stops, and requiring fewer transfers (e.g., by using more express buses for long-distance commuting). However, others argue that such agency-determined improvements are unlikely to persuade many with a choice to abandon cars unless the consumption of autos and roadways exceeds supply capacity. This condition, which appears symptomatically as traffic congestion, not only shrinks the time advantage of the auto/roadway mode but also brings route reliability and modal flexibility into question.

Supply of the auto/roadway mode is a product of automobile ownership and the amount of urban roadway miles provided. The consortium providing this mode has enormous combined resources to continue enlarging supply but shows little ability to manage interactions that contribute to auto/roadway demand. As a consequence, only aggregate dynamics of the market seem to govern the amount of roadway congestion, making the variable a market condition that no one controls. Furthermore, congestion can be deleterious to some forms of transit (such as buses, but not most rail systems) as well as to the adequacy of auto/road-way capacity.

Nevertheless, consumers clearly act on congestion in making modal choices because congestion affects both the number of feasible alternative auto/roadway routes (modal flexibility) and the differential in travel time between autos and transit. Mogridge (1997), Downs (1962), and others theorized, for example, that an increase in travel time by autos caused by congestion shifts demand from autos to transit until consumer indifference is reestablished to create a new equilibrium involving lower congestion. Confirming this in practice, the transit agency's general manager in Orange County observed that rapidly growing roadway congestion left transit supply "just trying to keep up with rider demand. We usually got criticized for operating empty buses. Now, we have people saying we gotta get more buses out there. We're packed in like sardines" (Reichert 1989: 4).

Since the problem of congestion cannot be resolved by adding capacity to the auto/roadway mode (Hansen and Huang 1997; Mogridge 1997), the narrowing of travel-time advantage for autos poses a long-term strategic opportunity for transit agencies. That opportunity is to increase transit's market penetration, load factor, and service capacity, a large part of which would have positive social-program consequences involving expanded route schedules and economic development spillovers. Congestion mainly affects the *strategic* market positioning of rival mode producers and does not directly implicate the cost structure of internal *operations*; thus the literature makes no clear assessment of whether or how congestion might affect an agency's operational efficiency. The expected multiple impacts of congestion on skewing the pattern of policy outcomes, therefore, may be stated as follows:

> H9: The more auto use exceeds roadway supply, creating congestion, the more likely a transit agency's policy emphasis will be on strategic organizational effectiveness (Outcome I) and social-program effectiveness (Outcome III), while leaving operational efficiency (Outcome II) substantially unaffected.

The second hypothesis has to do with the adoption of advanced transit-system technologies as they relate to consumer preference for modal attractiveness and travel time. The argument is made by Fielding (1987) and Wachs (1976) that transit's market position could be increased by making the transit mode faster and more aesthetically pleasing. Particularly for large urban areas where commutes are long, a strategy of investing in modern systems that match the imagery and speed of stylistic auto designs could bolster an agency's Outcome I effectiveness.

Transit technologies that emphasize high-speed futuristic designs and stylized passenger compartments are most often applied to fixed-route rail systems, specifically in either vehicle-replacement programs for heavy rail or new light-rail systems (Pickrell 1992). Buses have benefited from design improvements as well (especially on express routes to suburbs) but require much less technological sophistication and fewer advanced guidance systems. In addition, even though buses are more cost-efficient and have far greater route flexibility, rail-based systems are able to cover a greater linear distance at much higher speeds and usually over exclusive rights-of-way.

The rail alternative is especially appealing to those primary market consumers who are most likely to be enamored with high-tech solutions: suburban commuters. In St. Louis, for example, Bi-State's executive operations manager said, "People in suburbia use the light rail. The bus, however, is not viewed as a desirable alternative [to the auto]" (Sehr 1993: 15). As a consequence, many agencies operating both bus and rail service do not integrate the two by using buses to feed rail. In Washington, D.C., WMATA's assistant general manager said, "Most professionals here do not ride the buses. The buses unfortunately are considered to be for the poor folks and have a higher degree of personal risk" (Bassily 1993: 13).

Transit agency response to a preference for modal attractiveness may also have positive social-program effects. This is borne out by observed increases in urban land values along transit routes where rail (especially light rail) has replaced buses. Rail seems to impart a traditional image of permanence and connectivity for property adjacent to its routes and stops. In addition to having this positive collateral economic development effect (a social-program outcome) along routes (Boschken 1998b; Attoe 1988), a high-tech rail strategy may also aid mobility for transit-dependent users (another social-program outcome), especially if rail routes are subsidized for these disadvantaged users.

Transit-dependent users normally take the bus for local trips but have better access to the larger metropolitan area with the availability of rail (Wachs and Taylor 1997). In urban areas with a spoke-and-hub pattern, expanded rail routes may give new access to the core-city transit-dependent user seeking better employment and recreation opportunities in the suburban periphery (often referred to as "reverse commuting"). However, because of the much greater expense in operating and maintaining high-tech rail systems, the strategy may also depress operational efficiency (Pickrell 1992). The expected effect on skewing the pattern of policy outcomes is hypothesized as follows:

> H10: The greater the use of stylized or futuristic transit technologies (especially rail-based systems), the more likely the agency will emphasize strategic organizational effectiveness (Outcome I) and incidentally social-program effectiveness (Outcome III) but deemphasize operational efficiency (Outcome II).

Taken together, the two hypotheses advance the thesis that situational market conditions will skew the pattern of an agency's policy outcomes in reinforcing ways. Under conditions favorable to transit (e.g., congested roads, the existence of high-tech transit equipment), the agency will pursue an entrepreneurial strategy where budgets and market penetration grow, efficiency suffers, and social programs are served. An example of this is the strategic connection made in San Diego by MTDB's chief planner: "San Diego has been served principally by a bus system. But our light rail system has gotten a lot of support across the city from those who know how bad congestion is" (Lieberman 1989: 22).

Under unfavorable conditions (e.g., uncongested roads, the existence of unreliable or outdated transit equipment), the agency will adopt a subordination strategy that reduces budgets and market penetration, highlights efficiency, and diminishes social programs. Although this may seem to some an unlikely set of conditions, several agencies (especially in the Midwest) exhibit such an automobile-dominated but generally uncongested market environment. In St. Louis, for example, a Bi-State deputy transit director commented: "St. Louis is an auto-industry town. It's not like Boston or Chicago where the very infrastructure from day one was geared around public transportation. So we have developed a transit system that is complementary [to] and compatible [with] the auto rather than in competition with it" (Douglas 1993: 7).

Urban Spatial Structure

The populations of metropolitan areas differ greatly in their intraurban travel behavior and use of transportation modes. Some, like those in New York and Chicago, use public transit for many types of activities. Others, like those in Los Angeles and the San Francisco Bay Area, primarily use automobiles for most types of journeys. One cause of this variance is believed to be *urban spatial form* (Parsons, Brinckerhoff, Quade & Douglas 1996; Bourne 1982). The term refers to the geographic layout of the urban area as a whole, and specifically to (1) how concentrated or centralized activity sites are and (2) the way in which the location of home, work, and leisure activities are spatially arranged in relation to one another. Urban form is usually represented by two indicators: *density gradients* (visualized much like a geological topography map), involving both residential and employment locations; and *connectivity*, involving interaction between those locations as revealed by the variable uses of transportation routes and communications systems (Parsons, Brinckerhoff, Quade & Douglas 1996; Bourne 1982: 28–45; De Sola Pool 1982).

Differences in spatial form are perhaps best seen and compared when flying transcontinental routes, where a "bird's-eye" view of density gradients and connectivity reveals physical distinctions in the topography of American cities. At one extreme, for example, one can easily distinguish the *primary conical urban core* of Chicago tapering outward in concentric rings of residences and smaller secondary centers of greater Cook County (Atlanta, Philadelphia, and the New York metropolitan area share these features as well). At the other extreme is the *leveled polycentric cityscape* of southern California with its widely dispersed and nonintegrated activity centers (other urban areas with these features include Houston, Orlando, and the greater San Francisco Bay Area).

However, most cities today have spatial patterns that appear to lie somewhere between the extremes. Kansas City, for example, still has the residual of its "bombed-out" central core and first residential ring (developed more than a century ago), but the area also shows significant multinucleation from recent suburban residential and commercial developments. The Denver metropolitan area seems to be a combination of its older but still viable central business district formed around rail yards and a more recent multi-nucleation along a north-south axis, springing up from high-tech industry and an in-migration of upper-middle-class professionals. Even the greater Chicago area looks increasingly polycentric if one looks beyond Cook County to newer outlying areas such as Du Page County.

Conceptually, comparisons of urban form are made with reference to two polar models that are distinguished by several visual characteristics (Parsons, Brinckerhoff, Quade & Douglas 1996; Giuliano and Small 1991; Bourne 1982). The most commonly used is *spatial centralization* of human activities. Imagine an urban topography map with contours representing elevation: the contoured height of aggregated physical structures forms a cityscape shaped by variations in the stacking of commercial and residential floor space.

Reflecting the highest levels of centralization, the first and oldest model is of a monocentric or spoke-and-hub pattern. It has a center-peripheral configuration consisting of a single central business district (CBD) surrounded by concentric rings descending outward in terms of structural height, activity density, and property values. Its centralized conical form reflects the historical effects of transportation and communications technologies in the late nineteenth and early twentieth centuries, which reinforced a need for physical proximity and a common "downtown" core as the principal area of economic activity.

In cities that developed this spoke-and-hub form, human activities (including where people lived and worked, did errands, and engaged in a social life) clustered and concentrated along routes of public mass transit (Parsons, Brinckerhoff, Quade & Douglas 1996: part 1; Cervero and Landis 1995; Bourne 1982; Timms 1971; Burgess 1961). Between the Civil War and sometime before World War II, economic and technological considerations pushed transportation modes in the direction of fixed-route rail systems. Unable to easily move these routes, cities developed relatively linear and stable density patterns and land values emanating from a high-value common core and along transit corridors leading out from the CBD. Important features of its centralized organization are sector specialization of activities and areawide integration of its interdependent parts by the transportation "spokes" and primitive communications systems (e.g., central switchboards, message couriers, inventory delivery services).

The second, contrasting, model is of a "polycentric" cityscape (Giuliano and Small 1991; Gordon, Richardson, and Wong 1986; Leven 1982). It represents different degrees of spatial decentralization and integration of activities ranging from "corridors" and substantial clusters of subregional business centers to nearly undifferentiated dispersion (Parsons, Brinckerhoff, Quade & Douglas 1996). In its extreme form, it depicts an unstructured "urban sprawl" (Policy.com 1999), a level plane mostly devoid of specialized subareas that defies spatially parametric connectedness.

Appearing after World War II, the polycentric model resulted from three influences: (1) suburbanization, which often involved the growing together of small rural towns (Leven 1982); (2) the spatially liberating effect of automobiles (Bourne 1982; Meyer, Kain, and Wohl 1965) and more recently (3) high-technology communications and flexible production systems (Warren and Donaghy 1986; Castells 1985; Scott 1982). The combination greatly lessened the value of *physical proximity* in linking various activities and reduced the dependence of urban vitality on a CBD. Moreover, the influences created a pattern not of an integrated city-and-suburb (Rybcznski 1999) but of multi-nucleation, where the purpose of and distinctions between urban core and suburban periphery are blurred.

People came to perceive their cityscape as random fragments within a larger macrostructure, where a comprehensive integration of places was absent and an identity with other parts of the urban area were not commonly or universally shared. Orleans's ethnographic experiments with citizens of the Los Angeles basin (1967), for example, show that people's individual cognitive maps of their personal territory and movements within the basin included widely dispersed (often disconnected) landmarks and other spatial identities. In the aggregate, they appear to share little common ground except freeways, and a dispersion pattern with little areawide connectedness. Instead, people demonstrated a loose interdependence over the entire area, but not with regard to any sizable focal points or any particular subparts.

Moreover, the meaning of connectedness in the polycentric model was reshaped by three new decentralized types of urban journeys. First, many trips, especially work-related ones, involved "cross commuting" from one suburb to another without reference to a CBD. Second, increasing numbers of people settled in suburban communities where they could both work and live, thus reducing connectedness to the larger area as a whole. Some see this resulting from "edge-city" development (Garreau 1991) where "independent" residential-business cores spring up along the periphery of older cities. Third, as interurban freeways allowed for longer travel, a contingent of the population regularly crossed metropolitan boundaries into adjacent urban areas. All three travel patterns reinforced activity dispersal, a loss of intraurban connectedness, and a blurring of distinctions between urban and suburban periphery.

The Los Angeles basin is among the best representatives of this model as a dispersed urban form where no single center of activity dominates the region. The northern half shows some clustering of business activity (including the Los Angeles CBD and Wilshire Corridor), while the southern half (Orange and Riverside Counties) is much more highly dispersed. The basin experienced its principal development after World War II, when the auto and modern communications became dominant in journeys to work, errands, and leisure. As the metropolitan area grew from its multi-nucleated origin of small agricultural towns, the development pattern became a more randomized distribution of commercial strips and merchant residential subdivisions linked together by a latticework of wide boulevards and feeder roads.

The relevance of urban spatial form to the policy outcomes of transit agencies lies with an agency's ability to provide access to and deliver services to a high proportion of the urban population. Research shows that transit's market penetration is the result of how urban activities "are organized spatially" (Parsons, Brinckerhoff, Quade & Douglas 1996: part I, p. 4). Specifically, urban areas configured along the lines of the monocentric model with a dominant CBD or highly "corridored" concentrations of activity are more supportive of a transit agency's organizational prominence (Outcome I effectiveness) and social-program effectiveness (Outcome III) than areas characterized by the polycentric model (Cervero and Landis 1992; Bell 1991; Ley 1985).

Density gradient was found to be the most significant of the urban-form considerations; it particularly affects vehicle trip length between activity sites and the walking distance between vehicle stop (i.e., parking lot or transit station) and an activity site. With particular reference to travelers having a modal choice, "It stands to reason that mass transit needs 'mass' or density if substantial numbers of people are to ride trains and buses" (Parsons, Brinckerhoff, Quade & Douglas 1996: part I, p. 11). Moreover, most studies have found that shifts from a monocentric pattern to a polycentric configuration cause a significant decline in the centrality of transit for all kinds of intraurban journeys and thus lower patronage.

The shift also causes a change in how local politicians view the centrality of transit in relation to their constituents. Baltimore MTA's chief planner connected spatial form with transit popularity by saying, "Inside the Beltway, where the vast bulk of our service is, there is a general consensus among all elected officials that transit is good. . . . I think that changes somewhat as you get outside the Beltway, where service is much less dense. Politicians don't see us as that important in suburban areas" (Goon 1991: 24).

Most transit agency managers know of these economic and political variances in perceived transit value, but because they are backseat drivers in almost all metropolitan area land use policymaking, they have had little influence on halting suburban sprawl or maintaining a monocentric urban form. Orange County, located in the southern portion of the Los Angeles basin, is characteristic of unrelenting sprawl and subordinated mass transit. The agency's general manager reflected on this relationship:

> You cannot separate [transit] agency policymaking from land use if you want to make transit effective. [Even though local politicians run from the thought,] I still maintain if the agency doesn't have major participation in land use decisions, you're not going to make any progress in getting better use of transit. (Reichert 1989: 2)

Urban form is also thought to affect a transit agency's operational efficiency. The monocentric urban area is more centralized, with subarea specialization and concentrated linear connectivity. As a consequence, one study argues that it is easy to see how this pattern reduces the cost of providing service: "Shorter trips and trip times allow transit operators to provide the same quality and quantity [as in a polycentric pattern] with fewer vehicles and fewer driver hours" (Parsons, Brinckerhoff, Quade & Douglas 1996: part I, p. 11).

The multiple effects of urban spatial structure on skewing the pattern of policy outcomes, therefore, may be hypothesized as follows:

H11: The closer the spatial form of a transit agency's urban area fits the monocentric model, the more likely the agency's policy emphasis will be robust but evenly distributed among all three policy-outcome perspectives.

Conversely,

H12: The closer the spatial form of a transit agency's urban area fits the polycentric model, the more likely the agency will deemphasize all three policy perspectives.

Taken together, the two hypotheses advance the thesis that urban spatial form affects all outcome emphases, such that an agency in a monocentric area will more likely provide superior, widely used, and efficient services to both commuters and social-program users than an agency operating in a more decentralized area. Moreover, nearly all current urban growth in both monocentric and polycentric areas involves a decentralization of urban form. In Philadelphia (a monocentric city), for example, SEPTA's chief planner commented on the effect of this form of urban growth on transit: "We're decentralizing just like other metropolitan areas. That change, however, creates a dual challenge for a public transit agency to try to maintain service to the traditional commuter to the urban core and, at the same time, respond to these new suburban travel paths, most of which are cross-commuting all over the place. Suburban growth and development patterns are not transit-friendly" (Bickel 1993: 4).

However, the spatial form thesis does not speak directly to the *evenness* of effect on the three policy-outcome components and leaves open the question of how disproportional impacts might create an asymmetrical pattern of policy outcomes. Nevertheless, some threads of theory in managerial economics offer indirect insight based on scale. One concept says, for example, that concentrations of market demand provide economies of scale that may be used to keep prices affordable for a greater number of users. Applied to the spatial effects of urban form on outcome bias, this might suggest that the more monocentric the urban area, the greater the emphasis on an agency's organizational effectiveness, which consists in part of a market penetration measure. Economic scale would also explain a disproportional emphasis on operational efficiency. That is, for users, a monocentric urban form provides superior cost savings over urban sprawl because more passengers can be served with shorter routes and a denser or corridored route system. On the effectiveness of social programs, however, no compelling theory provides a hint. If urban form leaves social effectiveness unaffected, then, in combination with the other two outcomes, economies of scale might suggest a basis for pattern skewness favoring administration-centered outcomes.

Finally, with respect to skewing the pattern of transit-agency outcomes, it is possible that the market and urban-form theses are partially connected. Some research, for example, shows that a common denominator shared by market conditions and spatial form is consumer preference for *accessibility* (Handy 1995). Consumption of a transportation mode is dependent on (1) freeway congestion and parking availability, (2) the number of transit transfers required, (3) the proximity of transit stops to origin and destination points (all of which are market conditions), and (4) the proximal location of different activity sites to one another (the urban-form attribute of density). In addition, Pushkarev and Zupan (1982) and Leven (1982) found that transit technology and urban density were codeterminants of transit service levels, suggesting that Outcome I effectiveness (whose administration-centered perspective is heavily focused on suburban commuters) is emphasized by the use of a rail mode in monocentric areas. In a polycentric urban area, buses provide more route flexibility.

Operationalizing Market and Urban-Form Variables

For both the market thesis and the urban-form thesis, operationalization could include many different kinds of variables. Because the size of the data sample limits our model capacity to fewer than a dozen independent variables, choice among alternatives is important to achieving parsimony and model significance. Indeed, many potential variables for these theses are redundant and risk unnecessary exposure to collinearity. With this in mind, two variables were selected for the market thesis and one for the urban-form thesis.

The market thesis describes competition in the context of market conditions created by the interaction of supply and demand. A public agency's exposure to competition (in this case, a cell I market dominated by private sector suppliers) is determined by how consumers act on their preferences and by producers' ability to supply products or services to

TABLE **5.2** Agencies in Areas with the Highest and Lowest Roadway Congestion
Urban Public Transit, 1990

Ten Agencies with Highest Congestion	Z-Score	Ten Agencies with Lowest Congestion	Z-Score
1. SCRDT	2.33	42. NFTA	−1.76
2. MUNI	2.33	41. Utah Transit Authority	−1.31
3. Long Beach Transit	2.33	40. COTA	−1.26
4. AC Transit	1.43	39. Port Authority of Allegheny	−1.26
5. BART	1.43	County	
6. WMATA	1.43	38. IPT	−1.11
7. OCTA	0.88	37. VIA Metropolitan Transit	−1.01
8. M-DT	0.88	36. NFTA	−0.87
9. CTA	0.68	35. Metropolitan Transit Commission	−0.87
10. MMS	0.68	34. Jacksonville Transportation	−0.77
		Authority	
		33. SORTA	−0.67

NOTE: See Appendix A for agency names.

meet those preferences. From the agency's standpoint, the resultant market conditions may take the form of either (1) obstacles that moderate the competitive position of different product substitutes or (2) product characteristics that dominate consumer appeal.

In the case of transit, the measure indicative of the first type of market condition is *roadway congestion*. This variable represents a condition in which roadway demand exceeds capacity, thus altering the traveler's perceived modal flexibility and travel time differentials with transit (Bish and Nourse 1975; Downs 1962). It is the principal impediment for transit's main competitor—the auto/roadway consortium—and serves to improve the public agency's relative market position. The severity of the condition may affect whether transit can move from a subordinated position to a more equal footing with autos in the market.

The variable is a 1989 index of estimated roadway congestion for an urban area corresponding to the transit district jurisdiction. Developed by a Texas Transportation Institute study (Hanks and Lomax 1992), the index is calculated as a ratio of daily vehicle miles of travel per lane mile. Table 5.2 identifies in the sample those agencies with the ten highest and ten lowest levels of congestion in their metropolitan areas. Those with the most congestion are located in larger cities, especially on the

West Coast, and those with the least congested roadways are found in smaller cities, mainly in the Midwest.

In the second area of product characteristics, the variable used is transit's *technological image*. In reference to the stylistic attractiveness of the system's design and rolling stock, consumers factor into their choices whether the transit alternative is comfortable and technologically advanced. Evidence suggests that, when compared with autos, rail-based transit (both heavy and light rail) is viewed by the transportation consumer as stylistically more appealing than bus transit (Boschken 1998b; Pickrell 1992). Although some heavy-rail systems certainly fail the imagery test, rail still holds a stylistic superiority over a conventional bus system and therefore improves the market position of the agency in its bid to compete with the auto/roadway consortium.

To capture this technological effect on stylistic appeal, a surrogate derived from a transit system's modal mix is used. Data for the continuum-scaled variable were drawn from figures reported in FTA Section 15 tables as "passenger miles traveled by vehicle mode" (FTA 1993). The percentage of mileage driven by mode type was calculated as a continuous scale, which a frequency histogram showed to have three clustered peaks. From the histogram, variable values for technological image were then derived as a collapsed three-point scale, where 1 = bus system only, 2 = bus and rail combination, and 3 = rail system only. Because empirical formulas are difficult to construct for perceived or qualitative variables like imagery, the surrogate scale should be read cautiously as increasing levels of stylistic appeal for the system as a whole. Of the forty-two agencies, nearly three-quarters operate bus-only systems. The rest except for one (BART in the San Francisco Bay Area) operate a combination of bus and rail systems, some of which are integrated bus-rail systems (Chicago, Sacramento) and others are partitioned systems according to mode (San Diego, Washington, D.C.).

The second thesis of this chapter is about urban spatial form. It describes an impact on policy outcomes resulting from variation in the spatial arrangement of human activity. The literature distinguishes two polar models with in-between increments representing overall how activities are physically related to each other. The models incorporate a number of discriminating characteristics, which include distance between activities, specialized subregional segmentation of the urban area, the number and

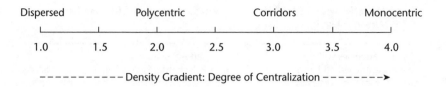

FIGURE 5.1 Urban Form: Scaling Centralization of Activities (42 Urban Transit Agencies)

relative size of concentrated activity masses, and the degree to which there is a hierarchy of dominance among centers. Combined, they reveal a comparative topology of cityscapes.

However, because the estimation of all these for a large statistical sample is costly, most research estimates spatial form using density gradients alone. Moreover, according to Parsons, Brinckerhoff, Quade & Douglas (1996), density gradients are the most important factor differentiating urban configurations and have the largest effect on transit patronage. Nevertheless, in order to incorporate as many of the characteristics of spatial form as feasible, this study adopts a variation of the density gradient method by creating a single intersubjective variable based on density mapping techniques and direct aerial observation of the forty-two transit districts.

This variable is called *urban form*, and as shown in Figure 5.1, was constructed as a seven-point continuous scale, along which four increments of centralization are identified. Derived from the works of Parsons, Brinckerhoff, Quade & Douglas (1996), Gordon, Richardson, and Wong (1996), Bourne (1982) and others, the scale increments are conceptually defined as (1) dispersed/sprawl (least centralized), (2) polycentric (dispersed but with numerous subregional concentrations randomly distributed), (3) corridors (more centralized, with a dominant CBD from which substantial corridors of specialized secondary centers radiate outward), and (4) monocentric (most centralized, in which a single large-scale CBD is surrounded by concentric rings of residential and small-scale commercial activity and where there is minimal dispersion of large secondary centers).

The variable provides a comparison between the spatial conical shape of urban areas found within each transit agency's operational juris-

TABLE **5.3** Agencies with the Highest and Lowest Centralization of Urban Form
Urban Public Transit, 1990

Twelve Agencies with Monocentric Urban Form	Score	Ten Agencies with Polycentric/Sprawl Form	Score
1. MUNI	4.0	42. PT	1.0
2. Jacksonville Transportation Authority	4.0	41. Long Beach Transit	1.0
		40. OCTA	1.0
3. CTA	4.0	39. GGT	1.0
4. Regional Transit Authority	4.0	38. Santa Clara County Transit	1.0
5. Mass Transit Administration	4.0	37. NFTA	1.0
6. GCRT	4.0	36. SCRTD	2.0
7. Tri-Met	4.0	35. AC Transit	2.0
8. SEPTA	4.0	34. Bi-State DA	2.0
9. Port Authority of Allegheny County	4.0	33. MTA	2.0
10. VIA Metropolitan Transit	4.0		
11. Pierce Transit	4.0		
12. MCT	4.0		

NOTE: See Appendix A for agency names.

diction. About 30 percent of the agencies exist in urban areas that fit the monocentric model, and about 15 percent operate in highly dispersed areas of urban sprawl. Table 5.3 identifies in the sample the twelve agencies operating in a monocentric urban form and the ten agencies operating under dispersed and polycentric conditions. Those in highly centralized spatial structures are located mostly in the East, but several are also found in the South and on the West Coast. Nearly all of the agencies operating in a polycentric or dispersed urban form are found in the West.

This discussion of market conditions and urban form concludes Part II of the study. This and the two preceding chapters put into play six rival theses for analyzing the socioeconomic, political, market, and urban-form determinants of pattern skewness in policy outcomes. Along with the theses, nine variables were operationalized to represent the rivals. Part III provides a comparative empirical analysis of the rivals to determine which offer the more durable, compelling, and significant explanations of bias in policy outcomes.

III   *Results, Analysis, and Implications*

6   Determining Policy Outcomes:
       What Matters Most?

Each of the six rival theses laid out in Part II provides a different explanation for the biasing of policy outcomes in public agencies. Although the theses are targeted at understanding determinants of the MSOI pattern as a whole, they speak in the form of hypotheses specific to the individual outcome perspectives that make up the overall pattern. In the course of those discussions, twelve hypotheses were drawn from the respective literatures on the upper middle class, regional wealth, the underclass, institutional exchange, market conditions, and urban form. With that comparative perspective, we turn now to empirically evaluating the hypothesized relationships. In this chapter, the analysis consists of (1) reviewing the basic tenets of the rival theses, (2) examining statistically the variance and independence of operational variables representing each thesis, (3) reporting initial full-model regression results on direct effects, and (4) reconsidering those results for variables potentially affected by collinearity.

In Chapter 2, the analysis of policy-outcome data for the forty-two agencies concluded that transit's different MSOI perspectives fit into an *interrelated pattern of outcomes*. In fact, after Outcome IV (reciprocal effectiveness) was eliminated (because it lacked sample variance after adjusting for urban scale), the three remaining outcomes were shown to be very significantly intercorrelated (see Table 2.3). Confirming that they may be considered components of an overall pattern of outcomes, the analysis also found two of the three cell relationships to be inversely (negatively) correlated. This means industrywide policy tradeoffs are made where an emphasis in one perspective tends to occur at the sacrifice or deemphasis of another.

In the transit sample, these tradeoffs are between an outcome of operational efficiency (cell II) on one side and the two strategic outcomes of organizational effectiveness (cell I) and social-program effectiveness (cell III) on the other. Consistent with this pattern, the one reinforcing (positive) relationship is between the two strategic perspectives, suggesting that, for transit at least, the larger cleavage in policymaking is not between administration-centered and social-centered outcomes but between strategic and operational perspectives. These empirical findings of an interrelated MSOI pattern set the stage for a review of the rival theses.

Rival Theses: Analysis of the Independent Variables

The six rival theses were developed according to four different groupings of social science literature. As summarized in Figure 6.1, these groupings are (1) socioeconomic influences (including an upper-middle-class [UMC] genre, local or regional wealth, and a poverty-stricken urban underclass); (2) the politics of intergovernmental exchange (involving an agency's autonomy in acquiring fiscal resources and engaging in statutory interactions with intergovernmental actors); (3) market conditions surrounding urban passenger transportation (involving roadway congestion and technological imagery of transit systems); and (4) urban spatial form, which physically structures metropolitan land use. The figure shows the previously hypothesized impacts on individual policy outcomes (i.e., whether they cause an outcome emphasis or deemphasis). In three theses, the literature was silent about one or more of the impacts on outcome perspectives, thus leaving us unable to hypothesize a relationship.

The first category is socioeconomic influences and includes theses about outcome skewness determined by conditions of an agency's metropolitan polity. Regarding the UMC genre, three hypotheses argued that a high proportion of UMC in the population would promote an asymmetrical pattern of outcomes favoring strategic emphases on organizational effectiveness and social-program effectiveness. With an appreciation for "abstracts," UMC persons project through their collective symbolic genre

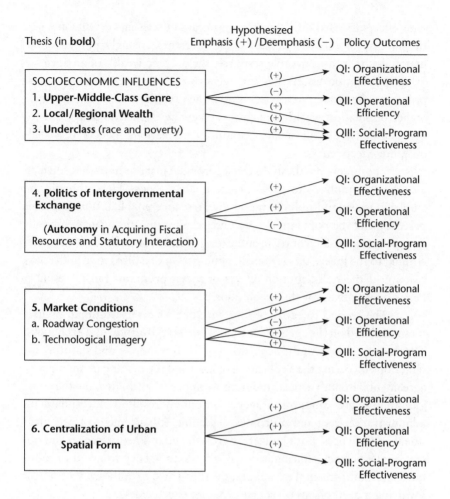

FIGURE **6.1** Rival Theses: Summary of Impacts on Policy Outcomes

cosmopolitan preferences for strong public institutions and effective so-cial programs, both of which indicate a sense of well-being in a global context of "world-class" cities. Because the presence of such underlying abundance makes waste a secondary issue, these more coveted strategic emphases would come at the expense of a deemphasis on operational efficiency.

In contrast to the UMC genre's comprehensive impacts on pattern bias, the two other socioeconomic theses pose a more limited impact, with effects focused only on social-program effectiveness (Outcome III). In the case of the wealth thesis, the literature strongly points to the hypothesis that, as a taxable resource, the average wealth of an agency's urban population establishes the agency's spending potential on social programs. According to a systems approach relating inputs to outcomes, higher population wealth will cause a skewing of the MSOI pattern toward emphasis on an agency's statutory obligations to achieve social-program effectiveness.

The underclass thesis, likewise, provides just one hypothesis, which also throws emphasis to social-program effectiveness. Here, though, the emphasis is demand-induced rather than resource-enabled. With a greater percentage of the population in an underclass status, the agency responds with programs sufficient to meet the level of need for welfare services. According to the thesis, this is done in anticipation of a disruptive underclass reaction if the redistribution efforts of social programs fail to result in better-quality lives for the urban poor.

The second category of literature defines an institutional-politics thesis centered on the agency's autonomy in intergovernmental exchanges. The thesis covers both the acquisition of fiscal resources and statutory interactions involving the application of laws and the making of interagency agreements. In both aspects of intergovernmental exchange, the thesis argues that greater amounts of agency autonomy result in an emphasis on administration-centered outcomes, including enhancement of organizational effectiveness (both budgetary growth and market presence) and operational efficiency. Since autonomy allows an agency to avoid or minimize intergovernmental exchanges, the thesis also hypothesizes a tradeoff involving a deemphasis on social-program effectiveness.

The third category addresses market conditions as a determinant of outcome skewness. Among the many possible factors of competition, two are included that cover supply capabilities and technology. In the case of roadway congestion, the thesis introduces limits on supply that transit's competitors are unable to overcome. As a supply-side condition, congestion is hypothesized to induce an emphasis on the agency's strategic outcomes of organizational effectiveness and social-program effectiveness. Because the literature is silent about any effects on operational efficiency, the asymmetrical pattern is formed by congestion's influence on these strategic emphases alone. The effects of technological imagery on strategic outcomes are argued to be similar to congestion, but in addition, adoption of high-tech alternatives comes with a tradeoff involving a deemphasis of operational efficiency.

The last category speaks to the effects of land-use configuration on policy outcomes. Although several aspects of land use may be involved, the common denominator in the literature seems to fall to a thesis about urban spatial form. An urban area's structure of human activities may be seen in part through the overall pattern and arrangement of physical artifacts that have been created over time to accommodate those activities. This spatial form varies from city to city, ranging from highly centralized and concentric urban patterns to level configurations of extensive metropolitan sprawl with few distinguishable concentrations of activity.

The literature indicates that an urban area's physical conical shape will determine the level of an agency's policy outcomes. That is, to the degree that urban activities are patterned around a central core, spatial form will cause all three outcome perspectives to be emphasized. In areas where activity patterns are dispersed urban sprawl, all policy outcomes of efficiency and effectiveness are likely to be reduced. Although spatial form is hypothesized to magnify or reduce all outcomes simultaneously, some threads of logic in managerial economics nevertheless suggest that its impact may be uneven. For example, enterprising agencies may take advantage of the economies of scale and greater access to customers afforded by a monocentric urban form. Since the managerial logic does not seem to extend to political considerations that drive social-program effectiveness, urban form may have a greater skewing effect on administration-centered outcomes.

The rival theses are operationalized by a model containing nine independent variables described in Part II. For empirical analysis, descriptive statistics and intercorrelations are reported in Table 6.1. Since the three socioeconomic theses are represented by factored variables, their values are automatically standardized with a mean of zero and a standard deviation of one. The remaining variables, although standardized as Z-scores in regressions, are reported here in their unstandardized values.

The sample of forty-two agencies is relatively small by large database standards, so it is especially necessary to be sensitive to multicollinearity effects on the models as a whole and in the potential for under- or overestimation of individual variables. Collinearity may distort the

TABLE **6.1** Rival Theses: The Independent Variables
Descriptive Statistics and Intercorrelations

Variable	Mean	s.d.	1	2	3	4	5	6	7	8	9
Socioeconomic											
1. Upper Middle Class	0.0	1.0	—								
2. Average Wealth	0.0	1.0	.86**	—							
3. Underclass Status	0.0	1.0	.17	.01	—						
Agency Autonomy in											
Intergovernmental Exchange											
4. Revenue (fiscal autonomy)	76.7	22.4	.14	.22	.01	—					
5. Capital (fiscal autonomy)	26.7	18.4	.37	.37	.00	.37	—				
6. Intergovernmental Interaction (statutory autonomy)	5.4	3.6	.32	.37	-.16	-.02	-.03	—			
Market Competition											
7. Roadway Congestion	1.1	0.2	.47*	.54**	-.53**	.13	.29	.34	—		
8. Technology Image	1.3	0.5	.29	.23	-.28	-.22	.23	.45*	.39	—	
Urban Spatial Form											
9. Spatial Centralization	2.9	1.0	-.24	-.42*	-.13	-.30	-.19	-.08	-.16	.26	—

NOTE: $N = 42$ agencies. Two-tailed significance: * = .01   ** = .001.

individual explanatory contribution (marginal effect) of highly associated variables in the model at hand, and in the extreme may cause false-negative results in the affected coefficients. In addition, severe collinearity causes models to be unstable in that statistical results can vary widely from sample to sample (thus raising questions about the reliability of generalizations).

Significant intercorrelations among independent variables, such as those representing the rival theses in this study, are often symptomatic of collinearity. As Table 6.1 indicates, six bivariate correlations exist, three of which are very significant (significance is greater than .001). The six include those between the UMC genre and wealth (r = .86), congestion and the UMC genre (r = .47), congestion and wealth (r = .54), congestion and underclass status (r = −.53), technology image and intergovernmental (IG) interaction (r = .47), and spatial form and wealth (r = −.42). Contained within these is a three-way intercorrelation cluster among the UMC genre, wealth, and congestion. However, the fact that some of the independent variables are correlated among themselves does not necessarily mean collinearity exists or is severe enough to matter in assessing the relative importance of each variable in explaining asymmetry in policy outcomes.

In fact, more precise "collinearity diagnostics" are used to pin down the degenerative effects of multicollinearity. One of these is the "variance inflation factor" (VIF), which measures how much variance in individual variables is inflated as a result of collinearity. A VIF value of 10 or higher is generally regarded as an indication of moderate to high degenerative effects of collinearity. A second diagnostic tool for corroborative purposes is the "condition index" (CI) used in combination with a matrix of "variance proportions" (VP). Together they measure the statistical stability of a correlation matrix of independent variables. A CI with a value greater than 30 is generally considered indicative of moderate to severe collinearity, which compromises the stability of the regression model. If the CI reaches this threshold level, the VP matrix is used to locate the variables contributing to the collinearity. Analysis of the matrix is considered unnecessary if the model's CI falls well below 30.

For this study, collinearity diagnostics were run on the nine independent variables composing the model of rival hypotheses. The VIF statistics for each of the variables were well below the threshold value of 10 and ranged from 5.6 (UMC genre and wealth) to 1.4 (revenue autonomy). In corroboration, the CI for the rival-theses model was 17.6, well below the threshold value of 30, and makes an analysis of the VP matrix unnecessary. In sum, the diagnostics appear to indicate that the problem is not severe enough to significantly compromise regression results, but, given the sample size, they justify a closer look at potentially affected variables later in this chapter.

Initial Analysis of Results

Table 6.2 reports initial results of OLS regressions for each of the three components of the MSOI pattern of policy outcomes. Each model includes the nine independent variables representing the four categories of rival theses. Results show each model as a whole (for Outcomes I, II, and III) to be very significant in contributing to an explanation of skewness in the pattern of policy outcomes (signif. of F = .000, .002, .000, respectively). Jointly they account for about 50 percent of the pattern dynamics, indicating a strong likelihood that few important variables have been left out of the models. Regarding the individual independent variables, however, regression results show a wide variance in the relative contributions of rival theses.

Among the socioeconomic theses, statistics for the UMC genre are in the direction predicted by the hypotheses, but the factor is truly significant only in the Outcome I model (signif. of t = .03). This result supports Hypothesis 1, which argues that the UMC genre encourages an emphasis on strategic organizational effectiveness (beta = .60, t = 2.23). Statistics are not at a level of significance (signif. of t = .71) to support Hypothesis 2 regarding a deemphasis on operational efficiency even though the sign is in the predicted direction (beta = −.11, t = −0.38). Results are near significance in the Outcome III model (signif. of t = .12), perhaps providing some tentative support for Hypothesis 3, which argued that the presence of a UMC genre will encourage an emphasis on social-program effectiveness (beta = .44, t = 1.60).

For the wealth thesis, the literature provides one of the oldest and most enduring concepts about what determines skewness in policy outcomes. Derived principally from general systems theory, the argument nevertheless speaks in a consistent voice for only one of the three compo-

TABLE **6.2** OLS Regressions: Initial Comparative Analysis of Rival Theses
Three Policy-Outcome Models, 42 Transit Agencies

	Dependent Variables								
	Outcome I			Outcome II			Outcome III		
Independent Variable:	beta	t	significance	beta	t	significance	beta	t	significance
Socioeconomic									
1. Upper-Middle-Class Genre	.60	2.23	.03	-.11	-0.38	.71	.44	1.60	.12
2. Population Wealth	-.27	-0.99	.33	-.21	-0.73	.47	-.15	-0.54	.59
3. Underclass Status	.06	0.35	.73	-.02	-0.09	.93	-.14	-0.81	.43
Agency Autonomy in Intergovernmental Exchange									
4. Revenue (fiscal autonomy)	-.26	-1.93	.06	.45	3.09	.00	-.03	-0.25	.80
5. Capital (fiscal autonomy)	.11	0.75	.46	-.14	-0.92	.36	.17	1.18	.25
6. Intergovernmental Interaction (statutory autonomy)	.26	1.83	.08	.19	1.20	.24	.01	0.06	.95
Market Competition									
7. Congestion	.10	0.53	.60	.17	0.86	.39	.27	1.46	.15
8. Technology Image	.02	0.15	.89	-.48	-2.77	.01	.19	1.17	.25
Urban Spatial Form									
9. Spatial Centralization	.42	2.92	.01	.05	0.31	.76	.30	2.04	.05
R^2	.59			.52			.58		
Adjusted R^2	.47			.38			.46		
F	5.04			3.82			4.95		
Significance of F	.000			.002			.000		

nents of the MSOI pattern. This hypothesis predicts a positive effect on Outcome III, where population wealth is expected to cause an emphasis on social-program effectiveness. Because contrary arguments exist for effects on administration-centered outcomes, no predictions were made, and the initial results indicate that no significant relationships exist. However, statistics for Outcome III are also not significant (signif. of $t = .59$) and thus do not support Hypothesis 4. Since this result is inconsistent with past research, the next section further examines the possible effects of collinearity on wealth.

As it does for wealth, literature on the underclass thesis provides a firm basis for only one of the three outcome components. In fact, although the underclass and wealth variables are statistically independent of each other ($r = .01$), Hypothesis 5 predicts that the underclass and wealth will cause similar emphases on social-program effectiveness. The initial regression results, however, indicate that the underclass is not significant in any of the policy-outcome models, including social-program effectiveness (Outcome III) (signif. of $t = .43$).

For the institutional exchange thesis, three independent variables were used to test hypotheses. Combined, their results provide either mixed or inconclusive support for the three hypotheses about agency autonomy in intergovernmental exchange. Statistics for the organizational effectiveness (Outcome I) model indicate revenue autonomy and IG interaction to be near significance (signif. of $t = .06$ and $.08$, respectively). However, the direction of each is the inverse of that predicted by Hypothesis 6 regarding the positive role of autonomy in encouraging an emphasis on strategic organizational effectiveness. Perhaps because there are few substantial alternative sources of revenue for transit operators beyond intergovernmental sources, the greater an agency's autonomy in acquiring revenue the more likely this revenue-demanding outcome will be deemphasized (beta $= -.26$, $t = -1.93$). Reinforcing this fiscal effect, the higher the statutory interaction required of the agency in intergovernmental exchange (representing lower autonomy), the more likely it will result in a deemphasis of organizational effectiveness (beta $= .26$, $t = 1.83$).

Statistics for the operational efficiency (Outcome II) model indicate only revenue autonomy to be significant (signif. of $t = .00$), but they strongly support Hypothesis 7, which argues that autonomy from inter-governmental exchange enhances the likelihood that the agency will emphasize operational efficiency (beta = .45, t = 3.09). In the case of revenue autonomy, this relationship may be due to the fact that fiscal conservation resulting from efficiency measures is more important when funding for operations is less available from intergovernmental sources (which may be more dependable than market sources, albeit with costly strings attached). Without significance for capital autonomy and IG interaction (signif. of t = .36 and .24, respectively), the broader results are inconclusive for supporting the hypothesis beyond the purely fiscal operational considerations.

Statistics for the social-program effectiveness (Outcome III) model do not support Hypothesis 8, which posits that lower autonomy promotes emphasis on social-program effectiveness. Although surprising given the vast federalist institutional literature that argues strong relationships should exist, none of the intergovernmental variables are near significance, and only the statistics for revenue autonomy show a directional sign consistent with that predicted by the hypothesis.

For the market conditions thesis, statistics for roadway congestion are in directions predicted by Hypothesis 9 for Outcomes I and III (no effect was predicted for Outcome II), but none of the relationships are significant. Congestion's effect on social-program effectiveness, however, is near significance (signif. of t = .15), perhaps providing some support for this part of the hypothesis and warranting a closer look in the next section, which analyzes the role of collinearity in regression statistics.

Like congestion, statistics for technology image are in directions predicted by Hypothesis 10 for all three outcome models, but significance is apparent only with technology's role in causing a deemphasis on operational efficiency (beta = $-.48$, t = -2.77, signif. of t = .01). Transit's adoption of futuristic technologies to be more competitive with autos seems to come with higher operational costs but not necessarily with the simultaneous emphases on strategic organizational and social-program effectiveness.

Finally, for the spatial form thesis, statistics significantly support two of three outcome emphases predicted by Hypothesis 11 and Hypothesis 12. Because an asymmetrical pattern would depend on whether urban form has equally strong effects on all outcome perspectives, the results provide a basis for concluding that this influence is one of the more powerful determinants of outcome skewness. The strongest effect is on emphasizing (and deemphasizing) organizational effectiveness (beta = .42, t = 2.92, signif. of t = .01), suggesting that agencies with greater institutional eminence and market presence are found in spatially more centralized metropolitan areas. Those tending to deemphasize organizational effectiveness (Outcome I) are more likely to be found in dispersed areas of urban sprawl. Less powerful but still significant is spatial form's impact on social-program effectiveness (Outcome III)(beta = .30, t = 2.04, signif. of t = .05), which suggests that the monocentric form enhances the likelihood of an emphasis on social programs and that sprawl tends to result in a deemphasis.

These initial regression results provide a picture of policy outcome determinants that in some cases are strongly supportive of theory, but in others raise serious doubts about the adequacy of certain theses. Moreover, they provide a starting point for addressing the question of "what matters most?" As summarized in Table 6.3, the initial results lead to the following ordering of significance in skewing the pattern of policy outcomes in transit.

Although no thesis clearly overshadows others, urban spatial form is the most important in explaining skewness in the outcome pattern as a whole. This thesis accurately predicted the most significant overall influence on the MSOI pattern. This significance is found first in spatial form's impact on emphasizing organizational effectiveness (signif. of t = .01), where monocentricity determines stronger market position and budgetary growth for the agency. Second but to a lesser extent, the variable's significance is also apparent in emphasizing social-program effectiveness (signif. of t = .05). Here the more centralized urban forms tend to promote allocation of more resources to transit-dependent users and to urban economic development. Because urban form holds greater significance for organizational effectiveness (Outcome I) than for social-program effectiveness (Outcome III) (and none for operational efficiency, Outcome II), the resulting asymmetric pattern consists of a primary and secondary skewness respectively toward these two strategic outcome perspectives.

Initial results suggest that the institutional exchange thesis may be

TABLE **6.3** What Matters Most? Initial Results of Direct Effects
42 Transit Agencies, 1987–1991

Rival Theses	Overall MSOI Pattern (Rank)	Individual Outcome Perspective (Rank, Significance)	Outcome Effect
Urban Spatial Form	#1	Outcome I (#1, .01)	Primary Emphasis
		Outcome III (#1, .05)	Secondary Emphasis
Institutional Exchange Power (Revenue Autonomy only)	#2	Outcome I (#3, .06)	Secondary Deemphasis
		Outcome II (#1, .00)	Primary Emphasis
Socioeconomic: UMC Genre	#3	Outcome I (#2, .03)	Emphasis
Market: Technological Image	#4	Outcome II (#2, .01)	Deemphasis
Market: Auto Congestion	#5	Not Individually Significant	—
Socioeconomic: Wealth	#6	Not Individually Significant	—
Socioeconomic: Underclass	#7	Not Individually Significant	—

NOTE: Outcome I = Administration-Centered Organizational Effectiveness; Outcome II = Administration-Centered Operational Efficiency; Outcome III = Political-Centered Social-Program Effectiveness.

the second most significant determinant of policy outcomes. Even though regression results are inconsistent with hypotheses, two of the three thesis variables are at or near significance. Fiscal autonomy in acquiring operational revenues has the most comprehensive effects in that the variable is very near significance in the deemphasis on organizational effectiveness (signif. of $t = .06$) and very significant to an emphasis on operational efficiency (signif. of $t = .00$). The effect of fiscal autonomy on organizational effectiveness is potentially corroborated by the near significance of IG interaction (signif. of $t = .08$), which suggests that the agency's eminence is enhanced by forming cooperative multilateral arrangements with intergovernmental actors.

Posing a basis for a revised thesis, these results suggest that intergovernmental exchange may be mostly a fiscal matter involving tradeoffs under conditions of limited funding options and scarce resources. That is, an agency's effectiveness in emphasizing its organizational presence seems to be enhanced when it gives up intergovernmental autonomy in exchange for operating revenues from federal, state, and local sources. By contrast, maintaining autonomy from intergovernmental exchange limits access to alternative operational funding and requires greater reliance on market sources, a dedicated tax base, and economizing. Under some assumptions in the intergovernmental literature, autonomy is thought to preserve administration-centered prerogatives in a conflict/consensus model of checks and balances. But the empirical results seem to point to agencies operating instead under a collaborative model involving the fiscal benefits of "strategic alliances," especially in getting relief from having to achieve operational efficiency to stretch scarce resources.

The socioeconomic thesis about an upper-middle-class genre is the third most important predictor of asymmetric policy outcomes. Although influence on the pattern as a whole consists of only one truly significant effect on Outcome I (signif. $t = .03$) and a second near significance on Outcome III (signif. of $t = .12$), statistics for all three outcome models are in the predicted direction. The disproportional significance initially suggests that this SES symbol holds more influence in promoting the eminence of professional public organizations than in projecting interest in social-program effectiveness. With respect to operational efficiency, the thesis might be recast to predict the genre's projection of a cue for *indifference* toward efficiency rather than a *proactive* preference for "conspicuous waste."

The fourth thesis posing significance is about the use of technological image in market competition. Although the market variable does not seem to figure into an agency's emphasis of strategic outcomes (contrary to thesis predictions), its statistics powerfully attest to its role in deemphasizing operational efficiency (signif. of $t = .01$). These results indicate that even though agencies often justify futuristic "high-tech" solutions (such as state-of-the-art rail transit systems) on grounds of improving organizational effectiveness (such as market share or ridership) and social-program effectiveness (such as urban economic development), such imagery-based solutions seem to have only one effect, that being an adverse impact on operational efficiency.

The remaining three thesis variables do not show significant initial results and are subjectively ranked according to the relative distance they are from significance. Ranked fifth is congestion, which statistics show to be at the center of an intercorrelation cluster. Ranked sixth is population wealth, which is strongly intercorrelated with the UMC genre. In seventh and last place is the underclass, which is correlated with congestion but not part of the three-way intercorrelation cluster. It may be that their interdependence is partially a source of their lack of individual significance in the models.

The Results Reconsidered

The initial results provide some important insights into which theses best explain what determines pattern bias in policy outcomes. However, it is important to note that when dealing with real-world or nonexperimental settings, results may be subject to potentially serious "instrument" errors in collecting data (many of which could not be corrected even if they were known), and in fundamental methodological limitations that are not easily rectified. Collinearity is a methodological example that poses a potentially difficult problem for this research design because of the study's focus on examining the relative contributions of different theses.

In this light, the initial ranking of thesis significance in Table 6.3 may prove to be misleading or inaccurate. An important reminder is that most of the variables lacking significance were ones most likely to be adversely affected by collinearity. Even though collinearity diagnostics show the problem to be within acceptable bounds, a prudent observer of the initial results would seek further examination. A principal method used for such analysis is "variable elimination" of candidates potentially contributing to collinearity. This procedure allows for the reciprocal deletion of suspected variables in subsequent reruns of regression models to determine the effect on significance of those variables remaining in the model. In the initial models, suspected variables implicated in collinearity include the UMC, wealth, underclass, congestion, and spatial form.

Taken in the initial order of significance and reporting only revised results involving significant changes, the most powerful variable implicated is urban spatial form. Although this variable is significantly intercorrelated only with wealth, the variable-elimination procedure actually shows it to have a more powerful collinearity effect on the UMC genre. When spatial form is removed from regression models, the significance of the UMC is substantially improved over initial results for Outcome I (significance of t is revised from .03 to .01) and Outcome III (significance of t is revised from .12 to .04). This would suggest more statistical support for the UMC thesis than was found in the initial results. By contrast, the deletion effect of spatial form on wealth (which was not initially significant to MSOI outcomes) brings wealth to significance only for organizational effectiveness (Outcome I)(initial significance of .33 moves to .04). However, this revised result does not support the wealth thesis, which predicts an effect only on social-program effectiveness (Outcome III).

Turning next to the sequential elimination of the UMC genre and wealth, we should expect to find reciprocal effects on each of these SES variables and on spatial form. However, when the UMC variable is removed, wealth shows a change in sign consistent with hypotheses for Outcomes I and III but remains insignificant. By contrast, urban form shows important changes in significance as a result of UMC deletion. Specifically, the significance of spatial form is substantially improved for Outcome I (where the initial significance of .01 is revised to .002) and more moderately improved for Outcome III (where the initial significance of .05 is revised to .02).

When wealth is eliminated from the models, little change occurs in the status of the UMC (further confirming no substantial collinearity effects between these two variables). Large improvements in significance, however, are found in spatial form. Showing magnitude of effect similar to that for UMC removal, the deletion of wealth changes the significance of spatial form's role in skewing Outcome I (where the significance of t is revised from .01 to .001) and Outcome III (where the significance of t is revised from .05 to .02).

From the variable-elimination analysis of these three variables, one important observation is that spatial form and the UMC appear to be potentially affected by reciprocal collinearity, which may cause the initial results to be distorted. By contrast, wealth has moderate effects on spatial form, but no reciprocal effects are apparent that would warrant seeing its role as different from that found in the initial results. Given the shifts in significance occurring from the variable-removal procedure, it would seem reasonable to say that (1) the spatial-form thesis may be even more powerful than initial statistics indicate, but (2) the UMC genre shows influence almost equal to spatial form and probably should be moved ahead of the intergovernmental exchange thesis in order of significance.

The last concern is about auto/roadway congestion, a market-

TABLE **6.4** What Matters Most? Revised Rankings of Direct Effects
42 Transit Agencies, 1987–1991

Rival Theses	Overall MSOI Pattern (Rank)	Individual Outcome Perspective (Rank)	Outcome Effect
Urban Spatial Form	#1	Outcome I (#1)	Emphasis
		Outcome III (#1)	Emphasis
Socioeconomic: UMC Genre	#2	Outcome I (#2)	Emphasis
		Outcome III (#2)	Emphasis
Institutional Exchange Power	#3	Outcome I (#3)	Deemphasis
(Revenue Autonomy only)		Outcome II (#1)	Emphasis
Market: Technological Image	#4	Outcome II (#2)	Deemphasis
Market: Auto Congestion	#5	Outcome III (#2)	Emphasis
Socioeconomic: Wealth	#6	Not Individually Significant	—
Socioeconomic: Underclass	#7	Not Individually Significant	—

NOTE: Outcome I = Administration-Centered Organizational Effectiveness; Outcome II = Administration-Centered Operational Efficiency; Outcome III = Political-Centered Social-Program Effectiveness.

conditions variable that shows significant intercorrelations with the three SES factors but is unrelated to other rival variables. In fact, the variable-elimination procedure produces some important additional information. When the UMC is removed, congestion becomes significant to social-program effectiveness (Outcome III)(the significance of t is revised from .15 in the initial results to .05) and becomes very significant to Outcome III when all three SES variables are eliminated (the significance of t improves from .15 to .003). However, a reciprocal effect on the SES variables is not apparent except for the UMC, which reaches significance for Outcome III with the deletion of congestion (the significance of t is revised from .12 to .04). This analysis reinforces a belief that the UMC may have a more formidable role in skewing policy outcomes than the initial results show, but also that congestion may as well. Although much of the information provided by roadway congestion about skewness may be contained in the UMC factor, congestion probably bears greater significance as a determinant than the initial results indicate and warrants consideration in the final analysis.

In summary, the variable-elimination procedure provides important additional information to the initial analysis of results. In answering the question about what matters most, it suggests that the initial findings might well be revised along the lines shown in Table 6.4. For urban spatial form, the revised analysis supports an even stronger basis for its number 1 ranking for direct effects than the initial analysis does. The case of the UMC thesis is also strengthened and would probably support a change in overall pattern rank from third to second. Although the UMC was initially significant only for organizational effectiveness (Outcome I), it may also be significant for social-program effectiveness (Outcome III). Since the institutional exchange thesis variables were not implicated in collinearity, their significance remains unchanged. However, the less clear support of their hypotheses and more limited areas of significance would support a change to third place. Although both market-competition theses retain their respective places, there is probably a basis for arguing that both congestion and technology image provide significant information to the analysis. The wealth and underclass theses, however, probably should be dropped from further consideration, at least regarding urban transit.

From this revised analysis of determinants, we are left with an intriguing scenario which suggests that asymmetry in the pattern of policy outcomes is the result of multiple influences, some of which have mutually reinforcing impacts while others are countervailing. From this, two contrasting pictures emerge. In the first, agencies appear more likely to emphasize organizational effectiveness (Outcome I), and secondarily social-program effectiveness (Outcome III) as a result of the metropolitan area's having a monocentric spatial form, a greater social presence of the upper middle class, and a widespread roadway congestion problem. The pattern's skewness toward these strategic emphases is further reinforced by an agency's formation of intergovernmental alliances where autonomy may be exchanged for secure revenue flows and mutual political support. However, this pattern skewness also includes a tradeoff involving a deemphasis on operational efficiency. This seems to result from an agency's forging intergovernmental alliances (reducing autonomy) and its use of futuristic high-tech transit solutions. As will be seen in Chapter 9, this profile is fully consistent with the conditions found in most of America's so-called "global cities."

By contrast, agencies appear more subject to deemphasizing strategic outcomes when their metropolitan areas are characterized by polycentric urban sprawl, a reduced social presence of the upper middle class, and less widespread roadway congestion. This austere pattern is further reinforced by an agency's high intergovernmental autonomy in fiscal matters and statutory interaction (perhaps reflecting an agency desire to "go it alone"). However, high autonomy along with the use of more traditional "low-technology" transit solutions (missing a futuristic image) also combine to determine a tradeoff favoring emphasis on operational efficiency. The profile of this characterization is more representative of non-global or regional-focused urban areas.

Although these two profiles may begin to look familiar to some in the transit industry, they do not yet explain how or why these relationships exist. This challenge is taken up in the next chapter.

The statistical results presented in Chapter 6 painted two contrasting scenarios about the makings of pattern bias in the policy outcomes of transit agencies. Yet, although these results support many aspects of the theses, the analysis to this point has not provided any unequivocal conclusions. The differences between the initial results (represented in Table 6.3) and the revised results (represented in Table 6.4) indicated that collinearity played some role in statistically clouding comparisons of the theses' relative importance in defining links to policymaking. Even though this was partly untangled by a variable-elimination procedure, the analysis does not fully account for how rival theses stack up in explaining pattern skewness. Specifically, the collinearity analysis may indicate but does not prove the magnitude of the *indirect* effects of intercorrelated determinants on policy outcomes. Hence this chapter uses a path analysis to take up the question of theory integration.

Policy Outcomes: A Causal Path Model

Most social science research on the determinants of policy outcomes has tested theses on the assumption that they represent competing independent concepts (e.g., Dye and Gray 1980; Lewis-Beck 1977). Indeed, the motivation for this research was stimulated by the scholarly tradition of comparing rival theses. However, a more robust view of the determinant relationships may require an analysis of underlying associations *among* determinant variables. Specifically, some rival-thesis variables may affect policy outcomes both directly (as examined in the last chapter) and indirectly through causal paths involving other independent variables. Hence the relative importance of those significant variables with both direct and indirect effects in explaining asymmetrical outcome patterns may be incomplete or understated.

The principal method used to examine a combination of direct and indirect effects is path analysis (Asher 1983; Lewis-Beck and Mohr 1976). The method is driven both conceptually and statistically, which for some makes the analysis more theoretically interesting but less empirically precise. Although path analysis requires subjective theoretical interpretation and model reduction consisting of only the *main* (i.e., parsimonious and substantively meaningful) causal routes, it allows one to see the independent variables against a more holistic backdrop of important secondary relationships. Hence the method not only provides a more comprehensive relative estimation of what theses matter most but also allows one to distinguish truly rival theses from those that are partially complementary. The analysis is done by first conceptualizing nonrecursive causal paths (i.e., those with no reciprocal or feedback linkages) that result from theoretical and substantive reasoning, and then using regression techniques to estimate the individual path relationships. Empirical analysis of these relationships usually employs the beta values of multiple regression (Lewis-Beck 1977).

A path analysis for the rival theses in this study is found in Figure 7.1. On the basis of the revised results of significance in Chapter 6, only five of the nine original independent variables are included here in regression models that estimate the *direct* path effects on policy outcomes. These are the UMC genre, intergovernmental revenue autonomy (one of the three institutional exchange variables), congestion and technological image (the two market-thesis variables), and spatial form. In addition, three more of the nine variables are included in regression models that only factor in the estimates of *indirect* effects on policy outcomes. These are the underclass, wealth, and intergovernmental interaction (a second institutional exchange variable). Intergovernmental capital autonomy (the

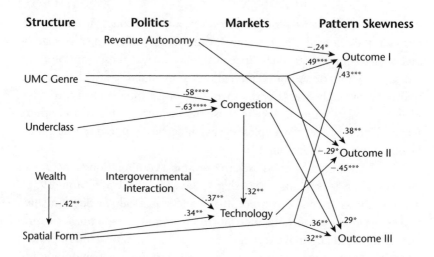

FIGURE **7.1** Path Analysis: Integration of Rival Theses (42 Transit Agencies, 1987–1991)
NOTE: Significance: * = .05   ** = .01   *** = .001   **** = .000
Main path coefficients = Beta values (standardized regression coefficients)

third institutional exchange variable) was found to have no significant direct or indirect effects on skewing policy outcomes and is thus deleted in the path analysis.

Analyzing the Paths

Looking first at the direct effects of rival-thesis variables, the statistical results vary slightly from those presented in Chapter 6 (Table 6.2) because the four insignificant variables of the original nine-variable model have been eliminated. Although significance increases for the five surviving variables across the three policy outcomes, in only one instance does a thesis variable become significant in a way it had not been originally. The upper-middle-class genre assumes significance previously absent in its effect on operational efficiency (Outcome II). It is noteworthy because this new significance (at the .05 level) and the effect's negative sign (beta = −.29) support the originally rejected hypothesis that the UMC genre causes a deemphasis on operational efficiency.

The UMC thesis had argued (in Hypothesis 2) that in addition to promoting institutional conditions for emphasizing strategic policy outcomes, the genre sets a behavioral standard for self-actualization made possible by living standards securely above subsistence levels (Maslow 1954; Clark 1998). A sense of security is found in economic abundance that diminishes a perceived role for efficiency in maintaining societal progress. To Veblen (1948), for example, a UMC person's high social status as a self-actualizer free from the "drudgery" of subsistence creates a motive for personal "conspicuous waste" and a devaluation of institutional efficiency. Along with the UMC's two strategic-outcome effects, these revised results appear to confirm the genre's influence on deemphasizing an agency's operational efficiency as a third vector skewing the pattern of policy outcomes.

The more important aspects of the path analysis, however, are the indirect effects, which involve to varying degrees all model variables except an agency's intergovernmental autonomy in acquiring capital. For three of those variables with significant direct effects, the path analysis shows that their indirect effects contribute additional influence in skewing policy outcomes. In order of significance, these include the UMC genre, urban spatial form, and auto/roadway congestion. Three other variables that have no direct effects but show significant indirect influences include the underclass, population wealth, and intergovernmental interaction (the statutory exchange variable).

The two most powerful indirect effects are found operating through roadway congestion, which is modulated by the UMC genre and the underclass variables. Interpreting the indirect role of the underclass is straightforward in that urban poor people do not have sufficient resources to own many cars or to engage in activities that require significant amounts of roadway travel. Although an underclass has no significant direct influence on policy outcomes, the presence of an underclass does reduce the level of traffic congestion (beta = -.63, signif. = .000). Reduced congestion would certainly benefit most people, but the indirect effect of the underclass on policy outcomes leaves a perplexing implication. Although the path only verges on statistical significance, it shows that *social services are provided at a rate inverse to needs of the urban poor* (the product of betas along this path to social effectiveness is -.23). The availability of transit services essential to regional economic development and mobility for the urban poor may be a beneficial result of congestion, but their effective provision depends on an urban area having fewer indigents in need.

The UMC genre has the opposite effect. Even though the UMC includes only a small proportion of any urban population, cities with higher concentrations of UMC have a greater problem with roadway congestion (beta = .58, signif. = .000). However, explaining the factor's significance for congestion first involves dispelling a common misconception. In transportation research, some argue that a wealth-based lifestyle and spatial form are the principal determinants of congestion. Those who have pointed to an affluent lifestyle as the primary cause of congestion base their contention on the premise that "the American dream is to live in a suburban single-family house on a half-acre lot with a three-car garage" (Kitamura 1988: 149). Kitamura's study and others like it show wealth to be a root cause of suburbanization (resulting in a polycentric spatial form); thus the implication is that wealth and spatial form combine to cause congestion.

The UMC thesis, however, raises a flag of caution by making an important distinction between wealth *alone* and the multi-attribute UMC. Although the exhibition of material affluence may be the preoccupation of those whose only SES characteristic is wealth, the UMC genre projects a more complex set of cosmopolitan tastes that place civic and cultural immersion (in volunteer work, the performing arts, art and educational venues, entertainment events, "city ambiance," and the like) at the forefront of the American experience. For those who have acquired the requisite resources of professional status, higher education, and income, the cosmopolitan urban experience may become their avocation. Moreover, the provision of such an experience seems to be limited to large global cities with the diversity to create a suitable "entertainment machine" (Lloyd and Clark 2000).

Of course, pursuing cosmopolitan interests may include suburban living for some UMC (especially those with young children), but just as many UMC (especially the growing numbers without children) may prefer the diversity and convenience of cultural and entertainment opportunities proximal to urban-core living. For example, a powerful UMC phenomenon contending with suburban living is "gentrification" and the pursuit of aesthetic opportunities emerging in revitalized big-city downtowns across the nation (Lloyd and Clark 2000; Smith 1996: chap. 5).

In contrast to the urban sprawl popularized by the press as the American dream/nightmare, the less-publicized UMC-inspired residential/entertainment developments in and around global cities (such as New York, Boston, Chicago, San Francisco, and San Diego) illustrate the different impacts on spatial form of wealth alone and a multifaceted cosmopolitan UMC lifestyle.

Equally significant, the UMC's penchant for aesthetic cosmopolitanism also confers a "transterritorial" consciousness of interests spread over a wide area (Boschken 1982). Enabled by transportation and communication technologies, their heightened awareness of social activities and entertainment venues in distant locations may undermine the "place boundedness" of spatial organization (Lloyd and Clark 2000: 3). Because the UMC's cosmopolitan pursuits are often not limited by distance or territorial boundaries (i.e., they are as likely to be across the metropolitan area and beyond as they are "just around the block"), they keep the UMC constantly on the go. With a penchant for showing up at an assortment of distant status-affirming events, the UMC often drive, logging many more than the average number of vehicle trips and miles per capita, irrespective of the urban area's spatial form.

By contrast, individuals whose socioeconomic status is defined only or principally by wealth have been characterized as more frugal, less cosmopolitan, and sedentary "millionaires next door" (Stanley and Danko 1996). Suburban communities are better suited for the more affluent who seek safe, self-contained amenities in a "family-values" atmosphere. Some of the UMC are also found in suburbs, but individuals of this genre seldom satisfy cosmopolitan yearnings with suburban aesthetics defined by country clubs and upscale shopping malls. As a consequence, wealth is strongly identified with suburbanization, but the UMC genre is not because the UMC habitat is often found in both the suburb and the culturally enriched core city.

Consistent with the distinction between these two SES identities, the data in this study indicate that the UMC genre strongly affects congestion but does not relate to spatial form in any particular way. In contrast, while the path analysis clearly shows wealth alone to contribute to polycentric sprawl (beta = $-.42$, signif. = .01), it does not show significant effects on congestion stemming from either wealth or spatial form. In sum, it is likely that a high-profile UMC genre creates a cultural and

economic environment within which larger numbers of non-UMC inhab-
itants participate by organizing and carrying on their lives according to
UMC status benchmarks; the result is more congestion.

The remaining four variables express indirect effects on policy outcomes through technological imagery. Since an agency's use of stylistic
technology is the most powerful predictor of a deemphasis on operational
efficiency (Outcome II), the variables that affect technology provide a useful extension to understanding the web of relationships that leads to this
aspect of outcome skewness. Congestion, which we saw above to be powerfully affected by class structure, is one of these technology determinants.
The more congestion, the greater the agency's market response, not just
in adding more transit service but also in matching stylish automobile
technologies with futuristic rail-based systems (beta = .32, signif. = .01).
Transit's use of stylistically appealing technical systems is partly a market-
directed response to competition from automobiles, especially when roadway congestion serves to level the playing field by making transit appear
relatively more attractive and publicly acceptable.

Spatial form, which is influenced by wealth (beta = −.42, signif. =
.01), is another of the rival theses implicated in the technology aspects
of market competition. Not surprising to most urban planners, the path
analysis indicates that the more monocentric the urban area, the more
likely it is that advanced technical systems involving rail will be used
(beta = .34, signif. = .01). Monocentric urban areas have concentrations
of housing, work, shopping, and other urban activities that allow transit
to use a fixed-route mode along rider-intensive corridors. Polycentric
areas cause a dispersion of origin and destination points, discouraging
high concentrations of user-rich locations.

This connection was not lost on Bi-State's strategic planner, who
was anxious about how St. Louis's new venture into rail would succeed
in this sprawling metropolitan area: "While we were operating just bus
service in the past, Metrolink [rail] is a big change. Its initial corridor
needs to be linked with other extension corridors, and we need to find a
way to build a network to make it successful" (Stauder 1993: 8). Ignoring this forethought, Los Angeles politicians went forward in the 1990s
with a multi-billion-dollar heavy-rail project to connect downtown Los
Angeles with Long Beach, the San Fernando Valley, and the Wilshire area.
After opening the San Fernando link in 2000, Mayor Richard Riordan

made an extraordinary speech declaring the costly system an utter failure and saying that, given the basin's freeway-determined spatial layout, the project should never have been built.

In addition to congestion, wealth, and spatial form, the statutory interaction of intergovernmental actors seems to matter to the agency's selection of technology. The greater the level of intergovernmental exchange required in the agency's policymaking process, the more likely stylistically attractive systems will be adopted (beta = .37, signif. = .01). Except for the extraordinarily high capital cost relative to buses, rail systems have widespread aesthetic and economic development appeal. First, as visible reminders of advanced technologies in the "new economy" and of revitalization in global cities, their fixed-route systems impart to the urban core a sense of stability, essence, and excitement. Second, although probably oversubscribed, the appearance and permanence of a rail system provides some physical affirmation of attempts to bring the parts of a metropolitan area together as an integrated whole. Third, while buses remain driver-based systems subject to some degree of union-management conflict, rail systems are managed by centralized, systemwide operations using advanced computerized logistics that minimize the discretion of drivers.

This techno-image of transit is especially persuasive to urban politicians and agency executives enamored by the permanence, connectivity, and futuristic character that rail systems impart to their respective jurisdictions. Many examples of this exist from Santa Clara County to Atlanta, but one of the lesser-known cases is St. Louis. In the post–World War II era, the city had lost large numbers of people to its burgeoning suburbs in surrounding counties. Until 1993 the metropolitan area's transit was provided entirely by a large 3,000-vehicle bus system operated by the Bi-State Development Agency (an interstate-compact authority consisting of four counties in Missouri and Illinois and the city of St. Louis).

During the 1970s and 1980s, the city launched a major redevelopment program to stem the out-migration and restore its centrality in the region. In addition to the National Park Service Arch, many civic buildings, and a stadium complex, it constructed its first rail project, called MetroLink. In interviews conducted for this study, several transit managers pointed to intergovernmental actors as the key to selecting the expensive rail alternative. In response to a question about where key policy ideas originate, the agency's strategic planner said, "The idea for MetroLink came from the mayor, who claimed it was needed to preserve the city" (Stauder 1993: 17). The general manager of operations said that other actors were also involved in intergovernmental exchanges that led to adoption of the rail idea: "The Metropolitan Planning Organization was very interested in the idea of light rail, as was the political community generally" (Sehr 1993: 13).

Reinforcing politicians' interest in rail as a stylistic enhancement to their jurisdictions is their belief in the secondary effect it has in remaking the look of the central business district and surrounding neighborhoods. Some economic evidence supports this view by showing that rail (instead of bus) systems may induce residential and business development, which increases the value of surrounding property adjacent to stations (Bernick 1996; Cervero 1995). The combination of rising property values and gleaming, newly constructed buildings imparts an image of sophistication and perhaps more access to the global economy. Consequently, intergovernmental actors (especially at the state and local levels) tend to favor rail over bus options in their exchanges with transit agencies regarding policy and planning.

Intraurban rail is also an identifying feature distinguishing the physical and political boundaries of one metropolitan area from another. In fact, in some areas with multiple competing political centers, investments in new rail technologies have become part of the arsenal politicians use in their struggles over regional dominance, autonomy, and identity. Transportation politics in the San Francisco Bay Area is a case of how highly politicized intergovernmental exchange results in a regionally nonintegrated set of rail-based systems. When BART began construction on its original master plan in the early 1960s, the agency envisioned the entire Bay Area to have a single system under its jurisdiction involving 200 miles of rail augmented by bus-feeder links.

What developed instead was a balkanized transportation network with poor interconnecting services, partly because of fights over political turf. At the center of this turf war were Santa Clara County politicians, who lobbied for their own rail system as a device to establish a metropolitan identity (Silicon Valley) separate from that of San Francisco or the region generally. By 2000, rail development in the Bay Area had become a political contest between South Bay politicians and regionwide interests, which led to a frenzy of new rail-based proposals even though the Silicon Valley light-rail system is not heavily used. Indeed, it is still known as a vastly overbudget and underutilized system that "comes from nowhere and goes nowhere."

From the transit agency's standpoint, there are also practical reasons for sacrificing its organizational autonomy for intergovernmental exchange if rail development is the popular mode du jour. For example, an agency may be more receptive to a stylistically attractive technology, even one with questionable operational function and that it fears will be little used, if it can enter into intergovernmental arrangements that spread the fiscal risk to others. Such was the case in Santa Clara County, where local politicians pressured agency administrators to understate cost and operating estimates for a new light-rail system, then reorganized the county authority into a multigovernment-sponsored "joint-powers" agency to finance the project with matching funds from a reluctant federal Department of Transportation.

A transit agency may also prefer the more glamorous but risky technologies if intergovernmental actors provide funds that could never have been arranged for a dapper bus system. Such was the case in St. Louis, where in the same year MetroLink was opened with a surplus of funds from a dedicated sales tax, the Missouri component of Bi-State's bus system was threatened with closure because of a long-standing funding disagreement with local jurisdictions and the state's reluctance to provide any funds for bus transit. Strategic alliance was readily acceptable for a glamorous technology but not for a boring functional one.

A similar expression of deference to techno-image solutions is found in the San Francisco Bay Area, where two existing systems share some jurisdictional overlap. BART (the system linking San Francisco to the East Bay by rail) has enjoyed much greater fiscal and political support than AC Transit (which links approximately the same areas by bus), even though BART is much more expensive and has a less flexible route structure than AC. Some predict that AC can survive as an independent agency only if it abandons its matrix route structure (beneficial to the East Bay urban poor) in favor of a feeder system to BART for San Francisco–bound commuters.

Feeding all of these examples was congressional policy that promoted expensive rail over most cost-efficient bus systems. Until the 1980s the federal Department of Transportation had two roughly comparable transit subsidy programs, one for annual operating expenditures and one for capital development. With passage of the federal Intermodal Surface Transportation Efficiency Act (ISTEA) in 1991, most operating subsidies were eliminated for large cities, and the capital funds program was liberalized to encourage intraurban rail development. In a study on the impacts of these policy shifts, Li and Wachs concluded that the new policy bias "may provide an incentive for local governments to invest in transit options that are capital intensive and in those that require high maintenance costs" (2001: 11). They argued further that their "data indicate that neither ISTEA nor TEA-21 [Congress's ISTEA reauthorization] would provide incentives for local governments to choose low capital-cost approaches. [In particular TEA-21 encourages] projects that maximize federal funding contributions [that] might not in the end be the most cost-effective ones" (p. 14).

Rival or Complementary Theses?

A more complete and robust interpretation of what matters in skewing policy outcomes includes viewing the rival theses as theories that may also complement each other in some key respects. Those that stand out in their indirect contributions are the UMC genre and the underclass, which seem to have profound but opposite indirect effects on social-program effectiveness through their influence on congestion. Also of special note are the combined indirect effects of congestion, intergovernmental exchange, and spatial form on operational efficiency, which occurs through an agency's mix of systems technologies. In addition, although market conditions surprisingly do not seem to exhibit any effects—direct or indirect—on organizational effectiveness, they are significant factors in overall pattern skewness through their direct and indirect effects on operational efficiency and social-program effectiveness. In short, in addition to the important rival dimensions analyzed in Chapter 6 as direct effects, the above path analysis brings to light a web of underlying relationships that offers a more complex and inclusive explanation of bias in policy-making than is provided by any individual thesis alone.

To translate the path results into an empirical analysis of total effects for each variable, the betas measuring the direct and indirect com-

,TABLE **7.1** Rival Theses: Total Causal Effects, Direct and Indirect
42 Transit Agencies (1987–1991)

Thesis Variable	Outcome I			Outcome II			Outcome III		
	Direct	+ Indir.	= **Total**	Direct	+ Indir.	= **Total**	Direct	+ Indir.	= **Total**
UMC Genre	.49	—	.49*	−.29	−.08	−.37*	.29	.21	.50*
Spatial Form	.43	—	.43*	.08	−.09	−.01	.32	—	.32*
Intergovernmental (IG) Revenue Autonomy	−.24	—	−.24*	.38	—	.38*	—	—	—
Technology Image	.14	—	.14	−.45	—	−.45*	—	—	—
Roadway Congestion	.05	—	.05	.17	−.14	.03	.36	—	.36*
Underclass	—	—	—	—	−.09	−.09	—	−.23	−.23
Wealth	—	−.18	−.18	—	.06	.06	—	−.13	−.13
IG Interaction (Statutory Autonomy)	—	—	—	—	−.17	−.17	—	—	—
IG Capital Autonomy	—	—	—	—	—	—	—	—	—

NOTE: Effects coefficients = Beta (standardized regression coefficients); spurious effects excluded;
* = total-effects coefficient significant at least at the .05 level.

ponents are summed from values shown in Figure 7.1. The indirect effects are determined by multiplying beta values for segments reported along the causal path leading to a policy outcome. For example, the indirect effect of the UMC on social-program effectiveness (Outcome III) occurs through roadway congestion and is calculated by multiplying .58 (beta for the UMC-congestion segment) by .36 (beta for the congestion-Outcome III segment), which equals a total indirect effect on social-program effectiveness of .21. When added to the UMC's direct effect of .29, the total-effect coefficient for social-program effectiveness equals .50 (significant at the .001 level).

The results of combining the direct and indirect effects for all rival-thesis variables are shown in Table 7.1 The figure divides the variables into those that exhibit at least one significant total impact on a policy outcome from those that have no significant impact on any component of the pattern of outcomes. The underclass variable has the only equivocal result but is not included as a significant component because it is only on the verge of significance for one outcome—social-program effectiveness (signif. = .07). Those included in the significant category have at least one very significant influence on policy outcomes. Hence the figure shows five of the seven original rival theses to have statistical support in their explanations about skewing the pattern of outcomes.

One surprising fact stands out in these numbers. Even though they contain many interesting insights about underlying causes of such provocative issues as roadway congestion and the choice of expensive, stylistically attractive systems technologies, the figures indicate that *only the indirect effects of the upper-middle-class genre alter the original findings of Chapter 6 in any major way.* Furthermore, by incorporating the UMC's indirect effects on policy outcomes via market-condition variables, the data support the UMC thesis in its entirety.

A Nontraditional View of Policy Outcomes Emerges

The traditional work on policy outcomes has been concerned primarily with whether an urban constituency's fiscal resources or its politics mattered more in predicting "who gets what." But the data in this study appear to stand the old debate on its head. The results show none of the traditional theses about local wealth, the underclass, and institutional politics to matter as much as the UMC genre, urban spatial form, and market conditions. Indeed, except for one of the institutional variables, the traditional theses are statistically insignificant in all three outcome models. This leaves us to ponder four points here, which are then taken up in detail in the next chapter.

First, the results may renew interest in social class and politics, which has been moribund since the vacuous "power-elite" thesis led to an empirical dead end in the 1970s. In fact, the path analysis gives valuable new insight into the importance of social class in policymaking and powerful new evidence that socioeconomic status matters in the governance of urban America. Adding fuel to a reemerging discourse on the nature and effect of social class on government policymaking (Clark and Lipset 2001), this study seems to affirm that social class matters a great deal in determining bias in the policy outcomes of public agencies.

Second, the results may also extend interest in urban spatial form as a predictor of policy outcomes. Although the thesis is widely applied in urban planning to developmental policy issues (i.e., community planning, public infrastructure), it is virtually silent in the literature on agency performance, administrative policymaking, and government accountability. We have long known that centralized urban areas offer greatly different life experiences than sprawled areas. Indeed, an emerging debate in urban studies pits the older "Chicago School" against a newer "Los Angeles School" (Miller 2000). But this study only scratches the surface on its usefulness to questions of policymaking bias and administrative reform.

Third, the total-effect results are not entirely confirming of a market thesis. Although the compelling allure of new and stylish technology has an unmistakable effect on deemphasizing an agency's operational efficiency, the effect of roadway congestion, which has long been assumed to matter in policymaking, is more equivocal. Although roadway congestion appears to be an important determinant of social effectiveness, it would have become even more significant to skewing the overall pattern of policy outcomes had its combined effect on operational efficiency been mutually reinforcing. Instead, congestion cuts both ways on operational efficiency (Outcome II) by acting *directly* as a positive influence but *indirectly* as a negative effect. This leaves the issue of how congestion matters open to a more complex market thesis than is currently postulated.

Finally, the remaining theses provide a mixed picture as well. For the causal paths operating through congestion, the underclass is immensely important to the congestion issue but by itself adds only marginal significance to the direct determination of just one policy outcome— social-program effectiveness. For all of the variables operating through technological image, none individually exhibits a magnitude of effect large enough to represent additional significance in skewing policy outcomes. However, because the choice of systems technology exhibits the most powerful direct effect on operational efficiency, those variables *in combination* that underlie its image-based selection criteria cannot be ignored. Without the larger joint influence of the urban setting, including congestion (market conditions), spatial form (physical realities), and intergovernmental interaction (politics), the market-conditions thesis on techno-imagery conveys a less robust story than it warrants.

8 Interpretations and Implications

For centuries, cities have been the cradles of advancement in the civilized world. Although we often toy with the idea of a technologically driven deconcentration of the human habitat, most of mankind's prospects and problems will probably continue to be urban. Indeed, we can expect that many if not most of the great American issues in the twenty-first century will have urban origins. Overwhelmingly framed by the needs and circumstances of a complex and globalizing population, some of these issues will be about enlarging the human potential and facilitating the freedoms of mobility and interaction. Others will concern the symptoms of socioeconomic exclusion and the treatment of equal access. Yet all will be about the struggle over change. Today it is in cities where we acknowledge the birth of a "new economy," and cities are where the future fortunes of mankind will be spawned and developed. In certain American core cities the socioeconomic effects of globalization are already clearly in evidence.

Because it is also in urban areas where government operates at a grass-roots level and where most of its vast assemblage of administrative agencies are located, it is in cities where policymaking bias and government responsiveness hold the greatest implications for Americans in this new world order. Whether the issue is education, community health, transit, urban infrastructure, or supporting access to the global economy, Americans will depend more on the delivery of public services than they have in the past. Whether serving an aging "boomer" population and working-age families, or planning for unborn generations, the quest for good government will remain the same—to render public institutions more responsive and equitable to multiple constituencies in an urbanized plural society.

What makes this book central to that discussion is its focus on the causes of policymaking bias in agencies providing services for large and diverse metropolitan populations. Certainly the contributors to bias may vary from policy area to policy area, but the implications of bias offer significant constants in most areas of policy. With this in mind, I conclude this book by venturing some interpretations and implications that may hold meaning for urban public agencies more generally. I do this by individually reexamining the rival theses according to some important and as yet unresolved conceptual controversies.

The Upper-Middle-Class Influence

In the path analysis of Chapter 7, statistics showed the UMC genre thesis to be unmatched by other rival theses in explaining asymmetry in policy outcomes. Nevertheless, an inferential question persists: does the UMC genre's influence simply reflect the political actions and civic engagement of directly involved actors, or does it operate through a separate independent venue as an impersonal anonymous agent? Some students of politics and certainly proponents of the institutional exchange thesis might find the anonymous path difficult to accept. Preferring instead to see the genre as just an inanimate SES icon, they might argue that symbolic representations of the upper middle class cannot influence policy outcomes apart from those persons acting politically.

Even Stone has said he prefers his "regime politics" thesis over his earlier symbolic "systemic power" notion:

> In my 1980 piece on systemic power, I answered the social justice [equality] question by saying that politics tends to reflect (not compensate for) inequalities in the distribution of social, economic, and organizational resources [i.e., pattern bias in policy outcomes]. Then, in Regime Politics I saw that this was not simply a passive structural inequality, but that Atlanta's business elite worked diligently and shrewdly to make use of and perpetuate their resource advantage. This "take"

was what moved me into thinking about urban politics in terms of [institutional] structure and agency. (Stone 2000)

Rejecting one thesis for the other, Stone became an ardent observer of regime politics, a model for which he is best known.

An argument for the UMC's required connection to direct political activity could be made in other ways as well. For instance, research shows that UMC individuals engage in political activity more than other SES groupings, and UMC participation is principally focused on making political contributions and contacting government officials (Verba, Schlozman, and Brady 1995; Brint and Levy 1999). This might suggest that the impact of elected officials on policy outcomes is mostly a UMC phenomenon of direct and visible proportions. Another and more compelling interpretation would accept the causal route as an indirect manifestation of UMC presence but also require involvement of direct political activity. For example, in conceptualizing a "linkage between passive and active representation," Meier and Stewart argue that "the social origins of [constituency] representatives mirror the social origins of the represented. . . . One way to assure policy congruence is if the representatives and the represented share the same policy relevant attitudes and values" (1991: 2).

This link could take the form of a two-stage process starting with Stone's contention that the UMC genre sets a city's political tone and cultural image by its anonymous "systemic power" (Stone 1980). In turn, elected leaders crystallize a vision for world-class status that "is tied to the city's image" (Pagano and Bowman 1995: xiv). This sequence of image formation and political application could provide a conduit whereby a regime of elected political entrepreneurs adopt a policy vision consistent with UMC preferences, at least where one-party domination provides an unobstructed opportunity for "credit claiming" (Feiock and Clingermayer 1986). Although these interpretations argue that the direct and active engagement of actors augments an indirect or passive influence of the UMC genre, their contentions are not borne out empirically by this study. Furthermore, in a separate analysis (Boschken 1998a), these and other direct-action political variables showed no statistical relationship with the UMC genre.

Yet another scenario would involve interest groups and their captive governmental actors. This study did not consider interest group variables as UMC proxies because interest groups are distinguished by their issue-specific nature (e.g., environmentalism, access for the disabled, abortion rights, nuclear proliferation) rather than SES. Issues fragment the UMC population into many and sometimes opposing factions, and few if any could be characterized as representing the UMC *qua monolithic UMC* (as does the UMC genre, which is a resource-based rather than an action-defined icon). Nevertheless, assuming that a UMC could exist as a distinct, forceful, and single interest group or entrepreneurial voice, three other conditions probably would also have to prevail.

First, to operationalize a set of monolithic UMC interests, its membership would want to act on its professional organizational norms (described in Chapter 3 as part of the UMC character) by seeking political influence through an institutional intergovernmental process. In a few key instances, this process might principally involve direct relations with the focal agency, but doing so across the board or in each case of interest would significantly tax even the UMC's considerable resources. Second, to more effectively manage its influence across a wide urban policy landscape, the UMC more likely would seek to capture a few agencies with broad intergovernmental authority, such as the Environmental Protection Agency or a local metropolitan planning organization (MPO), rather than numerous specialized service agencies. Third, for these UMC "sentry" organizations to be powerful intergovernmental gatekeepers and interveners in service-agency policymaking, each service agency would have to possess fairly limited autonomy.

On all three conditions requiring direct political action, a review of the intergovernmental exchange variables indicates two conclusions. First, in the analysis of Chapter 6, the UMC factor was found to be orthogonal to all intergovernmental (IG) variables, thus providing no supporting evidence of a causal route involving direct engagement. Second, though the UMC factor is significant in regression models, the path analysis fails to show a corresponding influence of political actors operating through intergovernmental processes. That is, the IG variables are either less significant than the UMC factor in the models, or they have an effect on policy outcomes opposite that of the UMC.

As a general conclusion regarding all the alternative political scenarios of direct action, the evidence seems to support the independent influence of an anonymous UMC genre. Even though UMC *individuals* certainly participate politically through interest groups and politicians regarding their particular concerns, Stone seems to be more accurate in his original conclusion that the influence of a UMC *genre* is "completely impersonal" and manifested as "systematic power [that] is not a general form of upper strata dominance through agenda control" (1980: 989).

Beyond the issue of how UMC influence fits on the causal map, another issue is how to more precisely interpret the power of the upper middle class. Although it is one of the oldest concerns in urban research, class power yields no obvious or definitive answers. Does it occur by a class of individuals deliberately but subtly acting to manipulate public policy through civic engagement in politics, or is the influence more the result of social deference to or mimicry of an SES symbol? Pointing to leverage in socioeconomic stratification, Stone (1980) originally saw an indirect and anonymous route involving the UMC genre's systemic power: "Because the [UMC] are strategically advantaged, their extraordinary influence is not so much exercised as it is selectively manifested in the predispositions and behavior of public officials" (p. 990).

Nevertheless, if influence is the central feature of the UMC ambiance, how does a nonverbal cueing process happen as described in Chapter 3? One plausible extension of Stone's sketch is a process involving the social construction of the UMC by policymakers. The theory "refers to the cultural characterizations or popular images of persons or groups" (Schneider and Ingram 1993: 334), and stems from cognitive psychology (see, e.g., Tajfel and Turner 1986). Along with Stone's description of political influence, social construction suggests that policymakers design agency outcomes to "fit" what they "anticipate" stereotype "target populations" want (Schneider and Ingram 1993).

To Berger and Luckmann (1966), however, two kinds of social constructs result in policy deliberations—images derived from the "face-to-face situation" with political actors, and ones from "remoter forms of interaction" where cognition of individuals or organized groups is not apparent (p. 30). In this latter instance, they say cognition is of "anonymous" characterizations of a "category" (i.e., the UMC genre) rather than of individually known actors with which the agency interacts: "Anonymity may become near-total with certain typifications that are not intended ever to become individualized" (p. 33). To them, then, the genre would be a distinctive cultural icon measured by anonymous symbolic characterizations of style, form, and content.

What remains dim is how the UMC as an impersonal abstract is reified to the point that it matters in policymaking. Part of the answer may lie in Stone's belief that policymakers favor UMC interests over others because this genre is perceived to hold a disproportional share of society's "diamond-shaped distribution of opportunities and resources. . . . Though they are the least numerous segment of the population, members of the upper strata possess resources strategically important to public officials [in furthering careers and agency growth]" (pp. 982, 984).

Stone contends that the UMC's influence on policymaking "flows more from the position they occupy than from the covert action they take" (p. 984). Echoing the thought, Pitkin reminds us that an actor's influence on policy may best be found in a person "being something rather than doing something" (1967: 67). It is possible to conclude, then, that just the perception of a UMC presence and their social position may be sufficient to create the *unspoken* influence of referent power. In concert, Berger and Luckmann claim: "Power in society includes the power to determine decisive socialization processes and, therefore, the power to *produce* reality" (1966: 119). In this sense, the anonymous UMC genre, acting as an icon of the inspirational good life, may be a political substitute for declining civic engagement in signaling to policymakers appropriate choices of emphasis in policy outcomes.

This possible replacement of direct civic engagement with an anonymous icon raises a final point about UMC impact on policymakers' perceptions. The statistical results for the UMC suggest it is a widely recognized genre in society, perhaps representing a predictable set of determinant public expectations. As a constant in a metropolitan milieu otherwise seen by policymakers as a chaotic state, this class genre may provide a stabilizing influence on those urban governments where the UMC are a significant population component. Like a directional beacon, the genre may offer a reliable context for policymaking and appear to reduce uncertainty about political consequences for public officials facing difficult policy choices.

If this UMC stabilizing phenomenon exists, further research needs to delve into the social-psychological origins of a UMC genre *within the agency.* Do bureaucratic structures and processes pose barriers to direct representation and foster more reliance on anonymous identities as political considerations? Are interpretations of the "general public interest" derived from the UMC's systemic power rather than from the "median voter" or pronouncements of bureaucratized civic associations? Is reliance on the genre reinforced by policymakers who themselves are mostly UMC and aspiring to fulfill the interests of their anonymous class? Taking up these questions, Lieberman suggests the causal route more appropriately involves "political [rather than social] construction [that] asks not only how group identities arise in a political setting but also how and why they become politically relevant" (1995: 440). In short, pursuing this line of inquiry may open a new venue of discovery about the role of class structure and bureaucratic decision-making.

Institutional Exchange in an Intergovernmental Setting

In combination, the three hypotheses of Chapter 4 predicted that agency intergovernmental autonomy encourages an emphasis on administration-centered policy outcomes (organizational effectiveness and operational efficiency) and a simultaneous deemphasis on social-centered programs. That is, intergovernmental autonomy leads to (1) the freedom to amass bigger budgets through enterprising economic behavior, and (2) achieving unfettered efficiency, partially by avoiding costly social programs required by mutual adjustment. In comparison with the substantial statistical support for the UMC thesis, the empirical results for intergovernmental autonomy were inconclusive, lending less support to the institutional exchange thesis.

Even though both theory and results suggest that agency autonomy matters in the skewing of policy outcomes, the lack of empirical confirmation of hypotheses gives renewed cause to question the application of "new institutionalism" to intergovernmental politics. Has the theory gelled to the point where it provides an integrated set of concepts? To more fully appreciate the generalizations this question evokes for the MSOI pattern as a whole, we look first at the contributing effects of intergovernmental autonomy on each policy component of the outcomes pattern.

For Outcome I, statistics show that the transit agency's organizational effectiveness is more likely to be emphasized when policymaking includes collaborative or negotiated arrangements with intergovernmental actors with whom the agency shares authority and on whom it depends for fiscal resources. This finding does not square with some aspects of new institutionalism found in political economy studies (e.g., Niskanen 1971), but it is consistent with a "rational behavior" explanation known in administrative science as "neoinstitutionalism" (Powell, Koput, and Smith-Doerr 1996; Gulati 1995; Parkhe 1993; Powell and DiMaggio 1991; Powell 1990). That branch of interorganizational theory argues that certain private industries exhibit conditions that promote strategic alliances. These conditions include (1) very high competition for scarce critical resources, including money and expertise, (2) very high existing or potential customer need for a product or service, (3) high uncertainty caused by the industry's chaotic change, and (4) interorganizational familiarity due to a history of exchanges.

Government agencies, including those in urban transit, may embrace similar strategic alliances. Certainly many transit executives claim that intergovernmental exchange is "a major challenge because you've got so many different governmental entities" (Gambaccini 1993: 15). But transit agencies may grow in stature as a result of alliances formed through intergovernmental exchange because collaboration allows for positioning and risk-sharing in a dynamically changing public economy. For example, public sector strategic alliances provide opportunities to grow the bureaucracy when (1) tax reductions increase competition for limited funding; (2) indirect governmental mandates sustain high demand for services (e.g., gas-tax transfers to alternative transportation modes, welfare-to-work programs, mandated corporate-employee alternative commuter subsidies); (3) programs like "reinventing government" and privatization introduce chaotic change potential; and (4) a history of dyadic working relationships makes intergovernmental exchange familiar and more predictable. In other words, all four conditions favorable to strategic alliance are present in urban transit. This circumstance makes it clear that public sector institutionalism is in need of considering some of its market-based cousins.

With respect to operational efficiency (Outcome II), an important finding was that revenue but not statutory autonomy is what matters most. Two possible refinements or interpretations of institutional theory may explain the anomalies between theory and results. First, in public enterprise theory (a branch not usually associated with new institutionalism), a rational entrepreneurial motive encourages a "minimax" strategy: the simultaneous minimizing of costs and maximizing of the organization's revenue stream.

Doig (1995), for example, attributes such behavior to the "engineering mind" of infrastructure executives who seek operational efficiency along with entrepreneurial "outreach" in the quest for leadership position and political control of their organizational domain. What may divert these aims are intergovernmental subsidies that come with spending requirements, a condition the autonomous public enterprise would not see fit to incur in the absence of fiscal inducements. Hence the more fiscally independent the agency, the more unfettered its opportunity to use engineers' neutral competence and bias toward efficiency.

The study's results support this argument in that intergovernmental autonomy seems to encourage an emphasis on operational efficiency. Parenthetically, though, the statistics fall short of supporting the other half of the minimax logic. The entrepreneurial side of the engineering mind also would call for the autonomous agency to emphasize revenue maximizing (an aspect of organizational effectiveness), which the study does not confirm. Instead the results indicate that, with fewer intergovernmental revenue sources and subsequently greater autonomy, organizational effectiveness will be deemphasized.

A second institutional argument (and one consistent with public choice) attributes transit inefficiency to an availability of federal Department of Transportation or state subsidies that for some agencies make up for farebox losses without regard to efficiency (Lave 1994; Cervero 1984). According to the chief planner for Baltimore's MTA, transit agencies see this intergovernmental situation in the context of "two universes," one that leaves budgeting to after-the-fact and another that begins the planning process with fiscal considerations. In the "non–fiscal constraint" universe, subsidies provide "enough money that we can try lots of new things" that may emphasize organizational and social effectiveness. In the contrasting "tight-budget restraint universe [where subsidizers are tight-fisted], we have self-imposed parameters we have to reach. Given those baseline conditions, are there things we could trim thereby opening up some dollars for us to try a few things?" (Goon 1991: 12, 14).

Niskanen generalizes the two-universe scenario, claiming that "bureaucrats have no incentive to be efficient" except under certain conditions dealing with scarcity (1971: 209). Subsidies remove the agency from a "budget-constrained region" when tight budgets would otherwise provide "a budget-maximizing incentive to identify and use more efficient production processes" (p. 210). Without initial fiscal constraints, agencies spend as much as they can without regard to efficiency, and federal or state subsidies (not indigenous wealth) often provide the means to do so.

A prime example consistent with the results is the link between intergovernmental exchange and the adoption of glitzy technologies. Along with the significance of revenue autonomy as a contributor to operational efficiency (signif. of $t = .01$), technological image also is significantly related (signif. of $t = .01$) but inversely so. These statistics may tell of contrasting motives in running a transit agency. On the one hand, SEPTA in Philadelphia may be forging strategic intergovernmental alliances to invest more in futuristic-looking technologies that will better position transit in competition with the auto/roadway system. By contrast, Orange County Transit in California has very high intergovernmental autonomy but only limited (and belatedly adopted) up-to-date technologies. As a result of its more limited fiscal and statutory support, the agency maintained a bus-only system that allows it to emphasize high relative efficiency.

With respect to social-program effectiveness (Outcome III), none of the intergovernmental variables attain significance in their effects. This is perplexing from an institutional exchange perspective because scarce fiscal resources held by intergovernmental actors for distribution to *compliant* agencies ought to provide powerful inducements for a social-program emphasis. But many infrastructure agencies harbor an "engineering mind" that derives satisfaction less from subsidization and more from great physical accomplishments for social welfare (Doig 1995). Civil engineers affirm their value to society by providing enhanced mobility for a transit-dependent population, inducing private collateral investment, or acting as linchpins in revitalizing a city (see, e.g., Attoe 1988). Since the engineering mind also demands accolades for its achievements, engineers may be more inclined to work alone through a single independent authority than to share acclaim with a balkanized or joint structure of urban politicians and city bureaucrats. Thus transit agencies may tend to resist political involvement or interference.

These desires of engineers are often incompatible with political necessity, and the struggle over aims may deny a consistent role for intergovernmental autonomy in implementing social programs. Indeed some of the great stories of public enterprise accomplishments tell of struggles to obtain public funding from politically inspired intergovernmental sources and victory in maintaining near-exclusive claims to the credit for enterprising behavior. The transit and seaport accomplishments of independent and engineer-dominated authorities in the New York City metropolitan area (Danielson and Doig 1982) and seaports on the West Coast (Boschken 1988) are classic examples of autonomy and societally beneficial motives working together. But there are also stories about autonomy being quashed by politicians' jumping on board after the fact to claim credit for great welfare accomplishments.

Given the individual effects of intergovernmental autonomy on each of the outcome components, what conclusions can be drawn about skewness in the overall pattern of policy outcomes? Despite some mixed messages, the application of institutional theory seems to provide some important understanding of how and why an asymmetrical pattern is endemic to transit agency performance. In a setting of many concurrent governmental authorities where economic and political aims conflict, paradoxes in judging governmental responsiveness and accountability will result. Besides the administration-centered outcomes preferred by agency management, public agencies must also perform according to "different social imperatives, including many that have only a tenuous relationship to economic ends" (Robins 1987: 78–79). Not all legitimate aims can be achieved in this plural setting, and arising from the struggle are tradeoffs representing a skewed pattern of outcomes. That pattern for the transit sample involves two tradeoffs: one between operational efficiency and organizational effectiveness, and the other between operational efficiency and social effectiveness (see Table 2.3). In seeking to address the issue of concept reliability, how consistent is the institutional exchange thesis in foretelling these tradeoffs?

The most expected of the two tradeoffs is the one between social programs and efficiency. To accommodate nonmarket political demands in conditions of scarce resources, a bias toward social-program buildup should positively affect social effectiveness and negatively affect operational efficiency. This is because the tradeoff for most social programs is based on regulatory or redistribution mandates rather than on an agency's economic or market calculus. In fact, some have argued that intergovernmental inducements and subsidies encourage agency management to think more "broadly" about balancing public demands with operational efficiency (Lave 1994; Guess 1990; Cervero 1984).

Downs and Larkey thus conclude that from *an efficiency perspective*, "politically justifiable—but inherently inefficient—decisions about which programs to operate and what constraints the program must satisfy are often a more important source of poor performance than bad management" (1986: 4). In public transit, Guess further argues that federal policy encourages "a contradictory quest" by use of subsidies that provide "means to generate increased ridership with an often serious disregard for the costs of service production" (1990: 1). This claim, however, is not substantiated by the evidence because none of the intergovernmental variables are near significance for social-program effectiveness. Since the results of this study show that intergovernmental exchange regarding revenue (the only institutional variable to show significance) has a depressing effect on efficiency but no effect on social effectiveness, claims of an exchange-induced tradeoff are not substantiated.

On the tradeoff between strategic organizational effectiveness and operational efficiency, the institutional exchange thesis is informative but equally inconclusive. Although descriptive statistics for the dependent variables indicate that the outcomes are paradoxical (see Table 2.3), the theory underlying two of the intergovernmental hypotheses implies that administration-centered strategic and operational policy aims ought to be mutually reinforcing. Furthermore, a comparison of impacts on Outcomes I and II shows that revenue-based intergovernmental exchange makes a significant contribution to the policy tradeoff and resulting outcome skewness (see Table 7.1). An agency with more intergovernmental autonomy will emphasize efficiency (beta = .38) at the expense of organizational effectiveness (beta = −.24). The opposite will occur with less autonomy. With new revenue opportunities afforded by the fiscal inducements of intergovernmental exchange, agency management sacrifices operational efficiencies to enhance strategic organizational effectiveness. Given the option, administrators emphasize organizational effectiveness because the concomitant growth in their budgets imparts the ability to increase salaries, power, and prestige (Niskanen 1971). Until the era of government downsizing and devolution, no comparable management motive existed for emphasizing efficiency.

This tradeoff, however, may be more sizable for infrastructure agencies than for welfare bureaucracies. The reason involves all three outcomes in creating the skewed pattern. For agencies with big plant and equipment requirements, access to large amounts of capital may be the most critical component in intergovernmental exchange. In order to continue bureaucratic growth in the absence of sufficient market-source revenue, the agency turns to intergovernmental sources, incurring significant social-program strings (irrespective of their social effectiveness) that cause inefficiencies. It would seem, then, that the more an agency pursues organizational effectiveness (growing the bureaucracy with the aid of intergovernmental exchange), the more operationally inefficient it is likely to become.

Beyond the question of thesis reliability, there is also the issue of theory integration and whether specific intergovernmental arrangements fit together. For example, what types of organizational groupings and their interactions does the institutional exchange thesis address? Are we formulating theory for the interaction of similar organizations (an industry of transit agencies) or dissimilar agencies (networks that include transit agencies, city governments, a state DOT, and the FTA)? Is the theory generalizable across both cooperative and competitive interactions?

As Table 8.1 depicts, intergovernmental exchange takes many forms, each involving separate attributes of interaction that affect agency policy outcomes differently. A type I setting, for example, involves market-response exchanges among agencies that provide the same public service. A type IV setting, however, involves cooperative behavior among dissimilar actors engaging in strategic alliances and interorganizational contracting. Postulating about the impacts of intergovernmental exchange on policymaking bias for all these types of relationships would require the incorporation of widely varying and probably conflicting premises and conditions. Moreover, in the case of transit alone, an agency could be engaged in intergovernmental exchanges involving all four types simultaneously. Can new institutionalism as an overarching thesis successfully account for all categories without the presence of major inconsistencies?

It is in raising this question that the results become more definitive: new institutionalism is a long way from composing an integrated body

TABLE **8.1** Institutionalism: Where Are the Limits of Theory Integration?
The Different Forms of Intergovernmental Exchange

Interagency Relationship	Organizations Involved in Exchange	
	Similar	Dissimilar
Competitive	TYPE I Intraregional competition between overlapping service area providers for funds and customers (BART and AC Transit)	TYPE III 1. Statutory: intergovernmental system of territory-based concurrent authorities 2. Fiscal: market competition around substitutes (transit and autos)
Cooperative	TYPE II Isomorphic behavior (mimicking) and interjurisdictional consolidations or integration of services	TYPE IV 1. Statutory: intraregional strategic alliances for economic development 2. Fiscal: networks of interagency and third-sector contracting

of interdisciplinary theory. Because urban scholarship has incorporated some but not all pieces of institutionalism offered by economics, sociology, and administrative science, the problem of integration is perhaps more acutely felt in intergovernmental politics and policymaking than elsewhere in the social sciences. Furthermore, although this study's evidence may be more confirming of the economic branch of institutional theory regarding intergovernmental fiscal dependency, it is not reassuring to political economy scholars who theorize about the concurrent distribution of constitutional (and statutory) authorities in a plural society (see V. Ostrom 1987; E. Ostrom 1986). The findings may be especially disturbing to those who argue that fiscal federalism is structured by statutory authority (i.e., concurrent government), where the two are postulated to have mutually reinforcing effects on policy outcomes. It may be that research needs to consider intergovernmental autonomy and exchange as involving many separate relationships that have different and often opposing effects on policy outcomes.

Beyond this, the results on intergovernmental exchange may warrant discussion about two other theory integration issues. First, institutional theory needs to incorporate more contextual considerations in order to be generalizable across different governmental service sectors. For example, the fiscal autonomy variables may be highly dependent on the nature of a public agency's charter, delivery technology, or service area. In transit, many agencies are chartered public enterprises using large-scale technologies to deliver a linearly integrated service. However, if a government sector consists mostly of general-fund agencies using low-complexity technologies, such conditions may make the institutional exchange thesis even less reliable.

Second, for agencies within a sector like transit, each basis for exchange (e.g., fiscal versus statutory) needs to be dealt with as potentially independent of the other. In fact, the intergovernmental variables in this study were statistically independent. Therefore, the treatment of institutionalism as an overarching concept about intergovernmental relations remains shrouded in complexity and ambiguity. Where are the limits of application? Although the common denominator among all branches and permutations of institutionalism seems to lie in a core idea about behavior toward "results, performance, outcomes, and purposefulness" (Frederickson 1999: 704), the types shown in Table 8.1 hold precious little else in common. Even though Frederickson claims institutionalism is limited to the study of agencies using "assumptions of cooperation, order, hierarchy, institutional responses to contextual influences, networks and governance" (p. 704), many others would argue that the "new" theory is also used to explain interactions based on conflict and competition (Shepsle 1989; Shepsle and Bonchek 1997; E. Ostrom 1995, 1986).

The evidence raises an even larger issue, though. Is this new institutionalism too broadly inclusive of social science theory, or is the problem one of theory integration? The complexity of intergovernmental exchange and its influence on agency policymaking invite institutional contributions to urban scholarship that unfortunately come from several antagonistic disciplines. Moving from the macro concept to mid-range theory and applied theory, there is an obvious bridging problem involving interdisciplinary competition. In administrative science, for example, much effort has been made to seal off the discipline from other "institutionalisms" by relabeling its mid-range version "neoinstitutionalism" and concentrating application on "isomorphism" (Powell and DiMaggio 1991: 1–62), which is a more narrowly focused concern about how and why organizations operating in a similar context evolve to a state where all exhibit a common behavior and structure.

Selznick (1996), in contrast, takes the position that scholars must avoid such attempts at "pernicious dichotomies" that denigrate other interpretations of institutionalism and get on with the effort to integrate an interdisciplinary theory. A few have tried to integrate the differences (Roberts and Greenwood 1997; Oliver 1991), but far more are pushing the envelope of their applied disciplines by making distinctions that render Selznick's suggestion for integration less feasible. With willingness across the social sciences to engage in invidious distinctions, can one expect urban scholars to make sense of it all for policymaking? Frederickson makes a grand attempt in his Gaus Lecture (1999), but one is left uneasy (even baffled) about how this paradigm better and more consistently informs us about the role of intergovernmental relations in policymaking. Urban affairs researchers have always been willing integrators of broader social science thought, but much work needs to be done to make the parochial pieces compatible before institutional theory will be a reliable contributor to the public management of American cities.

Competitive Market Conditions

The combined effects of competitive market variables on skewing policy outcomes strongly point to an explanatory role for the market thesis regarding tradeoffs between outcome perspectives. Take, for instance, the paradoxical relationship between operational efficiency and social-program effectiveness. On one side of the tradeoff, statistics indicate that transit's use of technological attractiveness to compete with the auto/ roadway consortium results in a deemphasis of the agency's operational efficiency. On the other side, statistics show that exposure to high levels of auto congestion encourages transit agencies to behave more entrepreneurially by emphasizing socially beneficial programs that promote mobility for the poor and community economic development.[1] For the tradeoff to exist, however, both variables of the market conditions thesis must be in play.

With regard to such competition-inspired tradeoffs, the path analysis in Chapter 7 shows that the combined market effects of congestion and technological attractiveness probably do not stand alone and may be more comprehensively understood in conjunction with background effects induced by intergovernmental exchange and urban spatial form. For example, the effect of transit technologies on policy outcomes is conditioned by the spatial distribution of a city's social and economic activities. Thus a rail-based system tends to be less efficient and less effective than a bus system in a nonparametric or sprawling metropolitan area, but is probably the superior alternative for a spoke-and-hub (monocentric) area.

The implication for policymakers is that technology choices should correspond or be congruent with the parameters of urban form. In polycentric urban areas, for example, transit may be able to improve its competitiveness by designing more attractive buses, but not by subsidizing the development of rail systems. Knowing this might have avoided the mistaken choice of intraurban rail for polycentric areas like Santa Clara County and more recently Los Angeles.

Two other major issues persist as well. The first is the role of entrepreneurial behavior. Do the modeled relationships between markets and policy outcomes exist because of a rational response of policymakers to competition, or do they occur simply by default of the auto/roadway alternative? The answer to this remains open to further study, and rival interpretations exist. Nevertheless, for some agencies with high organizational effectiveness, it is possible to conclude that their performance emphasis occurs purely as a result of very limited automobile viability in congested markets and not as a result of administration-centered entrepreneurial behavior. For example, in the city of San Francisco, where parking and roadway capacity are far below population needs (resulting in very restricted consumer choice), MUNI (the city's transit department) is a visible agency with high user rates as measured by the percentage of occupied seats on vehicles. Although appearing to emphasize organizational effectiveness, it offers notoriously poor service. Where choice is so limited, vehicles filled to capacity do not always reflect consumer satisfaction.

Nevertheless, most of this study's interviews with transit executives suggest that entrepreneurial behavior is consistent with the study's statistical findings on market determinants. For example, in the case of the paradox between efficiency and social-program effectiveness, interviews found that in most agencies market determination of the outcome tradeoff occurred with the proactive intermediation of management. In Washington, D.C., which has severe congestion and whose transit agency employs mainly advanced rail-based technologies, WMATA ranked first in social effectiveness and last in operational efficiency. Organizational response to this stark bias in policy outcomes was personified in a power struggle and fiscal crisis that brought David Gunn, a noted transit reformer and efficiency advocate, briefly to Washington in 1991 to reverse the agency's long-standing tradeoff.

During his three-year tenure as executive director, he was constantly compared with his predecessor, Carmen Turner, who had been one of the nation's leading champions of social effectiveness over efficiency. Illustrating the fundamental link between market conditions and managerial behavior, the agency's budget director laid out the circumstances that led to Gunn's shortened tenure:

> Carmen Turner was more socially attuned to what the area needed because she was a native of the District. She was born and raised here, identified with the black community, knew their concerns, and became a community leader. . . . [However,] Carmen, dear lady, was not a good administrator. In contrast, Gunn was all business. He really has no identity to this area and that makes a big difference. Carmen would never have been able to get rid of 300 administrator positions the way Gunn did. She would say: I know that person and he really needs a job. We can't do that. (Dotter 1993: 9)

Such comments demonstrate how powerful (albeit temporary) administration-centered perspectives can be when the pattern of policy outcomes become grossly unbalanced, but even more, they underscore the role agency policymakers play as intermediaries in maintaining a bias over time. Although consistent with the agency's market conditions (high auto congestion and use of advanced rail technologies), the emphasis on social programs and deemphasis on efficiency would not likely occur without the advocacy and proactive behavior of agency personnel in facing the paradox. In retrospect, Gunn appears only to have been hired to remedy a fiscal crisis brought on by the stark tradeoff, and he was too successful in fulfilling his original mandate to shift the bias. Urged on by disgruntled agency executives, the WMATA board of directors wasted little time in removing him and returning the agency to its traditional policy tradeoff consistent with market conditions.

The other major issue concerns the difference in significance of market variables in predicting organizational and social-program effectiveness. Why do market conditions have a larger positive effect on social programs than on organizational growth and stature? Although further research is certainly warranted, one speculation is that most agencies may be driven more by the public purpose of social mandates than by administration-centered desires for bigger market penetration or budgetary growth. According to the correlations found in Table 2.3, the two outcomes go hand in hand. However, when transit managers are presented with more favorable market conditions, they may overcompensate in social effectiveness to ensure that tradeoffs do not sacrifice the agency's public legitimacy. Moreover, some public managers prefer actions that respond to traditional public values and are frequently less versed in "profit-based" corporate behavior.

Nevertheless, some agencies indicate a growing tendency to favor strategic organizational effectiveness over social effectiveness. For example, transit in Los Angeles County has been accused of putting new, clean buses on white suburban express routes (as a market response to automobile-congested freeways) and older, poorly maintained buses on routes serving poor neighborhoods (de-emphasizing social effectiveness). Likewise, San Diego's principal transit agency divided itself spatially and organizationally to serve white suburbs, tourists, and cultural centers with a light-rail subsidiary and poor neighborhoods with a bus-system subsidiary. The two systems' routes are not well integrated, and the rail system has come to enjoy the greater visibility and fiscal support in response to market rather than social welfare considerations.

As important as a market connection to agency outcomes is for urban transit, empirical support for the market-competition thesis is not directly generalizable to most other public sectors. The unique conditions of congestion and modal technologies require hypotheses formulated specifically for transit. Nevertheless, the evidence presented in this research suggests that the general theory of market competition is transferable and may offer important insights for research in public sectors with at least some market exposure—county medical centers, for example.

Unlike their private counterparts, county medical centers are required by law to serve nonpaying patients. However, as cost-containment strategies by local government and health maintenance organizations (HMOs) emerged and sources of nonpaying clients multiplied, the proportion of welfare patients came to be a primary distinguishing factor between private hospitals (which emphasize administration-centered outcomes) and county medical centers (which must emphasize social-centered outcomes).

Although most county medical centers continue to be principally oriented toward social-centered outcomes, a few located in urban markets with high concentrations of private medical centers have designed ways to compete with them. Often done in the context of a strategic alliance with a university medical school, the county medical center markets itself as providing services at the cutting edge of research and technology. Sacramento County General Hospital, now operated as the U.C. Davis Medical Center, has gone one step further by organizing doctor medical groups as a private patient feeder system; the strategic alliance advertises widely through both print and broadcast media (including a weekly television program). Such public sector entrepreneurship designed to emphasize organizational effectiveness is far less common in areas that have fewer private medical centers because there is less competition.

The impact of competitive market conditions also may be found in agencies that are less similar to transit but still subject to competitive pressures. Take, for example, K–12 education: multiple public school districts vie for families whose choices about where to live are based in part on a district's reputation. In this case market competition may also be intensified by vouchers, charter schools, and private academies. Education research shows that these competition instruments influence school district policymaking, but it remains unclear how they skew the pattern of outcomes and whether markets are as important as other determinants, such as intergovernmental politics and population demographics.

Much was said during the era of Reaganomics, privatization, and reinventing government about the need to reform agencies, but many of the new-era results have proven less than satisfying (Miranda and Walzer 1994). Accountability and performance-based policymaking have been at the forefront of most discussions, but not much comparative empirical research has focused on how different reform models might alter policy outcome patterns for different agency stakeholders. The performance problem in the public sector traditionally has had little to do with publicness but almost everything to do with the monopolistic nature of many public agencies. This unfortunate oversight of market causation has been exploited by private firms seeking to claim managerial superiority in the delivery of public services. But this study shows that there is an important distinction not to be lost: "privatization" and "capitalism" may be interchangeable terms, but they are not synonyms for markets and competition.

Competition, but not necessarily privatization, will bring greater responsiveness to our governance structures. Indeed this study shows that public agencies act on competitive market conditions not only to fulfill consumer demands but also to achieve social-program mandates. Can privatization make the same claim? Shouldn't we expect the asymmetry in patterned outcomes resulting from competitive market conditions to be different from the skewed outcomes resulting from privatization? Won't tradeoffs be made in either case?

This research seems to suggest that the marketworthy public enterprise responding to competitive factors pursues a pattern that emphasizes both organizational eminence and social programs at the expense of operational efficiency. Although results are conflicting for transit (McCullough, Taylor, and Wachs 1997), more general research on privatization suggests the opposite pattern occurs when policy discretion is turned over to the profit-seeking firm. If so, then which pattern of outcomes do we want? Which is warranted for a plural society? Even though privatization seems more straightforward, maybe we get a better deal by finding ways to strengthen professional enterprise behavior in public agencies and immersing these organizations in competitive markets.

Urban Spatial Form

If not an integral part of urban market conditions, spatial form is certainly related to demand and supply in metropolitan passenger transportation. Nevertheless, its impact on policy outcomes varies from that of congestion and technology. Mainly through direct path influences, spatial form affects both an agency's organizational effectiveness and its effectiveness in delivering social programs. Although it exhibits positive influences on these strategic outcomes for agencies in traditional monocentric cities, its influence is not good news for those living in areas of metropolitan sprawl who favor viable public agencies.

In a nutshell, economically effective and socially responsive transit agencies are more likely to be found in cities with centralized forms. Asked what would help transit, SEPTA's (Philadelphia) planning director said, "What I preach is transit-friendly design—more compact development, higher density, creating nodes and places of community interest" (Bickel 1993: 21). Less strategically effective designs are typically found in spatially diffuse metropolitan areas where a dense central core of societal activities is small or nonexistent. This finding suggests yet another reason to be concerned about the dysfunctional effects of sprawl on the urban inhabitant's quality of life. When the effect of spatial form on policy outcomes extends beyond transit to other public sectors, the implications of irreversible urban decline are greatly magnified.

Given this, the heuristic question may seem obvious. Is it possible or desirable to recentralize the spatial configuration of cities through proactive planning, as some economic development scholars suggest (Goetz 1990)? Or is spatial form a policymaking precondition, as this research appears to indicate? If one believes that central-city renewal, restrictions on suburban growth, and integrated development planning will halt the corrosive effects of sprawl, then transit may remain a viable public service to market users and welfare clients alike.

However, this scenario requires transit agencies to acquire greater leadership authority and to play an activist role in metropolitan development planning. Such has been the case in the rebirth of core-city vibrancy in a few places, such as San Diego; but in nearly all transit agencies across the nation, management has sought a policy role in land use and has nearly always been rejected by local politicians. Recalling one such experience, Orange County's general manager said, "When I brought up the issue at an assemblage of local county officials, Oh my God, everyone disappeared from the room" (Reichert 1989: 2). Yet it seems clear that leaving land-use decisions and service-funding authority mainly to "home rule" cities of a metropolitan area will only further erode the dwindling potency of transit in determining the blend of an agency's policy outcomes, especially in emphasizing effective market responses to the auto.

But if one believes spatial form to be an unalterable precondition, then transit agencies are unlikely ever to be more than backseat observers of urban dynamics. For them to act proactively, they will need to look instead to strategic opportunities provided by new technologies and build information systems and other managerial resources necessary for reinventing the urban transportation business. This scenario would also require a reassessment of the methods used to compare and judge agency responsiveness. It might start with segmenting empirical comparisons of the nation's transit agencies according to their spatial environments in the same way that their comparisons are adjusted for urban scale.

Without further research, however, one cannot extrapolate the effects of spatial form on transit to other urban service sectors. Other sectors may be less sensitive to how a city is spatially configured, and even if they are affected by form, the relationships may be different from those for urban transit. Nevertheless, other sectors whose policy outcomes could benefit from further study include public health (e.g., hospital services, homeless care, ambulance services), safety and security (i.e., police, fire), public works (i.e., water, power, sewerage), and even K–12 school districts. Cumulatively, if urban spatial form matters to these sectors, the policy implications could be truly enormous and widespread. For one, the degree to which spatial form is a parameter could be an even more central question in the search for determinants of policy bias and government responsiveness.

For another, it would require a reassessment of how we think about contemporary administrative reforms. Most spring from a particular economic ideology (Savas 1987; Osborne and Gaebler 1992), and much reform has taken the approach of "one shoe fits all" without reference to contextual setting. Across the policy landscape (from education to transit), a uniform formula is often applied to metropolitan areas, regardless of whether spatial form is monocentric or sprawling. If this study's results are indicative, much of the attempt to make government more accountable would seem misguided and wasteful because the asymmetrical pattern of outcomes may be due in part to spatial form, which is not factored into most reform equations.

The decade of the 1990s brought many revelations about a new world order based on globalization. Not least among them is a fundamental rethinking of the role of cities as central connectors in this network of global interaction and exchange. At the 2000 Conference of the Urban Affairs Association, several panels were devoted to research on globalization and cities. At one of these, the question was asked: What is globalization? In response, Terry Clark ventured that, from a historical perspective, globalization appears to have been a cumulative process involving a three-stage sequence of economic, sociological, and political transformations. At the heart of this sequence is a realization that, in certain key cities, a new urban habitat is unfolding that would distinguish them from those that remained regional or national in focus.

From an American perspective, the first stage involved a geographic separation of goods-production locations from points of product consumption. Although self-contained regional economies (containing both producers and consumers of a product) had diminished in importance by World War II, by the late twentieth century the separation of production and consumption had taken on international proportions with the emergence of offshore sourcing of goods. Through a highly competitive system of remote multinational production sites (especially since 1960), this economic stage appeared as a concentration of demand on American soil offset by a global dispersion of supply (albeit skewed to the

Pacific Rim). Based on the premise that products could be made anywhere in the world without significant regard for per-unit transportation costs, it was a stage underscored by a phenomenal shift toward international trade made possible by a global "container revolution" in shipping (Boschken 1988).

Eventually, the economic stage yielded some of its visibility to a second transformation involving the rise of a more symbols-based cosmopolitan consumption, which was driven by demand for urban amenities and postmodern interest in cultural immersion (especially since 1980). The "global" lifestyle had arrived and brought with it mushrooming demand for culturally symbolic goods from all over the world, urban entertainment venues, and a host of "quality-of-life" services, as well as the free movement of foreigners, information, and ethnic lifestyles across national borders (Clark 2001). The celebration and consumption of wares at international festivals and an appreciation for ethnic restaurants, ethnic theater and music performances, culturally specific art exhibits, and multimedia trade shows are now central preoccupations of many Americans. So also are "buying trips" to such foreign destinations as London, Paris, Tuscany, Beijing, and Singapore, where at least a portion of the motive is cultural immersion.

More recently, these two stages appear to have given ground to a third involving a realignment of urban politics (especially since 1990), said to be founded on a "new political culture" of fiscal conservatism and social liberalism (Clark 1998). The politically important constituencies in many cities today seek "world-class" status that bestows membership in global interaction across traditional political boundaries. Being economically conservative, they tend to expect public policymaking priorities to favor "productive" developmental expenditures and to simultaneously deemphasize traditional welfare programs that might otherwise sustain blight and perpetuate an urban underclass. In a spirit of economic development, political support is often thrown to public-private partnerships that plan and carve out elegant postmodern habitats from economically declining urban cores. Affirmation is found, for example, in the comprehensive development of new multipurpose central districts with generously landscaped promenades threading together artfully designed high-rise business towers with entertainment and residential centers, all made regionally accessible by stylish, technologically advanced rail transit. Satisfying to a productivity-minded fiscal conservative, the reclaiming of core cities in this way reflects a forward-looking constituency determined to advance the competitive global position of its city, both symbolically and economically.

Being socially liberal, these same constituents also express deep commitment to their own personal freedoms and exhibit greater tolerance for and appreciation of foreign or ethnic cultures and variant lifestyles. As a consequence, many cities have developed social programs that invite and encourage the growth and integration of a multicultural community. Involving more than those segregated "island communities" (Park and Burgess 1967) of the city serving as cultural or lifestyle "showcases" (e.g., San Francisco's Castro District, Chinatown, and Little Italy), integration is also found in the "hybridizing" (Tajbakhsh 2002) of the city's legislative body, business districts, public spaces, and residential areas. Unlike earlier efforts at regentrification, ethnic and lifestyle diversity seems to have provided a robust source of cultural vitality, enlarging the civil liberties and international experiences for most of those immersed in it.

Not all American cities have shared equally in this transformation, and although most exhibit some traits of the three stages, few can claim comprehensive multidimensional changes that typically characterize the "global city." Disagreement over definitions may exist, but there are perhaps ten critical dimensions that distinguish such cities from their more regionally or nationally focused counterparts (see Table 9.1). Although any urban area may exhibit one or a few of the dimensions, a key overriding consideration is the extent to which a city's global connectedness is exemplified by the full spectrum of dimensions and the cosmopolitan synergy among them.

For example, large-scale cities may reach the status of "global" if they have in combination such distinctive attributes as culturally diverse and amenity-rich urban habitats, concentrations of world-renowned universities, centers of banking and advanced information-technology firms, massive global trade accounts and international shipping and embarkation centers (both maritime and airborne), and postmodern political leadership in setting developmental policy agendas. The quality of urban transportation and transit policy is also characteristic. Auto congestion is symptomatic of heightened mobility and the intensity of over-

TABLE **9.1** Socioeconomic Status: Coincidence or Influence?
Global-City Dimensions and Presence of the Upper Middle Class

Global-City Dimensions	UMC Characteristics and Political Culture
1. Integrated large-scale urban center	Urban form unrelated to UMC genre*
2. Amenity-rich infrastructure (cosmopolitan entertainment)	High income; university education
3. International banking and multimedia IT centers	Professional status; university education
4. World-renowned universities	Professional status; university education
5. Multicultural community	Political culture: Social liberalism
6. International embarkation point (seaport and/or airport)	UMC genre as a whole
7. Trade emphasizing transnational imports and exports	Professional status; university education
8. Postmodern political leadership in setting development agendas	Political culture: Fiscal conservatism
9. Severe auto/roadway congestion	UMC genre as a whole*
10. Integrated rail-transit system	UMC genre as a whole*

NOTE: * = Confirmed by path analysis in Chapter 7.

lapping activities but is at least partially offset when policy outcomes emphasize an accessible rail transit system that ties the larger urban area together as an integrated, competitive, economically functioning "platform" of globally connected activities.

Beyond this classification, however, Table 9.1 also makes the connection between the global city and this study's findings on the upper middle class. In observing the importance of UMC influence on policy outcomes in transit agencies, one is struck by the larger role this socioeconomic status group may have played in the development of each of the three stages of globalization and the global-city dimensions they spawned. Indeed, all but one of the ten dimensions can be traced (some by this study's path analysis) to corresponding characteristics of the UMC genre and its political culture. For example, large concentrations of information-technology firms, world-renowned universities, and a robust world trade account point both to multiple global connections and the presence of an employment base consisting largely of university-educated professional managers, technicians, attorneys, and other institutional actors.

The effects are probably reciprocal, but one cannot escape wondering if the UMC plays some pivotal and defining role in linking global-

TABLE **9.2** U.S. Global Cities and the Upper-Middle-Class Genre
Urban Areas Defined by Transit Agency Jurisdiction

Urban Area	Transit District	Number of Global-City Dimensions	UMC Factor Value
Global Cities			
New York	NYC MTC	10	−0.66
Washington, D.C.	WMATA	10	2.42
San Francisco	MUNI, BART, GGT	10	1.73
Boston	MBTA	10	1.23
Philadelphia	SEPTA	10	0.06
Chicago	CTA	10	−0.77
Atlanta	MARTA	8	0.81
San Diego	MTDB	8	0.52
Los Angeles	SCRTD	8	−0.18
Seattle	MMS	7	1.06
Nonglobal Cities			
Miami	M-DT	5	−1.33
San Antonio	VIA Metropolitan Transit	3	−1.06
St. Louis	Bi-State DA	2	−0.87
Cleveland	GCRT	2	−0.88
Indianapolis	IPT	0	−0.92
Phoenix	PT	0	−0.71
Buffalo	NFTA	0	−1.18
Milwaukee	MCT	0	−1.22

NOTE: See Appendix A for agency names.

ization and urban policy outcomes in cities where the genre exhibits a prevalent "systemic power." Such an implication is made by Clark, who argues that although globalization is transforming local processes, it "is not alone or a unique cause, but interacts with other factors like more education and income to *enhance* their effects" (2001: 4). It is probably not by coincidence that, along with professional status, these are the main characteristics of the UMC genre.

In a comparison of global and nonglobal American cities, Table 9.2 identifies the most obvious global-city candidates, six of which exhibit all ten of the global dimensions. Any definition, of course, does not allow us to be absolute in the distinction, and any city's status should be understood in the context of a continuous scale. Nevertheless, this multiple-factor comparison of global with nonglobal cities reveals at least anec-

dotal evidence of the comprehensive, multidimensional global connectedness required. Moreover, as evidenced by each city's UMC factor value,
those urban areas with the greatest number of global interfaces also tend
to have relatively higher concentrations of UMC.

This does not seem to be a coincidence either, because these managerial and technical professionals are at the forefront of international
awareness and experience. In the course of their transterritorial wander-
ings, these institutional architects appear to have cobbled together pieces
of a worldwide cultural milieu and global economy that extend far beyond local political boundaries and parochial interests. Drawn from great
geographic mobility, the UMC's systemic power may also be the decisive
influence in developing a city's postmodern business and employment opportunities and other dimensions of global connectedness.

Adding to this socioeconomic influence, foreign-born professionals with institutional credentials similar to the American UMC also tend
to seek out a global-city habitat when relocating their families in the
United States. For example, San Francisco and surrounding areas on the
peninsula and in the East Bay have large populations of foreign-born residents, including many South Asians (mainly Indians, many of whom are
engineers, scientists, managers, and doctors) who identify simultaneously
with specific U.S. locations and the heritage of their homelands. They not
only maintain large residences here and abroad, but also impart to the Bay
Area their unique consumer tastes and cultural practices. In combination,
the semipermanent presence of different foreigners (often of equivalent
SES to the American UMC) contribute to the immersion of all global-city
dwellers in an amenity-enriched, multicultural atmosphere.

Multiplying this transterritorial mobility many times and across
other global cities engenders an international emphasis on consumption,
which not only fosters changes in urban market demands but also poses
an often subtle political challenge for urban policymaking. This challenge
takes the form of competing values. In forming urban policy in a global
environment, what revision takes place in the meaning of social consciousness and a public agency's striving for social-program effectiveness?
Is it to help an indigenous underclass of disenfranchised citizens engulfed
in poverty, or is it to supplement the efforts of a city trying to become en-
franchised, at least symbolically, as a multicultural global habitat?

For many larger cities, globalization has stolen the stage from locally focused or parochial social issues. For example, economic development policies, which are often used to position a city for global connectedness, dominate much of today's urban politics, while concurrent and widespread homelessness is the cumulative result of diminished public attention to local family-support programs, mental health, housing for the poor, economic safety nets, and other "old liberal" programs. Global cities led the way in having both the highest average incomes in the United States and the highest percentage of families below the national poverty line.

This shift is particularly evident in urban transit. This study indicated that the larger relative presence and systemic power of the UMC corresponds to an agency skewing its policy outcomes toward more effective social programs. Yet, beginning in the mid-1980s, a change in the content of these social programs became apparent (especially in newly forming global cities). A greatly enlarged emphasis on technologically advanced systems (usually light rail) replaced a focus on infrastructure investment and noncommuter scheduling that principally aided the poor. Image-enhancing technological development in transit had become an instrumental feature of the cityscape, but in so doing may have caused some constituencies to sense a misalignment between their expectations and policy outcomes.

For example, in the globalization of Atlanta, the metropolitan area's five counties retained their individual original authority and policymaking discretion, which at times was used to enhance the wants of local constituencies at the expense of metropolitanwide interests. MARTA's general manager recognized the impact of this political misalignment on transterritorial mobility, saying, "On a daily basis, people cross our county and city lines paying no attention to changing jurisdictions. Yet they are governed by decisions that are locally made and parochial" (Gregor 1990: 6).

The need for an unimpeded right to travel is essential for a global city to become or remain competitive in a multicultural world order, but whom did Atlanta's misalignment affect the most? Was it more an impediment to UMC interests, or was it felt mostly by Atlanta's underclass? Moreover, is the misalignment spawned by territorial boundary or by a growing cleavage in constituency mindsets? Is there a political mismatch favoring the integrity of Atlanta's individual communities over transterritorial "invaders," or is the mismatch the result of a growing chasm between the city's residents holding a global cognitive map (predominantly the UMC) and other less-mobile, parochial-thinking Atlantans?

In noting the UMC genre as the most significant factor associated with bias in transit policymaking, one is tempted to see the degree of emphasis on social effectiveness as an incidental or collateral result of globalization. However, if the UMC has imparted a new meaning to social liberalism in its influence on making the postmodern global city, then won't an agency's policy emphasis on social programs reflect the new meaning as well? Invoking the question asked earlier, "Who gets what" from policymaking?, doesn't this connection bring a new reality to the prospects of urban life? Doesn't the use of symbol-bearing transit systems and collateral economic development illustrate the sacrificing of an urban underclass to favor the socially liberal interests of those at the forefront of the global economy?

These questions bring us back to the point at which this study began. The United States is not a nation of presumed equals, a circumstance that is reflected especially in the bias of policy outcomes fostered in response to a new world order. But this conclusion sparks yet another concern. By virtue of the roles played by the UMC in globalization, how will the global city habitat of the twenty-first century differ spatially and culturally from that of nonglobal cities? The answer may well depend on the evolution of the UMC household. Today, while UMC with children at home tend to prefer the security of suburban monocultural opportunities, those without children at home have every reason to prefer the quality of life and proximity of cultural amenities offered in large global cities.

After all, says Clark, these urbane UMC have shifted from being concerned mainly about "physical sustenance and safety" to being more interested in "belonging, self-expression, and the quality of life" (1998: 45). They believe that people should be able to buy what they choose and live whatever lifestyle suits them. They are more tolerant of individuals and groups that diverge from the mainstream than any previous generation. And those who are choosing global cities for their amenity-rich habitats are growing rapidly in number.

With regard to supporting public services, Lloyd and Clark (2000) argue further that, owing to Veblenesque consumption practices, lifestyle concerns of the UMC "are increasingly important in defining the overall

rationale for [all] urban social processes," including effective policy outcomes that focus on revamped urban cores and status-defining public
services such as technologically appealing transit systems. "A residential
population of [UMC] creates a social profile geared toward recreation
and consumption. They value the [monocentric] city over other forms of
settlement space because . . . it can become a cultural center offering diverse, sophisticated and cosmopolitan entertainment lacking elsewhere"
(pp. 4–5). Hence, as the empty-nest UMC come to make up more and
more of this socioeconomic profile in the twenty-first century, one may
expect core cities that matter to the global economy to adopt policies
that foster a more multifaceted, consumption-friendly, and monocentric
environment.

Yet in following the progressive logic of aging, one is left wondering if the global city is destined to become the end-stage habitat of aging UMC boomers. Will these culturally diverse and amenity-rich areas
evolve into downtown retirement communities for the current generation
of UMC boomers, or will the areas retain socioeconomic vitality by back-
filling with a continuous supply of younger UMC who will enjoy the convenience and accessibility of a global-city habitat? Will there be a place
for children in the global city, or are these monuments to postmodern civ-
ilization meant mainly for the convenience of global connectivity and the
pleasures of adult living?

Adding to this sketch, agency efficiency in delivering urban services
appears to be an outcome deemphasized by the UMC. Did the tax revolts
of the late twentieth century represent an abiding interest in operational
efficiency or mainly a personal loathing of unethical politicians and unre-
sponsive bureaucrats? With its globalized transterritorial membership, is
the upper-middle-class genre reflective of persons who are fiscally conservative toward government *efficiency* or mostly those who seek *productive*
urban policy? According to one analysis, most of the people represented
by this genre hold little esteem for the operations of traditional representative government; instead they seek new institutional mechanisms that
maximize tolerance of socioeconomic differences and personal autonomy
(Bishop 2000). Government efficiency is not a policy outcome central to
these quests and may resume its low priority in policymaking, especially
for agencies in UMC-influenced global cities. After all, how can one have
efficiency when novelty and Schumpeter's (1950) "creative destruction"

(the achievement of progress by driving out existing economic activity with innovation) are the overriding criteria for judging the value of today's institutions?

As compelling as social liberalism and good government are to most, not all urban observers looking at UMC influence over the global-city habitat see the bias in outcomes with enthusiasm. Indeed, one contrarian view warns of a clash between the UMC's symbolic world of self-actualization and certain urban realities that threaten that preoccupation. In reality, the world is a contradictory place where intractable inconsistencies and tradeoffs mar the otherwise ordered and symbolic world of those living comfortably beyond sustenance. With profound policymaking implications, this discontinuity between abstract consciousness and actuality has been met with attempts to construct facades and barriers that define, protect, and preserve the urban habitat for self-actualization. As a result, some critics of development are discerning the outline of a "two-tiered society" forged by the paradox of discordant but overlapping urban worlds and maintained by gated communities, restricted-access high-rises, public compounds admired principally for the aesthetics they promote, and the symbolic use of public spaces.

In the abstract, UMC political culture seeks tolerance and generosity toward all classes and groups throughout the world. But what happens when personified events intervene to threaten a symbolic world's prescribed order, paradigmatic assumptions, expressions of good intention, and personal security? From the perspective of genre characteristics, the threats of chaos and contradiction often appear reified in those who challenge meaning and perception—the cynical dissenters of political correctness, the cluttered cityscape of physical and social decay, the vagrant outside the door, the shadowy terrorist in our midst. Unlike the "lower tier," which fears the bill collector, poverty, child mortality, or insufficient health care and social security, those of the UMC genre are worried more about falling short in the face of professional challenge, the enemies of planned orderliness, and assaults on personal integrity. Given these vastly different cognitions, there seems little doubt who is served more by an urban agency's bias toward social-program outcomes. From the standpoint of policy content, the standard-bearing redesign of cityscapes and transit around the lifestyles of an educated and professional upper middle class would seem to make clear social liberalism's lack of empathy with society's lower tier. Indeed, one might make the point that tolerance without empathy is simply indifference.

It is not easy to make sense out of real-world existence in the face of such imposing contradictions without constructing some status-affirming physical evidence of order and pattern. In the case of UMC lifestyles, it also may be necessary to establish barriers that shield the mostly symbolic world in which the UMC increasingly live from the harsher physical reality endured by much of the rest of the population. Sealing off the contradictory reality becomes as essential to the UMC lifestyle as pursuing abstract self-actualization itself. One Chicago political scientist writes about this as it relates to his city:

> For Chicago's "haves," there is a new sector of privatized services and places. They move in the world of private schools, enclosed high-rent shopping malls, private parking garages, condominium and townhouse developments run by private governments, toll highways, private security guards. . . . But for the have nots, who didn't catch a ride on the neoliberal express, there is plenty of scarcity to go around. They are still dependent on public institutions. . . . In all of these issues, we see constituencies clashing over the direction of this city and its institutions." (McKenzie, 2001)

The same editorial could have been written about any of America's global cities where the systemic power of a UMC genre holds influence over the course of public policymaking and the design of urban services. By reference to their *being* rather than their *actions*, the genre prescribes demands on or the design of a world-class global city, which in part involves the construction of symbolic monuments and physical barriers that allow its members to carry on ordered, paradigmatic lives. Transit is an extraordinary example of the subtle way in which public services can be used to reify the abstract perception of urban global status and simultaneously to shield this symbolic existence and its devotion to social liberalism from the real world of fluid inconsistency.

Light-rail systems (and to a great extent modern heavy-rail systems in Washington, D.C., the San Francisco Bay Area, and Atlanta) provide a useful illustration. This newer mode is more technologically sophisticated than buses, but it is far more expensive and much less adaptable to changing urban activity patterns. Consistent with the fact that the UMC tend not to regularly ride transit of any kind, light rail's ridership remains persistently low, with a few notable exceptions. Yet it is immensely popular among mayors and many other urban politicians because its *presence* (more than its use) heralds something symbolic. Speaking to a UMC focus on global status, light rail imparts a sense of urban modernity, permanence of place, order, sophistication, and connectivity befitting enduring world-class cities.

It also acts as a barrier to entry by leapfrogging undesirable areas. In places fraught with socioeconomic problems (i.e., most large urban areas), light rail often serves as a consciously designed barrier to protect UMC activity enclaves from "nonconforming" parts of the cityscape. In many places since 1980 it has been designed to link upscale neighborhoods (including downtown high-rises, rail corridors, and more distant "edge cities") with corporate business centers, art and entertainment enclaves, and sports complexes. Because buses are used principally to provide access to lower-status neighborhoods and activities, bus routes are kept apart from rail mainly by minimizing common transfer points. In some areas, such as Atlanta, UMC enclaves in surrounding suburban counties have gone a step further by successfully blocking the entrance of regional rail transit to their communities, while at the same time lauding its presence in the central city (including its direct route to the airport) as a testament to the metropolitan area's global connectedness.

By implication, transit illustrates something even more fundamental about forging policy outcomes partly in the image of an SES genre composed of institutional symbolism and detached from concrete urban realities. In addressing the needs of a plural and increasingly transterritorial society, transit policymaking underscores the difficulty government has in responding to a society where some remain tied to "place" while others seem to have roots everywhere and yet nowhere.

For the UMC, it also points to the fragile meaning of social liberalism and to the inherent ambiguity faced by policymakers in translating the "interests" of an anonymous genre into policy design. With the decline of broad civic engagement, public officials may be left mainly with setting policy according to the UMC's visible show of institutional status, selection of socioeconomic activities, and choice of habitat. In the end, it may be inevitable that the bias of policy outcomes is framed by abstract images of a compelling lifestyle that is unattainable or unsustainable for a great many people.

Appendices

Appendix A

The Transit Agency Sample

The Transit Agency Sample

Case Number	Agency Name	Jurisdiction	Metropolitan Area	1990 District Population	System Size (Number of Vehicles)
1. Phoenix Transit (PT)		Maricopa County	Phoenix, Az.	2,122,000	296
2. Sun Transit (Sun Tran)		City of Tucson	Tucson, Az.	667,000	164
3. Long Beach Transit		City of Long Beach	Los Angeles, Ca.	429,000	150
4. Orange County Transit (OCTA)		Orange County	Los Angeles, Ca.	2,411,000	487
5. Southern California Rapid Transit District (SCRTD)		Los Angeles County	Los Angeles, Ca.	8,863,000	1,939
6. Sacramento Regional Transit		Sacramento County	Sacramento, Ca.	1,041,000	190
7. Metropolitan Transit Development Board (MTDB)		Southern Half of San Diego County	San Diego, Ca.	2,498,000	260
8. AC Transit		Alameda and Contra Costa Counties	San Francisco Bay Area, Ca.	1,356,000	657
9. Central Contra Costa County Transit (CCCTA)		Central Contra Costa County	San Francisco Bay Area, Ca.	414,000	80
10. Golden Gate Transit (GGT)		Marin, Sonoma, and San Francisco Counties	San Francisco Bay Area, Ca.	490,000	222

(*continued*)

The Transit Agency Sample

Case Number	Agency Name	Jurisdiction	Metropolitan Area	1990 District Population	System Size (Number of Vehicles)
11. Bay Area Rapid Transit (BART)	San Francisco, Alameda, Contra Costa, and San Mateo Counties	San Francisco Bay Area, Ca.	2,807,000	380
12. San Francisco Municipal Railway (MUNI)	San Francisco County	San Francisco Bay Area, Ca.	724,000	812
13. SamTrans	San Mateo County	San Francisco Bay Area, Ca.	650,000	259
14. Santa Clara County Transit	Santa Clara County, California	San Francisco Bay Area, Ca.	1,498,000	433
15. Regional Transportation District	6-County Area	Denver, Co.	1,848,000	689
16. Washington Metropolitan Area Transit Authority (WMATA)	5 Counties in Virginia, Maryland, and D.C.	Washington, D.C.	3,224,000	1,976
17. Jacksonville Transportation Authority	Duval County	Jacksonville, Fl.	673,000	145
18. Miami-Dade Transit (M-DT)	Dade County	Miami, Fl.	1,937,000	530
19. Metropolitan Atlanta Rapid Transit Authority (MARTA)	City of Atlanta and 5 Counties	Atlanta, Ga.	2,178,000	732
20. Chicago Transit Authority (CTA)	Cook County and City of Chicago	Chicago, Il.	5,105,000	2,888
21. Indianapolis Public Transportation (IPT)	City of Indianapolis Marion County	Indianapolis, In.	797,000	171
22. Regional Transit Authority	4 Parishes and New Orleans	New Orleans, La.	945,000	437
23. Mass Transit Administration	City of Baltimore and 2 Counties	Baltimore, Md.	1,855,000	880
24. Massachusetts Bay Transportation Authority (MBTA)	78 Cities in Greater Metropolitan Boston (5 Counties)	Boston, Ma.	4,058,000	1,459
25. Metropolitan Transit Commission	Hennepin and Ramsey Counties	Minneapolis and St. Paul, Mn.	1,518,000	837
26. Kansas City Area Transportation Authority (NFTA)	4 Missouri Counties and 3 Kansas Counties	Kansas City, Mo.	1,361,000	251

The Transit Agency Sample *(continued)*

Case Number	Agency Name	Jurisdiction	Metropolitan Area	1990 District Population	System Size (Number of Vehicles)
27. Bi-State Development Agency (Bi-State DA)	4 Missouri Counties, City of St. Louis, and 2 Illinois Counties	St. Louis, Mo.	2,309,000	636
28. Niagara Frontier Transportation Authority (NFTA)	Erie and Niagara Counties	Buffalo, N.Y.	1,190,000	384
29. Southwest Ohio Regional Transit Authority (SORTA)	City of Cincinnati and Hamilton County	Cincinnati, Oh.	866,000	360
30. Greater Cleveland Regional Transit Authority (GCRT)	City of Cleveland and Cuyahoga County	Cleveland, Oh.	1,412,000	758
31. Central Ohio Transit Authority (COTA)	City of Columbus and Franklin County	Columbus, Oh.	961,000	290
32. Tri-County Metropolitan Transportation District (Tri-Met)	Clackamus, Multnomah, and Washington Counties	Portland, Or.	1,175,000	518
33. Southeastern Pennsylvania Transportation Authority (SEPTA)	City of Philadelphia and 4 Counties	Philadelphia, Pa.	3,729,000	2,040
34. Port Authority of Allegheny County	Allegheny County	Pittsburgh, Pa.	1,336,000	846
35. Dallas Area Rapid Transit (DART)	14 Cities within Dallas County	Dallas, Tx.	1,853,000	753
36. Metropolitan Transit Authority (MTA)	Harris County	Houston, Tx.	2,818,000	805
37. VIA Metropolitan Transit (VIA)	Bexar County	San Antonio, Tx.	1,185,000	493
38. Utah Transit Authority	Salt Lake City and 4 Counties	Wasatch Front (Salt Lake City), Ut.	1,072,000	364
39. Tidewater Regional Transit	5 Cities	Greater Norfolk, Va.	962,000	233
40. Municipality of Metropolitan Seattle (MMS)	City of Seattle and Suburban Cities	Seattle, Wa.	1,507,000	1,414
41. Pierce Transit	Pierce County	Tacoma, Wa.	586,000	218
42. Milwaukee County Transit System (MCT)	Milwaukee County	Milwaukee, Wi.	959,000	452

Appendix B

Transit Performance Measures

The Twelve Performance Measures

Individual measures for transit performance run into the hundreds, most of them focused on aspects of operations (see APTA 1998; UMTA 1988; Fielding 1987; Perry and Babitsky 1986; Perry and Angle 1980; Altshuler 1979). Most are derived from data compiled by transit organizations in compliance with Section 15 of the Urban Mass Transportation Act, as amended in 1974. In Table B.1, transit measures for the MSOI framework are mapped according to policy outcome cells and in reference to transit constituency expectations. Although no conceptual limit exists on the number of measures to include, this study incorporated three in each cell, a total of twelve for the matrix. Note that all measures are stated as ratios, which allows interagency comparative equivalency adjusting for scale. These ratios are later divided into their component parts to create residual values generated by a regression technique using scale as the independent variable.

Outcome cell I is one of two administration-centered indices and is defined in terms of the agency's strategic positioning in the urban passenger transportation industry. It centers on the agency's effectiveness in acquiring organizational eminence, market position, and size. The most common economic performance measure consistent with this perspective is market share, but in transit this requires knowing the total number of vehicle trips in an agency's district area for all modes including autos. Such data are not routinely available or collected from a common source using conventional methodology. Lacking reliable market-share data, MSOI uses instead "market penetration," which the industry also calls "percent of population served." Although a less direct measure of strategic organizational effectiveness than market share, it measures an agency's ability to attract ridership and reflects relative market position.

The second cell I measure is "load factor," a performance indicator used by all passenger transportation industries. The measure indicates how much the service is used and is calculated as the number of passengers riding a vehicle relative to the total seats available. Like market penetration, it is an indirect symbol estimating how central transit is to customers given the market alternatives. The third measure is "budgetary growth," which acts as a macro indicator of resource acquisition. According to Niskanen, "budget maximization should be an adequate proxy even for those bureaucrats with a relatively low pecuniary motivation and a relatively high motivation for making changes in the public interest" (1971: 38). It measures year-to-year revenue changes from combined sources, and reflects the organization's accumulating (or declining) eminence in the community as determined by the farebox recovery rate (transit fare as a percentage of operating expenses), intergovernmental grantsmanship, and secondary fee-for-service sources (e.g., charter services, advertising).

Outcome cell II is the second administration-centered index and is focused on performance measures reflecting operational efficiencies. In transit, this is divided according to efficiencies achieved in operations, maintenance, and capital-equipment acquisition and replacement (system infrastructure). The first involves those unit costs incurred in running the transit route system, the largest component of which are vehicle operators' labor costs. The second measure is maintenance costs, which are a function of labor wage, age of the vehicle fleet, design quality of fleet vehicles, and incidence of public misuse (e.g., graffiti). System infrastructure efficiency measures the employment of capital facilities and equipment in the production of output and includes buildings (bus and rail barns), rail tracks, transit stop shelters, and vehicles (buses and rail cars) directly used in the system's operations.

Outcome cell III is one of two social-centered indices and is defined

TABLE **B.1** Constituency Interests and MSOI Matrix Measures
12 Performance Measures, Urban Transit, 1987–1991

Outcome Perspective Cell	Constituency	Constituency Interest	Fiduciary Agent	Primary Performance Focus	Statistical Measure
Administration-Centered					
I	Senior Management	Domain Eminence: Superior Market Share	Direct*	Market Penetration	Passenger Trips/ District Population
I	Senior Management	Domain Eminence: Superior Market Share	Direct*	Load Factor	Passenger Miles/ District Population
I	Senior Management	Domain Eminence: Resource Acquisition	Direct*	Budgetary Growth	Percentage Change in Revenue, All Sources
Administration-Centered					
II	Production Management	Minimize Route System Unit Costs	Direct*	Operations Efficiency	Operations Expense/ Vehicle Miles
II	Maintenance Management	Minimize Maintenance Unit Costs	Direct*	Maintenance Efficiency	Maintenance Expense/ Vehicle Hours
II	Financial and Engineering Management	Minimize Capital Costs	Direct*	System Infrastructure Efficiency	Operating Assets/ Vehicle Revenue Mile

(*continued*)

TABLE **B.1** (*continued*)

Outcome Perspective Cell	Constituency	Constituency Interest	Fiduciary Agent	Primary Performance Focus	Statistical Measure
Political-Centered					
III	Transit-Dependent Riders	Convenient Access to Metropolitanwide Economic Opportunities	FTA, State, and Local Officials	Mobility for Transit-Dependent Clients	Passenger Miles/Service Area (Sq. Mi.)
III	Nonworking Poor and Disabled Persons	Broad Area Access to Social Activities and Welfare Services	FTA, State, and Local Officials	Noncommuter Mobility Services	Off-Peak Vehicle Miles/Total Vehicles Miles
III	Regional Urban Population	Urban Revitalization and Economic Development	Metropolitan Government and Regional Interests	Economic Development Contribution	Annual Capital Investment/District Population
Political-Centered					
IV	Transit Hourly Workforce	High Standard of Living	Organized Labor: Local Unions	Wage Yield	Wage Expense/Vehicle Revenue Mile
IV	Federal, State, and Local Taxpayers	Tax Minimization	Ballot Measures and Legislatures	Subsidy Value	Vehicle Hours/Operating Subsidy
IV	Pedestrians and Motorists	Roadway Safety	FTA, State DMVs, and Legislatures	Vehicle Accidents	Vehicle Accidents/Vehicle Miles

NOTE: * = Constituency directly represents its interests.

in terms of the agency's social effectiveness in reaching program objectives mandated by external political authorities. The first measure is overall system "mobility afforded the transit dependent," defined by the Federal Transportation Administration (FTA) as "access to desired destinations" (Rosenbloom and Altshuler 1979: 136). Reflecting a route system's connectivity in an urban spatial network of residences and various social and economic activities, this measure combines geographic coverage and frequency (total vehicle miles driven on all routes) within a system's service area (in square miles). Service area covers the agency's urbanized tax base and is determined by an analysis of the 1990 census for each transit jurisdiction. An important but imperfect indicator of social-program effectiveness, it is silent on whether route coverage and intensity are suitably aligned temporally and spatially with patterns of social and economic activity.

The second measure is "noncommuter mobility" and looks at route extensiveness provided to transit-dependent riders who need access to nonemployment opportunities (e.g., grocery shopping, welfare services agencies, schools, community meetings). Many nonworking poor have widely dispersed origin and destination points and ride during off-peak hours when vehicles are less crowded with commuters riding express routes. To achieve high social-program compliance, an agency would need to encourage noncommuter riders by partially restructuring its route system during off-peak periods to provide greater access to more metropolitan areas (i.e., shifting route emphasis outside commuter corridors to a matrix structure). Measuring the extent of service provided to noncommuting clients, the indicator is defined as the number of off-peak vehicle miles driven as a percentage of total vehicle miles.

The third measure of the cell III index captures the interests of a metropolitan area's cities and special districts. As promoters of economic development, these governments seek expenditures by transit agencies as contributions to the creation of nontransit jobs and inducement of private sector capital improvements for a regional population. Transit agency capital budgeting often involves coordinated collateral development, and agencies engage in construction along transit corridors that provide positive externalities to the locales (Attoe 1988). "Economic development contribution" measures the level of an agency's capital investment program in terms of the size of its district population. Although such programs are imprecise and indirect in their impacts, spending more per capita on transit projects tends to have an increased multiplier effect (e.g., enhancement of urban property values in the vicinity, improvement of access to surrounding jobs, and retail activity).

Outcome cell IV is the second social-centered index and is defined with respect to the transit agency's external resource contributors who are not customers, clients, or client fiduciaries. Operational hourly employees (vehicle operators and maintenance workforce) are typically unionized and desire, among other things, high wages. "Wage yield" therefore captures what unionized employees earn for the amount of work produced (measured in mileage driven). Taxpayer initiatives and elected officials have tempered union legitimacy and have broadened the cell IV perspective to include a subsidy value measure. Third, motorists and pedestrians are concerned about potential harm from vehicle accidents. Accident rates according to the scale of operations, therefore, indicate the comparative level of this externality.

Calculating Empirical Values for the Twelve Measures

The twelve performance ratios reported in Table B.1 could be used as statistical measures to represent comparative performance of urban transit agencies, but ratios are generally considered less accurate than regression residuals. For the measures, both types of data take into account the effect of size or scale in agency performance, but the regression method is the more global technique, accepted for producing the best linear unbiased estimator of comparative data for policy outcomes. Using the size or scale component of each ratio as the independent variable, each of the twelve performance measures was regressed (as shown in Table B.2). This technique produced *residuals* for each agency representing variance from a measure's regression line (i.e., regression mean). Eliminating urban scale from the comparative analysis provides greater parsimony, and its significance is so widely accepted that it holds little theoretical interest in most urban studies.

Because the study is focused on outcome skewness, it looks at variance from the perspective of performance emphasizers in the sample. Determination of a performance scale is made for each of the twelve measures with reference to the sample's "frontier" of highest performers. That

TABLE **B.2** Regression Results for Urban Size and Metropolitan Scale
12 Performance Measures (Ratios), Urban Transit, 1987–1991

Performance Measure	R Squared	Significance (t)	Slope (Ratio Mean)
I *Organizational Effectiveness*			
1. Market Penetration	.54	.01	77.4
2. Load Factor	.96	.00	17.1
3. Budgetary Growth	.73	.00	0.25
II *Operational Efficiency*			
4. Operations Efficiency	.82	.00	2.30
5. Maintenance Efficiency	.86	.00	23.2
6. System Infrastructure Efficiency	.28	.05	17.8
III *Social-Program Effectiveness*			
7. Transit-Dependent Mobility	.18	.10	0.31
8. Noncommuter Mobility	.99	.00	0.76
9. Economic Development	.53	.01	38.5
IV *Reciprocal Effectiveness*			
10. Wage Yield	.92	.00	1.26
11. Taxpayer Subsidy	.71	.01	0.02
12. Vehicle Accidents	.80	.00	30.8

is, in visualizing a scattergram, think of agency variances as bounded by an "envelope" set at two standard deviations above and below the regression mean (an area containing 95 percent of the sample points). As an example, Figure B.1 provides a graphic representation of the economic development contribution measure.

As illustrated in the figure, data scatter along the fitted regression mean and are upwardly bounded by the frontier (on the positive side of the mean) representing the feasible outer boundary of superior performance. A similar boundary exists on the negative side of the regression line for performance laggards. The measure's value to be included in an index's calculation is determined by the distance each agency point lies from the regression mean (positive for emphasizers, negative for deemphasizers). Notice that three agencies are outliers and one of those (the Washington, D.C., Metropolitan Transit Authority) is clearly a hyperperformer regarding capital budget expenditures contributing to metropolitan economic development potential. Although representing less than 5 percent of the sample, true outliers were retained in the sample but ad-

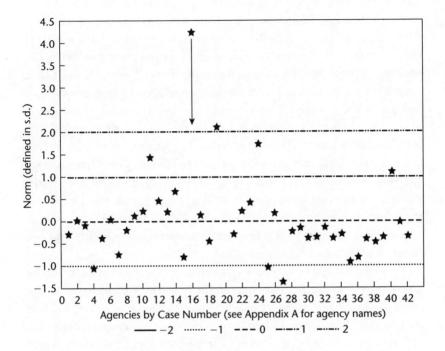

FIGURE **B.1**   Scattergram Example: Data Envelope for Economic Development (Envelope Set at 2 s.d., 42 Transit Agencies, 1987–1991)

justed back to their nearest envelope boundary. This prevented problems of missing data and eliminated any undue influence of their original status as outliers.

This regression technique creates data that allows the analysis of agency performance on a given measure to be understood globally relative to all agencies in the sample. Moreover, the regression residuals represent the unexplained variance in each measure after the explanatory power of agency size or metropolitan scale has been removed. That is, the agency residual variances scattered along the regression line are the result of causes yet to be determined. As shown in Table B.2, variance in some of the twelve measures can be explained principally by agency size or metropolitan scale alone (as represented in the table by high R-squared values). Others leave open considerable room for determinants of individual performances unrelated to size or scale.

In the case of outcome cell I, scale seems to account for nearly all the variance among agencies in the load factor measure but for a much lower amount of the variance in market penetration and budgetary growth. As a result, the outcome index for this cell captures most of its variance from the residuals of these two latter performance measures. In the case of outcome cell II, variances in operations and maintenance efficiency are significantly accounted for by scale, but sufficient residual variances remain to examine the thesis-based determinants of this study. Nevertheless, residuals of system infrastructure efficiency will have a larger influence because scale is only marginally significant to variance in this measure. In the case of outcome cell III, scale is mainly the determinant of variance for noncommuter mobility but weighs considerably less in accounting for variance in transit-dependent commuter mobility and economic development contribution.

Outcome cell IV becomes a special case. Variances in its three measures are very significantly accounted for by scale. This leaves less room for thesis-based determinants to have much influence in explaining variance in this cell's index. Indeed, in preliminary analysis of independent variables for the study, none were near significance in the cell IV regression model. Scale alone seems to explain any real variance in outcome emphasis. Hence, in the examination of outcome skewness in the MSOI framework, this cell was eliminated from further analysis.

The final stage in determining values for the four indices of MSOI involved standardizing values (dividing each measure's values by its standard deviation) for the twelve measures, which has the effect of reducing them to a common scale format. This is done so that each of the four outcome-cell indices is a summation of its three performance measures, which are of equivalent magnitude providing scale-equivalent contribution to the index variance. The resulting data for the analysis of outcome skewness exhibit near normal frequency distributions and satisfied three statistical tests showing the four indices to be independent in both means and variance. ANOVA indicated statistically significant differences in index means (F value = 13.77 for four groups with three degrees of freedom). The F-test comparing the two cell indices with the greatest differences in variance indicates significance (F = 4.85 at the .05 level). Finally, a principal components analysis shows that the indices are distinctly different—three cell indices were required to explain 94 percent of the variance.

Reference Matter

Notes

Chapter 4

1. An interest group thesis is not pertinent to this study for two reasons. First, the presence of interest groups has no singular or monolithic influence toward any particular policy emphasis. Instead, the interest group literature speaks of group mobilization, not government behavior (Moe 1987). For example, some groups mobilize to advocate administration-centered aims and others mobilize to demand policy congruency to social-centered mandates. Second, the intergovernmental exchange thesis incorporates an indirect influence for interest groups by viewing them as empowered by a representative governmental process and enacted through intergovernmental exchanges. Agencies and politicians within a network of concurrent authorities may be said to act as proxies for a range of interest groups (Buchanan and Tullock 1965).

This proxy argument is made in two lights. First the *number and variety* of perspectives in any intergovernmental network reflect the presence of interest groups. Wise, for example, contends that "government organizations are created and configured . . . according to ideas that policy participants (interest groups based . . .) have about how the [public] organization will respond to the variables of interest" (1990: 148). Second, the argument is made that agencies form their authorities according to different *scales* of public demand (ACIR 1993; Boschken 1982, 1976; Warren 1966). The multiple levels of governmental actors account for interest groups having different territorial scope (i.e., some are local, others are regional or national). With an eye to multiscale interest group inclusion, the ACIR argued that multiple "units of government, when used concurrently, reflect complementary expressions of public preference, not contradictory principles of organization" (1987: 53).

Even so, interest groups may directly influence focal-agency policymaking when their proxy is with that agency, examples of which include the focal agency's clients (involving both political and market exchanges), supporters (political affiliations), and activist internal management (Bozeman 1987; Meltsner 1976). But in emphasizing transactional exchange, the institutional perspective does not see interest groups determining outcomes from outside the web of government or from some amorphous, latent, or detached environmental position, as is often found in the interest group literature (Cigler and Loomis 1991; Lowi 1969; Truman 1951).

To the contrary, institutionalism views a focal agency's policymakers as reflections of a particular supportive and "politically powerful group" who select "the right types of bureaucrats" who will follow policy emphases congruent with the interest group's preferences (Moe 1990: 135). Hence, the proxy argument limits the intergovernmental network to exchanges with governmental authorities, where interest groups play out their influence through a structure of political representation and transactional exchange.

Chapter 8

1. Parenthetically, traffic congestion may also have contributed to an emphasis on organizational effectiveness, but the results show no significant effect. It is not completely clear why this relationship is not statistically significant, but part of the answer may lie in how the MSOI index for Outcome I is constructed. Remember, rail service is unhampered by roadway congestion in its ability to operate at prescribed speeds and on schedule. This ability to respond to frustrated drivers results in higher passenger loads and deeper market penetration (two of the Outcome I measures). But buses may be constrained in their market response because they experience the same roadway congestion (and resulting delays) that autos do. Since MSOI components are constructed to measure *agencywide* policy outcomes, they cannot distinguish between one program performance and another (e.g., rail and bus). Hence, it is possible that no relationship with organizational effectiveness registers statistically for the agency as a whole because many agencies have some mix of dual modes where congestion forces buses and rail service in opposite directions of impact. For MSOI analysis, this may cancel a positive impact on the agency's overall organizational effectiveness.

References

Aberbach, Joel D., Robert D. Putnam, and Bert A. Rockman. 1981. *Bureaucrats and Politicians in Western Democracies*. Cambridge, Mass.: Harvard University Press.

ACIR (Advisory Commission on Intergovernmental Relations). 1987. *The Organization of Local Public Economies*. Washington, D.C.: Advisory Commission on Intergovernmental Relations.

———. 1993. *Metropolitan Organization: Comparison of the Allegheny and St. Louis Case Studies*, SR-15. Washington, D.C.: Advisory Commission on Intergovernmental Relations.

Agranoff, Robert, and Michael McGuire. 1993. "Theoretical and Empirical Concerns for Intergovernmental Management and Policy Design." Paper presented at the 89th Annual Meeting of the American Political Science Association, Washington, D.C., September 2–5.

Altshuler, Alan. 1979. *The Urban Transportation System*. Cambridge, Mass.: MIT Press.

Altshuler, Alan, and William B. Parent. 1999. "Breaking Old Rules: Four Themes for the 21st Century," online at www.harvard.edu/innovat/4themes21st.htm, February 24, pp. 1–3.

American Public Transit Association (APTA). 1998. *Transit Fact Book*. Washington, D.C.: APTA.

Ansoff, H. Igor, and R. G. Brandenburg. 1971. "The Language for Organizational Design." *Management Science* 17: 705–31.

Arrow, Kenneth J. 1977. "The Organization of Economic Activity: Issues Pertinent to the Choice of Market Versus Nonmarket Allocation." In Robert H.

Haveman and Julius Margolis, eds., pp. 67–81. *Public Expenditure and Policy Analysis*. Chicago: Rand McNally College.

Asher, Herbert B. 1983. *Causal Modeling*. 2d ed. Beverly Hills, Calif.: Sage.

Ashforth, Blake E., and Fred Mael. 1989. "Social Identity Theory and the Organization." *Academy of Management Review* 14: 20–39.

Attoe, Wayne, ed. 1988. *Transit, Land Use and Urban Form*. Austin, Tex.: Center for the Study of American Architecture.

Barnard, Chester I. 1938. *The Function of the Executive*. Cambridge, Mass.: Harvard University Press.

Barnum, Darold T., and John M. Gleason. 1979. *Measuring the Influence of Subsidies on Transit Efficiency and Effectiveness*. Washington, D.C.: Urban Mass Transportation Administration.

Bassily, Fady P. 1993. Interview by Herman Boschken and Suann Shumaker with the assistant general manager for rail services, Washington Metropolitan Area Transit Authority, at agency headquarters, September 1.

Bell, Daniel. 1960. *The End of Ideology*. New York: Free Press.

———. 1976. *The Coming of Post-Industrial Society*. New York: Basic Books.

———. 1991. "Office Location: City or Suburb?" *Transportation* 18: 239–59.

Benson, Kenneth J. 1975. "The Interorganizational Network as a Political Economy." *Administrative Science Quarterly* 20: 229–50.

Berger, Peter L., and Thomas Luckmann. 1966. *The Social Construction of Reality*. New York: Doubleday.

Bernick, Michael. 1996. Transit Villages: Tools for Revitalizing the Inner City. *Access* (Berkeley, University of California Transportation Center), no. 9: 13–17.

Bickel, Richard G. 1993. Interview by Herman Boschken and Suann Shumaker with the director of long-range planning, Southeastern Pennsylvania Transportation Authority, at agency headquarters, September 2.

Bish, Robert L., and Hugh O. Nourse. 1975. *Urban Economics and Policy Analysis*. New York: McGraw-Hill.

Bishop, Bill. 2000. "The Changing Face of American Politics," *Austin 360 News*, online at www.austin360.com/statesman/editions/today/news_4.html.

Boschken, Herman L. 1976. "Organizational Logic for Concurrent Government in Metropolitan Areas." *Academy of Management Review* 1: 5–13.

———. 1982. *Land Use Conflicts*. Champaign: University of Illinois Press.

———. 1988. *Strategic Design and Organizational Change*. Tuscaloosa: University of Alabama Press.

———. 1992. "Analyzing Performance Skewness in Public Agencies." *Journal of Public Administration Research and Theory* 2: 265–88.

———. 1994. "Organizational Performance and Multiple Constituencies." *Public Administration Review* 54: 308–12.

———. 1998a. "Institutionalism: Intergovernmental Exchange, Administration-

Centered Behavior, and Policy Outcomes in Urban Agencies." *Journal of Public Administration Research and Theory* 8: 585–614.

———. 1998b. "Upper Middle Class Influence on Developmental Policy Outcomes." *Urban Studies* 35: 627–47.

Bourne, Larry S. 1982. *Internal Structure of the City*. New York: Oxford University Press.

Bozeman, Barry. 1987. *All Organizations Are Public*. San Francisco: Jossey-Bass.

Brint, Steven. 1984. "New Class and Cumulative Trend Explanations of the Liberal Political Attitudes of Professionals." *American Journal of Sociology* 90: 30–71.

———. 1994. *In an Age of Experts: The Changing Role of Professionals in Politics and Public Life*. Princeton, N.J.: Princeton University Press.

Brint, Steven, and Charles S. Levy. 1999. "Professions and Civic Engagement." In Theda Skocpol and Morris P. Fiorina, eds. *Civic Engagement in American Democracy*. Washington, D.C.: Brookings Institution Press.

Buchanan, James N., and Gordon Tullock. 1965. *The Calculus of Consent*. Ann Arbor: University of Michigan Press.

Buckley, James F. 1991. Interview by Herman Boschken and Suann Shumaker with the assistant general manager for operations, Baltimore Mass Transit Administration, at state agency headquarters, August 28.

Bureau of the Census. 1992. *Census of the Population*. CD file 1A. Washington, D.C.: U.S. Department of Commerce.

Bureau of the Census. 1999. "Poverty Thresholds: 1990," online at www.census.gov/hhes/poverty/threshld/thresh90.html.

Burgess, Ernest W. 1961. "The Growth of the City." In G.A. Theodorson, ed., *Studies in Human Ecology*, pp. 37–44. Evanston, Ill.: Northwestern University Press.

Burgess, Ernest W., and Donald J. Bogue. 1967. *Urban Sociology*. Chicago: University of Chicago Press.

Burt, Ronald. 1987. "Social Contagion and Innovation: Cohesion Versus Structural Equivalence," *American Journal of Sociology* 92: 1287–1335.

Cameron, Kim. 1986. "Effectiveness as Paradox." *Management Science* 32: 539–53.

Campbell, John P. 1977. "On the Nature of Organizational Effectiveness." In Paul S. Goodman and Johannes M. Pennings, eds., *New Perspectives on Organizational Effectiveness*, pp. 13–55. San Francisco: Jossey-Bass.

Castells, Manuel. ed. 1985. *High Technology, Space, and Society*. Beverly Hills, Calif.: Sage.

Catoe, John. 1989. Interview by Herman Boschken and Suann Shumaker with the manager of transportation operations, Orange County Transportation District, at agency headquarters, July 26.

Cervero, Robert. 1984. "Effects of Operating Subsidies and Dedicated Funding on Transit Costs and Performance." *Urban Analysis* 8: 37–53.

———. 1990. "Profiling Profitable Bus Routes." *Transportation Quarterly* 44: 183–201.

———. 1997. "Tracking Accessibility." *Access* (Berkeley, University of California Transportation Center), no. 11: 27–31.

Cervero, Robert, and John Landis. 1992. "Suburbanization of Jobs and the Journey to Work: A Submarket Analysis of Commuting in the San Francisco Bay Area." *Journal of Advanced Transportation* 26: 275–97.

———. 1995. "The Transportation–Land Use Connection Still Matters." *Access* (Berkeley, University of California Transportation Center), no. 7: 2–10.

Cherlow, J.R. 1981. "Measuring Values of Travel Time Savings." *Journal of Consumer Research* 7: 360–71.

Chisholm, Donald W. 1989. *Coordination Without Hierarchy*. Berkeley: University of California Press.

Chubb, John E., and Terry M. Moe, 1990. *Politics, Markets, and America's Schools*. Washington, D.C.: Brookings Institution Press.

Cigler, Allan J., and Burdett A. Loomis, eds. 1991. *Interest Group Politics*. Washington, D.C.: CQ Press.

Clark, Terry Nichols. 1994a. "Race and Class Culture: The New Political Culture." In Terry N. Clark, *Urban Innovation*. Thousand Oaks, Calif.: Sage.

———. 1994b. *Urban Innovation*. Thousand Oaks, Calif.: Sage.

———. 1996. "Structural Realignments in American Politics: Less Class, More Race, and a New Political Culture." *Urban Affairs Review* 31: 367–403.

———. 1998. *The New Political Culture*. Boulder, Colo.: Westview.

———. 2001. "Amenities Drive Urban Growth." Paper presented at the Annual Meeting of the American Political Science Association, San Francisco, August 28–31.

Clark, Terry Nichols, and Lorna Crowley Ferguson. 1983. *City Money: Political Processes, Fiscal Strain and Retrenchment*. New York: Columbia University Press.

Clark, Terry Nichols, and Edward G. Goetz. 1994. "The Antigrowth Machine." In Terry N. Clark, ed., *Urban Innovation*, pp. 105–45. Thousand Oaks, Calif.: Sage.

Clark, Terry Nichols, and Seymour Martin Lipset. 2001. *The Breakdown of Class Politics: A Debate on Post-Industrial Stratification*. Baltimore: Johns Hopkins University Press.

Coleman, James S. 1990. *Foundations of Social Theory*. Cambridge, Mass.: Harvard University Press.

Dahl, Robert A. 1961. *Who Governs?* New Haven, Conn.: Yale University Press.

Danielson, Michael N., and Jameson W. Doig. 1982. *New York: The Politics of Urban Regional Development.* Berkeley: University of California Press.

Dawson, Richard E., and James A. Robinson. 1965. "The Politics of Welfare." In Herbert Jacob and Kenneth Vines, eds., pp. 398–401. *Politics in the American States.* Boston: Little, Brown.

De Sola Pool, Ithiel. 1982. "Communications Technology and Land Use." In Larry S. Bourne, ed., pp. 450–458. *Internal Structure of the City.* New York: Oxford University Press.

DiMaggio, Paul J., and Walter W. Powell. 1983. "The Iron Cage Revisited: Institutional Isomorphism and Collective Rationality in Organizational Fields." *American Sociological Review* 48: 147–60.

Doig, Jameson W. 1983. "'If I See a Murderous Fellow . . . ': The Wilsonian Dichotomy and the Public Authority Tradition." *Public Administration Review* 43: 292–304.

————. 1995. "Politics and the Engineering Mind." In David C. Perry, ed., *Building the Public City*, pp. 21–71. Thousand Oaks, Calif.: Sage.

Doig, Jameson W., and Erwin C. Hargrove, eds. 1987. *Leadership and Innovation.* Baltimore: Johns Hopkins University Press.

Doig, Jameson W., and Jerry Mitchell. 1992. "Expertise, Democracy and the Public Authority Model," in Jerry Mitchell, ed., pp. 17–29. *Public Authorities and Public Policy.* New York: Greenwood Press.

Domhoff, G. William. 1967. *Who Rules America.* Englewood Cliffs, N.J.: Prentice-Hall.

Dotter, LaMar. 1993. Interview by Herman L. Boschken and Suann Shumaker with the budget director, Washington Metropolitan Area Transit Authority, at agency headquarters, September 2.

Douglas, Juliette. 1993. Interview by Suann Shumaker with the deputy general manager for human relations, Bi-State Development Agency (St. Louis), at agency headquarters, November 2.

Downs, Anthony. 1957. *An Economic Theory of Democracy.* New York: Harper & Row.

————. 1962. "The Law of Peak-Hour Expressway Congestion." *Traffic Quarterly* 16: 393–409.

Downs, George, and Patrick Larkey. 1986. *The Search for Government Efficiency.* New York: Random House.

Dye, Thomas R. 1966. *Politics, Economics and the Public.* Chicago: Rand McNally.

————. 1998. *Understanding Public Policy.* 9th ed. Upper Saddle River, N.J.: Prentice-Hall.

Dye, Thomas R., and Virginia Gray. 1980. *The Determinants of Public Policy.* New York: Lexington-Heath.

Easton, David. 1965. *A Framework for Political Analysis*. Englewood Cliffs, N.J.: Prentice-Hall.

Ehrenreich, B. 1989. *Fear of Falling*. New York: Pantheon.

Elliot, James R. 1965. "A Comment On Inter-Party Competition, Economic Variables, and Welfare Politics in American States." *Journal of Politics* 27: 185–91.

Eulau, Heinz, and Paul D. Karps. 1977. "The Puzzle of Representation: Specifying Components of Responsiveness." *Legislative Studies Quarterly* 2: 233–54.

Farney, Dennis. 1994. "Elite Theory: Have Liberals Ignored Have-Less Whites at Their Own Peril?" *Wall Street Journal*, December 14, p. A1.

Federal Transit Administration (FTA). 1993. *Data Tables for the 1992 Section 15 Report Year*. Washington, D.C.: U.S. Department of Transportation.

Feiock, Richard C., and James Clingermayer. 1986. "Municipal Representation, Executive Power and Economic Development Policy Adoption." *Policy Studies Journal* 15: 211–30.

Fielding, Gordon. 1987. *Managing Public Transit Strategically*. San Francisco: Jossey-Bass.

Fisher, G.W. 1964. "Interstate Variation in State and Local Expenditure." *National Tax Journal* 17: 57–74.

Fisher, R.J., and S. Rickeson. 1994. *The Transit Opportunity in IVHS*. Washington, D.C.: Federal Transit Administration.

Frederickson, H. George. 1999. "The Repositioning of American Public Administration." The 1999 Distinguished Gaus Lecture of the American Political Science Association. *PS: Political Science & Politics* 32: 701–11.

Freeman, Edward R. 1984. *Strategic Management: A Stakeholder Approach*. Boston: Pitman.

Freidson, Eliot. 1986. *Professional Powers*. Chicago: University of Chicago Press.

Fried, Robert C. 1971. "Communism, Urban Budgets and the Two Italies: A Case Study in Comparative Urban Government." *Journal of Politics* 33: 1008–51.

Friedman, Thomas L. 2000. *The Lexus and the Olive Tree*. New York: Anchor Books.

Gambaccini, Louis J. 1993. Interview by Herman Boschken and Suann Shumaker with the chief operations officer, Southeastern Pennsylvania Transportation Authority, at agency headquarters, September 2.

Garreau, Joel. 1991. *Edge City*. New York: Anchor Books Doubleday.

Goetz, E.G. 1990. "Type II Policy and Mandated Benefits in Economic Development." *Urban Affairs Quarterly* 26: 170–90.

Giddens, A. 1973. *The Class Structure of the Advanced Societies*. London: Hutchinson.

Giuliano, Genevieve, and Kenneth A. Small. 1991. "Subcenters in the Los Angeles Region." *Regional Science and Urban Economics* 21: 163–82.

Goodnow, Frank J. 1900. *Politics and Administration.* New York: Macmillan.

Goon, Kenneth A. 1991. Interview by Herman Boschken and Suann Shumaker with the director of planning, Baltimore Mass Transit Administration, at state agency headquarters, August 28.

Gordon, P., H.W. Richardson, and H.L. Wong. 1986. "The Distribution of Population and Employment in a Polycentric City: The Case of Los Angeles." *Environment and Planning A* 18: 161–73.

Gottdiener, M. 1986. "Culture, Ideology and the Sign of the City." In M. Gottdiener and A.P. Lagopoulos, eds., *The City and the Sign: An Introduction to Urban Semiotics*, pp. 209–16. New York: Columbia University Press.

Gouldner, Alvin. 1979. *The Future of Intellectuals and the Rise of the New Class.* New York: Seabury Press.

Gregor, Kenneth M. 1990. Interview by Herman Boschken with the general manager, Metropolitan Atlanta Rapid Transit Authority, at agency headquarters, May 7.

Grizzle, Gloria A. 1984. "Developing Standards for Interpreting Agency Performance." *Public Administration Review* 44: 128–33.

Gruber, Judith. 1987. *Controlling Bureaucracy.* Berkeley: University of California Press.

Guess, George M. 1990. *Public Policy and Transit System Management.* New York: Greenwood.

Gulati, Ranjay. 1995. "Does Familiarity Breed Trust?" *Academy of Management Journal* 38: 85–112.

Gunn, David L. 1993. Interview by Herman Boschken and Suann Shumaker with the general manager, Washington Metropolitan Transit Authority, at agency headquarters, September 1.

Gustafsson, Gunnel. 1983. "From Issue to Metapolicy." *World Policy* 1: 20–34.

Hahn, Harlan, and Sheldon Kamieniecki. 1987. *Referendum Voting: Social Status and Policy Preferences.* New York: Greenwood.

Handy, S. 1995. "Understanding the Link Between Urban Form and Travel Behavior." Paper presented at the Annual Meeting of the Transportation Research Board, Washington, D.C., January 22–28.

Hanks, James W., and Timothy J. Lomax. 1992. *1989 Roadway Congestion Estimates and Trends.* Research Report 1131–4. College Station, Tex.: Texas Transportation Institute.

Hansen, Mark. 1975. "Do New Highways Generate Traffic?" *Access* (Berkeley, University of California Transportation Center), no. 7 (Fall): 16–22.

Hansen, Mark, and Yuanlin Huang. 1997. "Road Supply and Traffic in California Urban Areas." *Transportation Research* 31: 205–18.

Hartz, Louis. 1955. *The Liberal Tradition in America*. New York: Harcourt, Brace & World.

Hummon, David M. 1992. "Community Attachment." In I. Altman and S. Low, eds., *Place Attachment*, pp. 253–78. New York: Plenum.

Jones, David W. 1985. *Urban Transit Policy: An Economic and Political History*. Englewood Cliffs, N.J.: Prentice-Hall.

Kantor, Paul, Hank Savitch, and Serena Vicari Haddock. 1998. "Social Progressivism and Market-Centeredness in Development Policy." Paper presented at the Annual Meeting of the American Political Science Association, Boston, September 3–6.

Kaufman, Jerome, and Anthony Jacobs. 1987. "A Public Planning Perspective on Strategic Planning." *Journal of the American Planning Association* 53: 23–33.

Kerr, Clark. 1963. *The Uses of the University*. Cambridge, Mass.: Harvard University Press.

Kitamura, Ryuichi. 1988. "Life-Style and Travel Demand." In Transportation Research Board, *A Look Ahead: Year 2020*, Special Report 220, pp. 149–89. Washington, D.C.: National Research Council.

Larwin, Thomas F. 1989. Interview by Harman Boschken and Suann Shumaker with the general manager, Metropolitan Transit Development Board, San Diego, Calif., July 25.

Lave, Charles. 1994. "It Wasn't Supposed to Turn Out Like This." *Access* (Berkeley, University of California Transportation Center), no. 5: 21–25.

Lazar, David. 1995. "Social Network Methods in the Study of Political Influence." Paper presented at the 1995 meeting of the American Political Science Association, Chicago, August 31–September 2.

Leven, Charles L. 1982. "Growth and Nongrowth in Metropolitan Areas and the Emergence of Polycentric Metropolitan Form." In Larry S. Bourne, ed., *Internal Structure of Cities*, pp. 585–93. New York: Oxford University Press.

Levy, Frank S., Arnold J. Meltsner, and Aaron Wildavsky. 1974. *Urban Outcomes*. Berkeley: University of California Press.

Lewis-Beck, Michael S. 1977. "The Relative Importance of Socioeconomic and Political Variables for Public Policy." *American Political Science Review* 71: 559–66.

Lewis-Beck, Michael S., and Lawrence B. Mohr. 1976. "Evaluating Effects of Independent Variables." *Political Methodology* 3: 27–47.

Ley, D. 1985. "Work-Residence Relationships for Head Office Employees in an Inflated Housing Market." *Urban Studies* 22: 21–38.

Li, Jianling, and Martin Wachs. 2001. "How Subsidies Shape Local Transit Choices." *Access* (Berkeley, University of California Transportation Center), no. 18: 10–14

Lieberman, Robert. 1995. "Social Construction (continued): Comment." *American Political Science Review* 89: 437–41.

Lieberman, William. 1989. Interview by Herman Boschken and Suann Shumaker with the director of planning and operations, Metropolitan Transit Development Board (San Diego), at agency headquarters, July 25.

Lindblom, Charles E. 1977. *Politics and Markets.* New York: Basic Books.

Lineberry, Robert L. 1977. *Equality and Urban Policy.* Beverly Hills, Calif.: Sage.

Lineberry, Robert L., and Edmund P. Fowler. 1967. "Reformism and Public Policies in American Cities." *American Political Science Review* 61: 701–16.

Lloyd, Richard, and Terry Nichols Clark. 2000. "The City as an Entertainment Machine." Paper presented at the Annual Meeting of the American Sociological Association, Washington, D.C., August.

Logan, John R., and Harvey L. Molotch. 1987. *Urban Fortunes: The Political Economy of Place.* Berkeley: University of California Press.

Lowi, Theodore J. 1969. *The End of Liberalism* New York: Norton.

Maslow, Abraham. 1954. *Motivation and Personality.* New York: Harper.

McAdams, J. 1987. "Testing the Theory of the New Class." *Sociological Quarterly* 28: 23–49.

McCullough, W. B.D. Taylor, and M. Wachs. 1997. "Does Contracting Transit Services Save Money?" *Access* (Berkeley, University of California Transportation Center), no. 11: 22–26.

McKenzie, Evan. 2001. "Is the New Political Culture Only Middle Class?" Column in the *Chicago Journal*, online at www.FAUINET@ listserv.nd.edu (December 3).

Meier, Kenneth J., and Joseph Stewart Jr. 1991. "Active Representation in Educational Bureaucracies: Policy Impacts." Paper presented at the Annual Meeting of the American Political Science Association, Washington, D.C.

Meltsner, Arnold J. 1976. *Policy Analysis in the Bureaucracy.* Berkeley: University of California Press.

Meyer, J.R., J.F. Kain, and M. Wohl. 1965. *The Urban Transportation Problem.* Cambridge, Mass.: Harvard University Press.

Miles, Robert H. 1980. *Macro Organization Behavior.* Santa Monica, Calif.: Goodyear.

Miller, D.W. 2000. "The New Urban Studies." *Chronicle of Higher Education* 46, no. 50 (August 18); online at www.chronicle.com/free/.

Mills, C. Wright. 1956. *The Power Elite.* New York: Oxford University Press.

Mindlin, Sergio, and Howard Aldrich. 1975. "Interorganizational Dependency." *Administrative Science Quarterly* 20: 382–92.

Miranda, Rowan A., and Norman Walzer. 1994. "Growth and Decline in City Government." In Terry Nichols Clark, ed., pp. 146–67. *Urban Innovation.* Thousand Oaks, Calif.: Sage.

Mitchell, Gwendolyn. 1993. Interview by Herman Boschken and Suann Shumaker with the assistant general manager for public service, Washington Metropolitan Transit Authority, at agency headquarters, September 1.

Mitchell, Jerry, ed. 1992. *Public Authorities and Public Policy*. New York: Greenwood.

Moe, Terry M. 1987. "Interests, Institutions, and Positive Theory: The Politics of the NLRB." *Studies in American Political Development* 2: 236–99.

——. 1990. "The Politics of Structural Choice." In Oliver E. Williamson, ed., *Organization Theory*, pp. 116–53. New York: Oxford University Press.

Mogridge, Martin. 1997. "The Self-Defeating Nature of Urban Road Capacity Policy." *Transport Policy* 4: 5–23.

Mumford, Lewis. 1961. *The City in History*. New York: Harcourt, Brace & World.

Murray, Charles. 1999. "And Now for the Bad News." *Wall Street Journal*, February 2, p. A22.

Niskanen, William A. 1971. *Bureaucracy and Representative Government*. Chicago: Aldine-Atherton.

——. 1975. "Bureaucrats and Politicians." *Journal of Law and Economics* 18: 617–43.

Nivola, P.S. 1979. *The Urban Services Problem*. Lexington, Mass.: Lexington Books.

Nutt, Paul C., and Robert W. Backoff. 1997. "Crafting Vision." *Journal of Management Inquiry* 6: 308–28.

Oliver, C. 1991. "Strategic Responses to Institutional Processes." *Academy of Management Review* 16: 145–79.

Olson, Carrol. 1990. Interview by Herman Boschken with the assistant general manager for finance, Metropolitan Atlanta Rapid Transit Agency, at agency headquarters, May 9.

Orleans, Peter. 1967. "Urban Experimentation and Urban Sociology." In National Academy of Sciences, *Science, Engineering and the City*, pp. 103–17. Washington, D.C.: National Academy of Sciences.

Osborne, D., and Ted Gaebler. 1992. *Reinventing Government: How the Entrepreneurial Spirit Is Transforming the Public Sector*. New York: Plume.

Ostrom, Elinor. 1986. "An Agenda for the Study of Institutions." *Public Choice* 48: 2–24.

——. 1995. "New Horizons in Institutional Analysis." *American Political Science Review* 89: 174–78.

Ostrom, Vincent. 1973. *The Intellectual Crisis in American Public Administration*. Tuscaloosa: University of Alabama Press.

——. 1987. *The Political Theory of a Compound Republic*. 2d ed. Lincoln: University of Nebraska Press.

Ostrom, Vincent, Charles M. Tiebout, and Robert Warren. 1961. "The Organization of Government in Metropolitan Areas." *American Political Science Review* 55: 831–47.

Pagano, Michael A., and Ann O'M. Bowman. 1995. *Cityscapes and Capital*. Baltimore: Johns Hopkins University Press.

Park, Robert E., and Ernest W. Burgess. 1967. *The City: Suggestions for the Investigation of Human Behavior in the Urban Environment*. Chicago: University of Chicago Press.

Parkhe, Arvind. 1993. "Strategic Alliances Structuring: A Game Theoretic and Transactional Cost Estimation of Interfirm Cooperation." *Academy of Management Journal* 36: 794–829.

Parsons, Brinckerhoff, Quade & Douglas. 1996. *TCRP Report 16: Transit and Urban Form*. Vol. 1, pt. I. Washington, D.C.: National Perdon, Albert H. 1989. Interview by Herman Boschken and Suann Shumaker with the assistant general manager for planning and public affairs, Southern California Rapid Transit District, at agency headquarters, August 10.

Perdon, Albert H. 1989. Interview by Herman Boschken with the Assistant General Manager of Planning, Southern California Rapid Transit District, August 10.

Perry, James L., and Harold L. Angle. 1980. *Labor-Management Relations and Public Agency Effectiveness*. New York: Pergamon Press.

Perry, James L., and Timlynn T. Babitsky. 1986. "Comparative Performance in Urban Bus Transit." *Public Administration Review* 46: 57–65.

Peters, Tom, and Robert Waterman. 1982. *In Search of Excellence: Lessons from America's Best-Run Companies*. New York: Harper & Row.

Peterson, Paul E. 1981. *City Limits*. Chicago: University of Chicago Press.

Pfeffer, Jeffrey. 1990. "Incentives in Organizations: The Importance of Social Relations." In Oliver E. Williamson, ed., *Organization Theory*, pp. 72–97. New York: Oxford University Press.

Pfeffer, Jeffrey, and Gerald R. Salancik. 1978. *The External Control of Organizations: A Resource Dependence Perspective*. New York: Harper & Row.

Pickrell, Don H. 1992. "A Desire Named Streetcar." *Journal of the American Planning Association* 58: 158–76.

Pinchot, Gifford. 1910. *The Fight for Conservation*. New York: Doubleday Page.

Pitkin, Hannah F. 1967. *The Concept of Representation*. Berkeley: University of California Press.

Policy.com. 1999. "Sprawl: The Growing Pains of Suburban America." (Research Issue of the Week); online at *www.policy.com/issuewk/1999/0426*.

Powell, Walter W. 1990. "Neither Market nor Hierarchy: Network Forms of Organization." In L.L. Cummings and B.M. Staw, eds., *Research in Organizational Behavior*. Greenwich, Conn.: JAI Press.

Powell, Walter W., and Paul J. DiMaggio. 1991. *The New Institutionalism in Organizational Analysis*. Chicago: University of Chicago Press.

Powell, Walter W., Kenneth W. Koput, and Laurel Smith-Doerr. 1996. "Interorganizational Collaboration and the Locus of Innovation." *Administrative Science Quarterly* 41: 116–45.

Pressman, Jeffrey, and Aaron Wildavsky. 1973. *Implementation*. Berkeley: University of California Press.

Pushkarev, Boris S., and Jeffrey M. Zupan. 1982. "Where Transit Works: Urban Densities for Public Transportation." In H. S. Levinson and R. A. Weant, *Urban Transportation: Perspectives and Prospects*. Westport, Ct.: Eno Foundation.

Quinn, R., and Kim Cameron. 1983. "Organizational Life Cycles and Shifting Criteria of Effectiveness." *Management Science* 29: 33–51.

Quinn, R., and John Rohrbaugh. 1983. "A Spatial Model of Effectiveness Criteria." *Management Science* 29: 363–77.

Rainey, Hal G., Robert W. Backoff, and Charles H. Levine. 1976. "Comparing Public and Private Organization." *Public Administration Review* 36: 233–44.

Reich, Robert. 1991. *The Work of Nations: Preparing Ourselves for 21st Century Capitalism*. New York: Alfred A. Knopf.

Reichert, James P. 1989. Interview with Herman Boschken and Suann Shumaker with the general manager, Orange County Transit District, at district headquarters, July 26.

Riesman, David. 1961. *The Lonely Crowd*. New Haven, Conn.: Yale University Press.

———. 1964. *Abundance for What?* Garden City, N.Y.: Doubleday.

Roberts, Peter W., and Royston Greenwood. 1997. "Integrating Transaction Cost and Institutional Theories." *Academy of Management Review* 22: 346–73.

Robins, James A. 1987. "Organizational Economics: Notes on the Use of Transaction-Cost Theory in the Study of Organizations." *Administrative Science Quarterly* 32: 68–86.

Rohrbaugh, J. 1981. "Operationalizing the Competing Values Approach." *Public Productivity Review* 5: 141–59.

Rosenbloom, Sandra, and Alan Altshuler. 1979. "Equity Issues in Urban Transportation." In Alan Altshuler, ed., pp. 135–47. *Current Issues in Transportation*. Lexington, Mass.: Lexington Books.

Rosenthal, Stephen J. 1984. "New Directions in Evaluating Interorganizational Programs." *Public Administration Review* 44: 469–76.

Rybczynski, Witold. 1999. *A Clearing in the Distance: Frederick Law Olmsted and America in the Nineteenth Century*. New York: Scribner.

Savas, E.S. 1987. *Privatization: The Key to Better Government*. Chatham, N.J.: Chatham House.

Sayre, Wallace S., and Herbert Kaufman. 1965. *Governing New York City*. New York: W.W. Norton.

Schick, Allen. 1970. "The Road to PPB." In Fremont Lyden and Ernest G. Miller, eds., *Planning, Programming, Budgeting*, pp. 25–52. Chicago: Markham.

Schneider, Anne, and Helen Ingram. 1993. "Social Construction of Target Populations." *American Political Science Review* 87: 334–47.

Schneider, Mark. 1989. *The Competitive City*. Pittsburgh: University of Pittsburgh Press.

Schumpeter, Joseph A. 1950. *Capitalism, Socialism and Democracy*. New York: Harper Torchbooks.

Scott, Allen J. 1982. "Production System Dynamics and Metropolitan Development." *Annals of the Association of American Geographers* 72: 185–200.

Scott, William G., and David K. Hart. 1979. *Organizational America*. Boston: Houghton-Mifflin.

Sehr, Thomas. 1993. Interview by Suann Shumaker with the deputy executive director and general manager of operations, Bi-State Development Agency (St. Louis), at agency headquarters, November 2.

Selznick, Philip. 1948. *TVA and the Grass Roots*. Berkeley: University of California Press.

Selznick, Philip. 1996. "Institutionalism Old and New." *Administrative Science Quarterly* 41: 270–77.

Sharkansky, I., and R.I. Hofferbert. 1969. "Dimensions of State Politics, Economics, and Public Policy." *American Political Science Review* 63: 867–79.

Shepsle, Kenneth A. 1986. "Institutional Equilibrium and Equitable Institutions." In H. Weisberg, ed., *Political Science: The Science of Politics*, pp. 51–81. New York: Agathon.

———. 1989. "Studying Institutions: Some Lessons from the Rational Choice Approach." *Journal of Theoretical Politics* 1: 131–47.

Shepsle, Kenneth A., and Mark S. Bonchek. 1997. *Analyzing Politics: Rationality, Behavior and Institutions*. New York: W.W. Norton.

Sherman, Roger. 1967. "A Private Ownership Bias in Transit Choice." *American Economic Review* 4: 1211–17.

Simon, Herbert. 1995. "Guest Editorial: Upon Acceptance of the Dwight Waldo Award." *Public Administration Review* 55: 404–5.

Skocpol, Theda, and Morris P. Fiorina. 1999. *Civic Engagement in American Democracy*. Washington, D.C.: Brookings Institution Press.

Smerk, George M. 1979. "The Management of Public Transit." In George E. Gray and Lester A. Hoel, eds., *Public Transportation*, pp. 422–42. Englewood Cliffs, N.J.: Prentice-Hall.

Smith, Neil. 1996. *The New Urban Frontier*. New York: Routledge.

Stanley, Thomas J., and William D. Danko. 1996. *The Millionaire Next Door:*

The Surprising Secrets of America's Wealth. New York: Pocket Books/Simon & Schuster.

Stauder, Susan. 1993. Interview by Suann Shumaker with the special assistant for strategic planning, Bi-State Development Agency (St. Louis), at agency headquarters, November 2.

Steffens, Lincoln. 1931. *The Autobiography of Lincoln Steffens*. New York: Harcourt, Brace.

Steers, Richard M. 1975. "Problems in the Measurement of Organizational Effectiveness." *Administrative Science Quarterly* 20: 546–58.

Still, Bayrd. 1974. *Urban America: A History with Documents*. Boston: Little, Brown.

Stone, Clarence N. 1980. "Systemic Power in Community Decision Making." *American Political Science Review* 74: 978–90.

———. 1989. *Regime Politics*. Lawrence: University Press of Kansas.

———. 2000. E-mail response to FAUINET members regarding commentary on Barbara Ferman's *Challenging the Growth Machine*; online at www .FAUINET@listserv.nd.edu)(February 4).

Suarez-Villa, Luis, and Wallace Walrod. 1997. "Operational Strategy, R&D and Intra-Metropolitan Clustering in a Polycentric Structure." *Urban Studies* 34: 1343–80.

Susman, W.I. 1984. *Culture as History*. New York: Pantheon.

Tajbakhsh, Kian. 2002. *The Promise of the City: Space, Identity and Politics in Contemporary Social Thought*. Berkeley: University of California Press.

Tajfel, H., and J.C. Turner. 1986. "The Social Identity Theory of Intergroup Behavior." In S. Worchel and W.G. Austin, eds., *Psychology of Intergroup Relations*, pp. 7–24. Chicago: Nelson-Hall.

Thompson, James D. 1967. *Organizations in Action*. New York: McGraw-Hill.

Tiebout, Charles M. 1956. "A Pure Theory of Local Expenditure." *Journal of Political Economy* 64: 416–27.

Timms, Duncan. 1971. *The Urban Mosaic*. Cambridge, England: Cambridge University Press.

Tri-Met County Metropolitan Transporation District, Portland, Ore. 1994. Unsigned note attached to this study's agency questionnaire and returned to Herman Boschken.

Truman, David B. 1951. *The Governmental Process: Political Interests and Public Opinion*. New York: Alfred A. Knopf.

Tsui, Anne S. 1990. "A Multiple-Constituency Model of Effectiveness." *Administrative Science Quarterly* 35: 458–83.

Turk, H. 1970. "Interorganizational Networks in Urban Society." *American Sociological Review* 34: 1–19.

Turner, J.C. 1985. "Social Categorization and the Self-Concept: A Social Cognitive Theory of Group Behavior." In Edward J. Lawler, ed., *Advances in Group Processes*, Vol. 2, pp. 77–122. Greenwich, Conn.: JAI Press.

Urban Mass Transportation Administration (UMTA), Office of Grants Management. 1988. "Compendium of National Mass Transportation Statistics: 1985 Reporting Year." Washington, D.C.: U.S. Government Printing Office.

Van Sickel, Kay. 1989. Interview by Herman Boschken and Suann Shumaker with the manager of planning, Orange County Transit District, at district headquarters, July 26.

Veblen, Thorstein. 1948. *The Portable Veblen*, edited by Max Lerner. New York: Viking.

Verba, Sidney, Kay Lehman Schlozman, and Henry E. Brady. 1995. *Voice and Equality*. Cambridge, Mass.: Harvard University Press.

Wachs, Martin. 1976. "Consumer Attitudes Toward Transit Service: An Interpretive Review." *Journal of the American Institute of Planners* 42: 96–104.

Wachs, Martin. 1985. "Planning, Organizations, and Decision Making: A Research Agenda." *Transportation Research* 19A, nos. 5/6: 521–31.

Wachs, Martin, and Brian D. Taylor. 1997. "Can Transportation Strategies Help Meet the Welfare Challenge?" UCTC Report 364. Berkeley: University of California Transportation Center.

Wagner, Richard E., and Warren E. Weber. 1975. "Competition, Monopoly, and the Organization of Government in Metropolitan Areas." *Journal of Law and Economics* 18: 661–84.

Waldo, Dwight. 1948. *The Administrative State*. New York: Ronald Press.

Walsh, Annmarie Hauck. 1978. *The Public's Business*. Cambridge, Mass.: MIT Press.

Warren, Robert O. 1966. *Government in Metropolitan Regions*. Davis: Institute of Governmental Affairs, University of California.

Warren, Robert O., and Keiran Donaghy. 1986. "Telecommunications and the Use of Urban Land." Paper presented at the Canadian Institute of Planners National Conference, Vancouver, B.C., July 20–23.

Whyte, William. 1956. *Organization Man*. New York: Anchor.

Wiebe, Robert H. 1967. *The Search for Order*. New York: Hill and Wang.

Williamson, Oliver E., ed. 1990. *Organization Theory*. New York: Oxford University Press.

Willoughby, W.F. 1919. *The Government of Modern States*. New York: Appleton-Century.

Wilson, Frank J. 1990. Interview by Herman Boschken and Suann Shumaker with the general manager, Bay Area Rapid Transit District, at district headquarters, March 29.

Wilson, James Q., and Edward C. Banfield. 1964. "Public-Regardingness as a Value Premise in Voting Behavior." *American Political Science Review* 58: 876–87.

Wilson, Woodrow. [1887] 1941. "The Study of Administration." *Political Science Quarterly* 2: 1–37.

Wingo, Lowdon, ed. 1963. *Cities and Space: The Future Use of Urban Land*. Baltimore: Johns Hopkins University Press.

Wise, Charles R. 1990. "Public Service Configurations and Public Organizations." *Public Administration Review* 50: 141–55.

Yamaguchi, Kazuo. 1996. "Power in Networks of Substitutable and Complementary Exchange Relations." *American Sociological Review* 61: 308–32.

Index